# The ANTIQUES Guide to

# *Decorative Arts in America*

## *1600-1875*

With an introduction by Alice Winchester

Illustrated with 192 drawings
by Pauline W. Inman
and
434 photographs

E. P. DUTTON NEW YORK

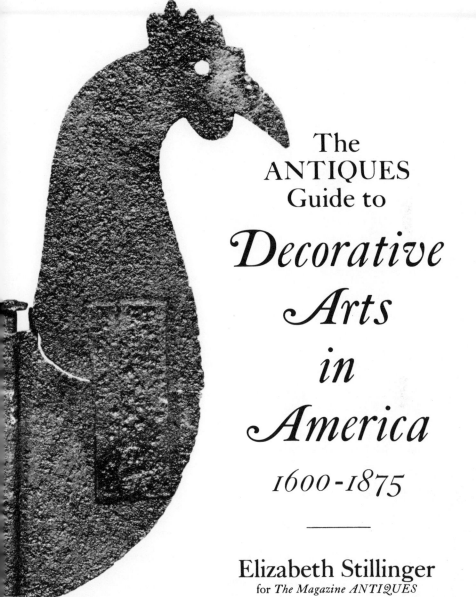

# The
# ANTIQUES
# Guide to

# *Decorative*
# *Arts*
# *in*
# *America*
## *1600-1875*

## Elizabeth Stillinger
### for *The Magazine ANTIQUES*

THIS BOOK IS DEDICATED TO
THE MEMORY OF
HELEN COMSTOCK
FROM WHOSE "CHRONOLOGY OF CRAFTS"
IT GREW

# Contents

*vii*

# *Introduction*

This is a book about relationships—the relationships of our American antiques to their own time and to each other. It is designed to outline the development in each of the main branches of craftsmanship and to suggest as well how each of these branches is related to the others and how all are related to the major trends in history and art.

That is a large order for a small book, but the text and pictures are arranged in such a way as to make the point clear and to make the book itself easy to use. It is primarily a general introduction to a broad field. At the same time its treatment of the subject both in cross section and in parallel lines provides a helpful reference for those with specialized knowledge.

The period covered, from the days of earliest settlement in the American Colonies until after the Civil War in the United States, is divided into quarter centuries and each is treated in a separate section. Within each section significant events of the period are reviewed and the character of the decorative arts is sketched in. Against this historical and stylistic background is traced the development during the quarter century in each of the crafts considered: furniture, silver and other metals, ceramics, and glass. This presentation brings out the relationships of styles, forms, and craftsmen within each category and among all the categories, from period to period. In each section drawings and photographs illustrate characteristic examples in every craft, representing the significant aspects of style and form.

Thus virtually at a glance one is reminded that in the second quarter of the eighteenth century, for example, when George II was reigning in England and Louis XV in France, furniture in the Queen Anne style was being fashioned by Job Townsend in Newport and by William Savery in Philadelphia; stoneware was being made in New York, redware in New England, delft and salt-glazed wares in England; Caspar Wistar established his glasshouse in South Jersey; and silversmiths in the American Colonies were still making pear-shape teapots in the style introduced in the previous quarter century. One can also make a rapid review of the development within a single craft through the centuries: the gradual shift in silver and furniture styles, for instance, from baroque to rococo to neoclassic, and on to revivals of these styles; or the expansion of ceramic production, by means of new techniques, to include hard-paste and soft-paste porcelain, transfer-printed wares, creamware, Parian ware and many other inventions.

The objects considered here are the useful and decorative things that are known to have had a place in American homes of an earlier day and that have been widely sought by American collectors of antiques in our own day. In the categories of furniture and silver, the emphasis is on what was made in America; in the other categories, many types made elsewhere and imported here are included. This is admittedly an arbitrary distinction but it is one sanctioned by the collecting habits of many Americans in the twentieth century, and it has indeed a certain historical validity. The crafts of the cabinetmaker and the silversmith were highly developed here by the early eighteenth century, so that, while furniture and silver made in England were prized and imported in quantity, native craftsmen were able to supply the needs—and even to meet the most exacting demands—of many Americans. In the field of glass, nothing of a quality to compare even faintly with fine German or English ware was made here until Stiegel's operations in Pennsylvania just before the Revolution and Amelung's in Maryland soon after it. And in ceramics, not until the mid-nineteenth century did Americans offer anything like competition to the versatile and highly productive earthenware potters of England or the makers of sophisticated porcelain in Germany and France and in China.

This book, then, aims to bring out historical and stylistic relationships among the major types of decorative arts made and used in America up to about a hundred years ago. Limited as it is in scope, it does not pretend to be a complete treatment of the period styles and their development. Nor does it claim to elucidate the mysteries of the techniques practiced by the craftsmen in producing our antiques, though it does furnish a good deal of incidental—and useful—information about them. There are many books in print that consider each of the categories represented here in far more detail, and they should be consulted by anyone seeking fuller information. What is offered here is, in effect, a perspective view.

Among the matters that the reader seeking further specialization will want to pursue is that of the identity of the craftsmen involved. Leaders in each craft are listed in the text on each period, but makers of the objects illustrated are named only when those objects are labeled or marked. A collector naturally wishes to be able to name the maker of his Chippendale table or his pewter porringer, but the great majority of our antiques are unmarked, and attribution can usually be made only on the basis of stylistic analogy—and that is a hazardous business. As our knowledge of early craftsmen and how they worked increases, old attributions are constantly being revised and new questions raised. We still know all too little about the manner and degree of specialization practiced by our early craftsmen. For example a piece of furniture attributed to Thomas Affleck of Philadelphia may incorporate the work of several specialists—turner, joiner, carver, finisher; how much of it was actually made by Affleck himself or even in his shop?

Because the 13 American Colonies belonged to England, the strongest influence on their decorative arts was English. That is apparent in the pages that follow—in the objects illustrated and in the references to English crafts. But it should not be forgotten that almost from the first several countries of continental Europe were represented here, by individuals and by groups. Most of these people maintained their national character and to a significant degree perpetuated their native traditions of craftsmanship while contributing to what we claim as American decorative arts. In some cases, such as that of the Germans who settled in Pennsylvania, what they made is part of what we call American folk art. Examples of these national expressions are illustrated and mentioned here in connection with the appropriate categories and periods.

Fine art–folk art; city–country; high style–low style: these and other terms are often used in the effort to differentiate among the decorative arts in terms of quality or degree. This book is not the place to establish distinctions of that kind, but they should be recognized. It is not quite true, as is often said, that American decorative arts are simpler than European or that country work is simpler than urban. But they are different. There is a time lag between Europe and America, and between city and country. There are also differences in traditions of design, methods of work and intention.

This book grew out of a more condensed presentation—a chart, in fact—called *Chronology of Crafts,* which was prepared for *The Magazine* ANTIQUES by Helen Comstock and first published in *The Antiques Treasury* (Dutton, 1959). Its purpose was to provide a quick survey of parallel developments in the major crafts in America and to place them in their historical context. The purpose of this book, which was prepared for ANTIQUES by

Elizabeth Stillinger, is similar, but broader and deeper. She has clothed the skeleton *Chronology* with the flesh and blood of informative, interpretative text and profuse, pertinent illustration so that it has ceased to be a two-dimensional chart and has acquired the third dimension of depth. There are many books about antiques, general and specific, broad surveys and studies in depth, but we know of no other that covers so much ground in just this illuminating way.

—ALICE WINCHESTER
Editor, *The Magazine* ANTIQUES

*1600-1700*
# The
# Jacobean Style

*Map of New England,*
*from Captain John Smith's*
**DESCRIPTION OF NEW ENGLAND**
*(London, 1616).*

# Historical Background

JAMES I, 1603–1625; CHARLES I, 1625–1649;

COMMONWEALTH, 1649–1659 (OLIVER CROMWELL, 1653–1658);

CHARLES II, 1660–1685; JAMES II, 1685–1688;

WILLIAM AND MARY, 1689–1694; WILLIAM III, 1694–1702.

LOUIS XIII, 1610–1643; LOUIS XIV, 1643–1715.

In the New World the seventeenth century was one of great hardship, but one also of continuous growth and achievement. English settlers arrived in Jamestown, Virginia, in 1607, and in Plymouth, Massachusetts, in 1620. The same period saw the Dutch in New Amsterdam; the French in Quebec; and the Spanish in Florida, the Southwest and California. By midcentury settlements had grown up in Connecticut, Maryland, Rhode Island, Delaware, New Jersey, and Pennsylvania (where Swedes settled along the Delaware River). After 1650 North and South Carolina were settled, and the British, in a bloodless coup, took New Netherlands from the Dutch, renaming it New York.

When they first saw it, the beauty of the Chesapeake Bay area "almost ravished" the men who came to found Jamestown. Pleasure in the tall trees, fair meadows, fruit, flowers, fish and game, joyously recorded in George Percy's *Observations,* was eradicated by the dreadful sickness, famine and Indian hostility that turned their hopeful venture into a nightmare. The disinclination to work among a number of Colonists, poor planning and internal dissension contributed to the enormous hardship of the first several years. Captain John Smith, one of the colony's most effective leaders, describes life at Jamestown:

> Many were the assaults and Ambuscadoes of the Savages, and our men by their disorderly straggling were often hurt, when the Savages by the nimbleness of their heels well escaped. What toil we had, with so small a power to guard our workmen by day, watch all night, resist our enemies and effect our business, to reload the ships, cut down trees and prepare the ground to plant our corn &c. I refer to the reader's consideration. [Smith's *The Generall Historie of Virginia, New-England* . . . , London, 1624.]

The purpose of the Virginia Company was to find silver, gold and a passage to the South Sea, but it was John Rolfe who discovered Virginia's real treasure: tobacco. With the planting of tobacco and other crops, and the arrival in 1619 of 90 "pure and spotless" young women (sent out by the Virginia Company to become wives of Jamestown Colonists) who were "willinglie and lovinglie" received and bought at auction by the settlers, the colony took on a more permanent air. That same year, a cargo of black slaves was landed at Jamestown, establishing an institution that served for almost 200 years as the foundation of a way of life quite different from that of the Middle Atlantic and New England colonies.

Slaves enabled planters to farm enormous tracts of land, gather wealth and acquire political power. A few great landowners gradually deprived small farmers and others of their political and economic rights and at the same time burdened them with heavy taxes. Bacon's Rebellion of 1676 was an effort on the part of these disenfranchised citizens to dramatize their grievances by avenging themselves on hostile Indians, from whose attacks the government was not protecting them, and then marching on the governor himself. Governor Berkeley and the wealthy planters remained unsympathetic, Bacon died of malaria and the revolt petered out, but it remains a vivid chapter in the history of the American struggle for equality.

Life in New England was just the opposite: instead of a few great plantations worked by slaves, there were many farmers, fishermen, merchants and artisans doing their own work with their own—and perhaps a few hired or indentured—hands. Villages and towns were important community centers and fostered social intercourse, if not equality, among citizens of all stations of life. Manners, morals and even a man's innermost thoughts were regulated by Puritan lawmakers. Those who indulged in such debauched pursuits as playgoing, dancing round a maypole, sleeping during sermons, overdressing, playing shuffleboard or quoits were not only frowned upon but penalized. The famous diarist Judge Samuel Sewall recorded from 1674 to 1729 events and attitudes which are of great interest to the student of life in Puritan New England.

By midcentury Massachusetts had done much toward establishing a reputation for intellectual and moral leadership: Harvard was founded in 1636, a law was passed requiring supervision of schooling and apprenticeship, and the Stephen Daye Press of Cambridge printed the *Bay Psalm Book*.

Later literary works from New England were Anne Bradstreet's *The Tenth Muse;* Increase Mather's *A Brief History of the War with the Indians,* 1676; Burke and Howe's *The New England Primer,* 1690; and Cotton Mather's *Memorable Providences Relating to Witchcrafts and Possessions,* 1689, reflecting the witchcraft superstition then current in New England.

In 1682 William Penn arrived in the New World. Like the other middle colonies, Pennsylvania stood temperamentally as well as geographically between the North and the South. "To be furious in religion is to be irreligiously religious," said Penn, who set out to establish an open, tolerant society. Small farms in nearby counties, various arts and industries (such as the first paper mill in the Colonies, set up near Germantown by the Rittenhouse family) and a vigorous shipping industry soon made Philadelphia the richest city in the Colonies.

One of the most lucrative shipping routes was a triangular one, to Africa, the West Indies and back home. Rum was shipped to Africa and traded for black slaves, who were then taken to the West Indies and traded for sugar and molasses to take home to make more rum. Merchants in all the sizable Atlantic seaboard cities were apparently able to reconcile their consciences with engaging in the slave trade, for many American fortunes were made this way.

England, viewing Colonial initiative with apprehension, passed a series of Navigation Acts, that of 1651 being the earliest, designed to limit Colonial manufacture and to assure British supremacy in the shipping of goods between the mother country and her dependencies (the second measure was to prevent the Dutch from sharing in the carrying trade between England and America). The idea was for England to get raw materials such as sugar, tobacco, rice and indigo (the latter two cultivated on great plantations in North and South Carolina) in return for supplying manufactured goods to the Colonists.

For much of the seventeenth century the French presence in North America consisted of fur traders, explorers and missionaries. In 1682 the trader and explorer La Salle went down the Mississippi, claiming for France all the lands drained by the great river from its source to the Gulf of Mexico. He named the region Louisiana in honor of his king, Louis XIV. In France itself, Louis revoked the Edict of Nantes in 1685, depriving French Protestants, or Huguenots, of the freedom from persecution the Edict had guaranteed them. Thousands of Huguenots fled France for England and America. A German migration occurred during the same period, and many of the Palatine Germans chose to build their new homes in Pennsylvania.

Obviously, the Colonies were flourishing by the end of the century. Immigrants of all kinds, in search either of freedom from oppression or confinement or just of greater scope for their abilities, flocked to the New World. Many of them contributed to its spiritual growth as well as to its population.

# Development of the Style

For early settlers, time and energy were just sufficient to provide food, shelter and the barest household necessities. As time passed and more Colonists arrived, life gradually became easier, so that by about midcentury it was possible to devote some attention to household furnishings that pleased the eye besides serving practical purposes.

There was by no means a great increase in the variety of objects, however, for houses were small and furniture especially was often designed for more than one use. Shapes were simple and straightforward, and materials were, on the whole, inexpensive and sturdy. Wood, pewter, horn, iron and earthenware were favored for everyday objects, while a few very highly prized pieces of brightly decorated pottery from Europe or a piece or two of silver, if the wealth of the householder permitted, might be reserved for display and use on special occasions.

Since the majority of the first Colonies were English, the main stylistic impulse in early Colonial times was that of Elizabethan and Jacobean England, and objects from this period are large with

*An arrangement of seventeenth-century furnishings.* Smithsonian Institution.

bold geometrical ornament. There was not much variation on basic themes: stools, tables, chests, cupboards, spoons, plates, bowls, cups and candleholders are the kinds of necessary things that were made. And during the first few decades of settlement, when there was little of the specialization that developed in later periods, it was not unusual for a family to make most of its own housewares and furnishings.

The Dutch were the other major early colonizers of the eastern coast of the new continent. They settled in New York and

New Jersey, and their crafts were based on the broad, sturdy Dutch prototypes they remembered from their homeland.

Toward the end of the century, as the early years of labor bore the fruits of increased leisure and affluence, larger, better-finished houses were built, and the demand for a wider variety of household objects grew. In the late 1600s the William and Mary style was gradually taking hold and there began to be much greater diversity in materials, decorative techniques and forms. With the William and Mary style, too, came exotic influences from the Continent and the East.

# Furniture

Almost nothing remains from the first few decades of settlement. By about 1640, however, solid furnishings with a certain amount of sophistication were being produced, and it is from that period that our earliest surviving pieces come. According to Wallace Nutting, these examples are perhaps as interesting to us as a result of "the admiration which we have for a people who paused in a wilderness to embellish their households" as for their intrinsic artistic merit.

Furniture made in seventeenth-century America was principally of oak (used widely in England) and pine. The main constructive and decorative techniques were turning (shaping on a lathe), joining (constructing by means of mortise-and-tenon joints), carving, and painting in black (ebonizing) and other colors. Typical decorative elements include applied bosses (round or oval knobs) and spindles, arcaded and geometric panels, ball turnings, and massive baluster supports. Furniture forms were limited to seats, tables and basic articles for storage.

Houses of this first century of settlement were small and

*Gateleg table holding vessels*
*that might have been used in Colonial America.*
White Horse Tavern, Newport, R.I.

crowded, and such space-saving items as trestle tables and chair tables were important. The former was a detachable board which rested on trestles, or footed supports, joined by a central stretcher. At dinnertime it was moved to the center of the room and joint stools or forms (plain backless benches) were pulled up to either side; the master and mistress might have presided from chairs placed at either end of the table. After dinner the board could be taken off and the base moved to the side of the room. The chair table was a chair with a hinged back which could be tilted over the arms to make a table. The stretcher table, which takes its name from the box stretchers that connected and strengthened its legs, was much in use, and drop-leaf tables of various sorts were also being made.

Chests, benches, settles and stools were the chairs of all but the most important members of the household. The joint (or joined) stool was a useful seat with attractive turned legs. It looks like a table and is in fact a small stretcher table. There were several early types of chairs: the Brewster, named for Elder William Brewster of the Plymouth colony, has turned members both above and below the seat; the Carver chair, named for Gover-

*Cromwellian side chair,*
*ball turnings; maple;*
*woolwork upholstery original.*
Mrs. Francis P. Garvan.

*Wainscot chair*
*carved in low relief, oak.*
Wesleyan University.

nor John Carver of the same colony, is similar but has vertical spindles only in back, not below the seat or arms. The wainscot chair, perhaps the most impressive of all seventeenth-century types, was of oak with a paneled back which was often lavishly carved. The slat-back was another early form, with turned uprights and a series of horizontal slats for the back; sometimes these curved outward, providing more comfort. The Cromwellian chair,

*Arcaded chest, oak.*
Metropolitan Museum of Art.

which became popular in England during Oliver Cromwell's protectorate, also provided a degree of comfort: though it had no arms, its seat and back rest were upholstered.

There were no closets in early seventeenth-century houses, so such items as chests, court cupboards and press cupboards were necessary. The earliest chests were low lidded boxes whose legs were a continuation of the corner posts, or stiles, of the chest itself. Some were simply boards nailed together by the men of the family; others were more elaborately constructed by a joiner, carved in low relief or decorated with applied moldings. Court and press cupboards were rarer, because they were more difficult to

*Court cupboard, geometric moldings,*
*ebonized baluster supports, rare inlay; oak with pine shelves.*
Wadsworth Atheneum.

make and decorate. The court cupboard had an enclosed section for storing clothes or linens with an open shelf either above or below it, while the press cupboard had an enclosed cupboard section above and drawers below for more storage. Both types were owned by the more affluent Colonists, and they were used to display the proudest family possessions, such as silver tankards or plates, or imported pottery.

In the late 1600s the chest began to lose favor and the chest of drawers, a much more convenient storage receptacle, took its place. The process was gradual: at first one or two drawers were added beneath the conventional chest to make a form now popu-

*Press cupboard,*
*applied bosses and spindles; oak and pine.*
Concord Antiquarian Society.

larly called a "blanket chest"; later the rows of drawers increased, until finally the chest became merely a frame for the drawers.

Although regional variations in furniture are most often discussed in connection with the eighteenth century, there is a group of seventeenth-century chests made in the Connecticut Valley that have distinctive regional characteristics. From the Hartford region came "sunflower" chests, so called because of the peculiar sunflower and tulip design carved on them. From the vicinity of Hadley came a somewhat different type of chest, ornamented with an allover pattern of flowers and sinuous vines carved in very low relief.

*Hadley chest signed*
*by Nicholas Disbrowe, pine.*
Photo Parke–Bernet Galleries, Inc.

*Bible or desk box, oak.* Wadsworth Atheneum.

Related to chests are two smaller articles: the Bible box and the spice cabinet. The first was a small box to hold valuables or books, often the Bible; it was decorated in much the same way as the chest, and it was kept in a place of honor. Sometimes such boxes had slanting lids so that they could be used as desks or reading stands. The spice cabinet is really a miniature chest used to store spices, which were great luxuries in this period; it was also used sometimes as a dressing box.

By the 1680s a wider variety of forms, often fashioned of maple, was being made in America: Hartford and Hadley chests, butterfly and stretcher tables, and chests of drawers belong to this time. Decorative details, too, were more varied and included ball and vase-and-ring turnings.

Little is known of furniture makers before 1700, but Nicholas Disbrowe of Hartford and Thomas Dennis of Ipswich are two joiners who produced fine furniture in the last quarter of the century.

England, meanwhile, had progressed from the Jacobean through the Cromwellian (or Commonwealth) style in the 1650s and the Carolean (or Restoration) style in the period from 1660 to 1690. Walnut replaced oak as the predominant wood, while Oriental lacquer, painted beech and marquetry reflected developing sophistication fostered by greater contact with Europe and the Far East. All these materials were fashioned not only into already

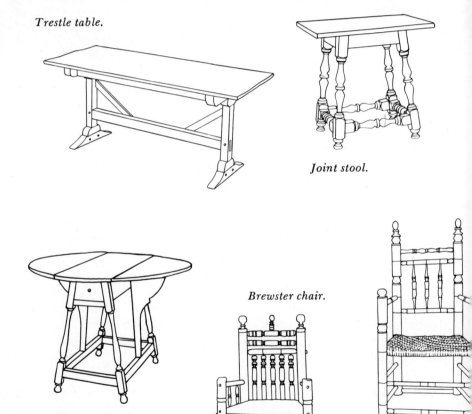

*Trestle table.*

*Joint stool.*

*Brewster chair.*

*Butterfly table.*

*Carver chair.*

existing types of furniture but also into several new ones: daybeds, tall-back chairs, high chests, fall-front desks, tall-case clocks and upholstered wing chairs (1670s). With 1690 came the William and Mary style, showing foreign influence in the Flemish scroll; ball, bun and Spanish feet; cup and trumpet turnings. Daniel Marot, whose designs were an important element in the development of the baroque style in England, worked there from 1694 to 1698.

*Blanket chest, Long Island type showing Dutch influence.*

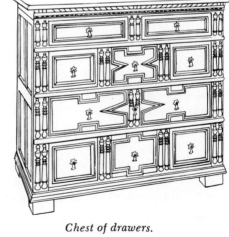

*Chest of drawers.*

*Slat-back chair.*

# Silver

The earliest datable piece of American silver was made after 1650, indicating a concern in the first half of the century with occupations more basic to survival than silversmithing. As life grew easier, silversmiths became busy and highly respected members of the Colonial community: they served as bankers, converting coins into useful objects that proclaimed the wealth of their owners and, at the same time, safeguarded them against theft. Silver could be easily identified because each piece was made and decorated to order.

Spoons, beakers, caudle and dram cups, tankards, porringers and other practical items were the earliest forms. In New England these were fashioned in the "Puritan" style, whose beauty lay in the outlines of the form itself—strong, simple and well proportioned. Toward the end of the century the Stuart and William and Mary styles brought more elaborately decorated types of silver into fashion. Standing cups, sugar boxes, and flat-topped, tapering cylindrical tankards were added to the silversmith's repertoire. Characteristic, too, were the decorative techniques of embossing, or repoussage (raised designs made by hammering the metal outward from the inside of the object), engraving, gadrooning, and the use of cast details.

Among New England forms the earliest spoon was the "slip end," which had a deep fig-shape bowl and narrow handle with a diagonally sliced end. Next came the Puritan spoon, with shallower oval bowl and a flattened handle. The trifid-end spoon succeeded this type; its flat three-lobed handle and ridged oval bowl back were sometimes ornamented with scrolling foliage. Forks were mentioned in inventories, but none survives except the sucket fork, a combination fork and spoon used to serve sweetmeats.

Drinking vessels include the very popular tankard. Straight, tapering bodies with flat covers and scroll handles ending in a shield make up the characteristic New England tankard of this period. Beakers, used both at home and at church, were made in two shapes: one was straight-bodied and flat-bottomed, and the other was flared at the lip and had a molded base. Standing wine cups were used chiefly as communion vessels, and the earliest type was tall and slender with baluster stem.

The caudle cup was another typical drinking vessel, for serving various spiced wine drinks such as caudle, posset and syllabub. It was a two-handled cup, sometimes covered, and either smooth-surfaced or decorated with flat-chased flower or other designs. Many people willed such cups to churches, so more have survived than might otherwise have done so. Dram cups, small, shallow two-handled bowls, were in wide use for the service of distilled spirits. And the punch bowl, indispensable to "the custom . . . to pass around the table a great bowl of punch from which each guest was obliged in turn to drink . . ." is another characteristic seventeenth-century product. The earliest were straight-sided and decorated with flat chasing. It is likely that large caudle cups were also used for serving punch.

The porringer, a shallow bowl for berries, cereals and a wide variety of other foods, was a very popular form. The earliest were, again, straight-sided with simple handles. Toward the end of the century the bowl became rounded and the handle grew much more elaborate.

Among other pieces made in New England in this first century were salvers, baptismal basins, standing and trencher salts, candlesticks and chafing dishes, but only one or two examples, if any, of each of these forms have survived.

New England silver has come down to us in the greatest quantity, but New York was a thriving silver-making center, too, with many talented smiths of both Dutch and French ancestry at work. New England and New York silver products of this period

*Tankard by Robert Sanderson, Boston.*
Museum of Fine Arts, Boston.

*Tankard by Charles LeRoux*
*with medal inset*
*and other New York features.*
Privately owned.

reveal the differences they were to maintain throughout the next century. Those of New England can, generally speaking, be said to be spare and slender, while those of New York were more massive and frequently more boldly ornamented.

The New York spoon differs from that of New England in being made in two parts: a round hammered bowl was attached to a handle cast in the shape of an animal, hoof or caryatid, in the Dutch manner. By 1690 the trifid handle had come into fashion, though it was broader than its New England counterpart. The sucket fork was also popular in New York.

The tankard, a very typical New York form, displays a basi-

*Two-handled, lobed punch bowl, New York.*
Metropolitan Museum of Art.

cally English shape and Dutch or Swedish ornament consisting of a coin or medal set into the cover, lavishly ornamented handle and handle end, spiral corkscrew thumbpiece and leaf molding on base. The mug was very much like the tankard, except that it did not have a cover. Tumblers were small, with straight sides and rounded bottoms. Beakers, here as in New England, were used in homes and churches alike, and the New York type had a wide, flaring lip and rich, engraved ornament.

Unique to seventeenth-century New York is a small group of two-handled lobed bowls that express the worldly, pleasure-loving nature of the Dutch merchants and traders who settled the Hud-

*Caudle cup with*
*embossed decoration, by John Coney.*
Harvard University.

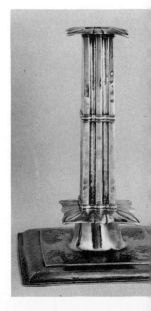

*Candlestick, square pillar,*
*one of a pair by Jeremiah Dummer, Boston.*
Yale University Art Gallery,
Mabel Brady Garvan Collection.

son River Valley. These richly decorated bowls were apparently not made elsewhere in the Colonies, and according to John Pearce, they "drew their design inspiration from the Dutch version of a north European type."

Of smaller two-handled cups very few survive. Many of the other earliest New York forms, such as standing salts and baptismal basins, are equally scarce or have not come down to us in even one example.

America's best-known early smiths were John Hull and Robert Sanderson of Boston, partners who set up the Colonies' first mint in 1652. John Coney, Jeremiah Dummer, Timothy

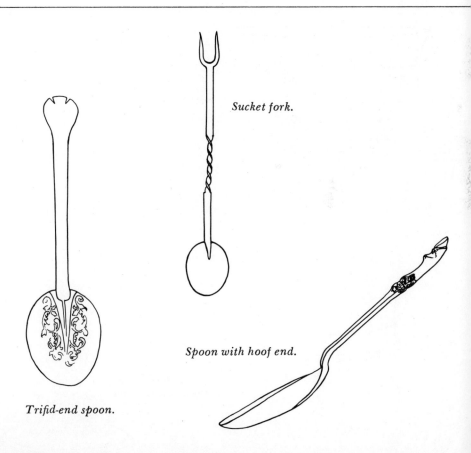

Sucket fork.

Spoon with hoof end.

Trifid-end spoon.

Dwight and Edward Winslow were also working in Boston; Jurian Blanck, Jacob Boelen, Jesse Kip, Bartholomew LeRoux, Gerrit Onkelbag, Cornelius van der Burgh, and Jacobus van der Spiegel were New York smiths; and toward the end of the century César Ghiselin and Johannis Nys worked in Philadelphia.

England, of course, produced a much greater quantity and variety of silver in the seventeenth century. From 1600 to 1625 forms and motifs were imposing and ornate, of late Renaissance derivation with German influence. By 1625, in the early Stuart period, simpler "Puritan" silver was fashionable, but during the

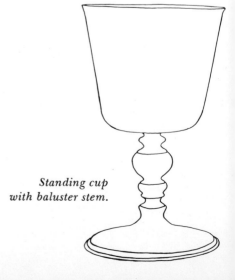

*Beaker with engraved ornament, New York.*

*Standing cup with baluster stem.*

Commonwealth (1649–1659) much domestic silver was melted down. The Restoration of 1660 reestablished not only the Stuarts, but also interest in beautiful decorative objects. Many new forms were made and handsomely adorned with floral embossing, matted ornament and engraved chinoiserie; about 1685 fluting and gadrooning became popular as well. Dutch influence predominated until 1685, when it was overshadowed by the French influence exerted by Huguenot smiths. The Britannia standard, requiring a higher percentage of pure silver in the alloy, went into effect in 1697.

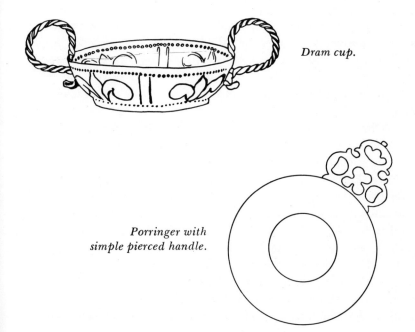

*Dram cup.*

*Porringer with
simple pierced handle.*

# Ceramics

The earliest American table, kitchen and dairy wares were made of either pottery or wood (also called "treen"—that is, made from trees). Pewter eventually replaced treen, but the pleasantly shaped and colored red earthenwares, or redwares, that served the first settlers continued to be made and used well into the nineteenth century.

Redwares were first made in Jamestown, Virginia, where fragments of bowls, pots, cooking vessels, plates and other forms have been unearthed.

New England was a great center for the production of redwares from the beginning and continued so for many generations. Charlestown, near Boston, became the home of the potter Philip Drinker in 1635. That same year William Vincent (later called Vinson) arrived in New England, as did another potter, John Pride. The market for the useful wares these men produced was consistently good, so their descendants and apprentices were able to carry the craft successfully into later generations. Another member of a New England potting family was James Kettle (later

Kettell) of Danvers. The site of the pottery where he worked from about 1687 to 1709–10 is the earliest New England pottery site to have been located, and shards found there indicate that Kettle was a careful and experienced craftsman.

The material with which these early potters worked was common brick clay, available almost everywhere along the Atlantic coast. It was of red or reddish-brown color, and forms were usually glazed inside and sometimes all over with a clear lead glaze which gave a sheen to the body color. Glaze colors varied as a result of impurities in the clay or in the glaze itself and of fluctuations in kiln temperature. The resultant uneven and streaked surfaces in shades of orange, green, brown and red are an effective decoration for these earthy wares. Occasionally manganese was added to the glaze to produce a brown or brilliant black which was used for such tablewares as mugs, jugs, pitchers and teapots. Another intentionally produced color was green, but the copper oxide necessary for the process was expensive, so green glaze was infrequently used.

Additional decoration was achieved by means of trailed slip or incised or tooled lines. Slip was liquid clay which was trailed in freehand patterns onto the surface of the pottery to create bright, cheerful designs.

Redware forms were always simple and serviceable: plates, bowls, mugs, jugs, cooking and baking dishes, and milk pans. Their "preeminent qualities," according to the authority Lura Woodside Watkins, were "sturdiness and repose," and they were made year in, year out, with very little alteration. The potter, whether he plied his trade continuously or occupied himself otherwise part of the time, required a minimum of equipment; all he needed was a mill for purifying the clay and a horse to operate it, a potter's wheel and a few basic wooden tools, and a kiln.

Of these early redwares hardly anything except a handful of shards survives. They received constant and rough usage, and because they were so easily replaced, no one gave a thought to preserving them. Fortunately, since they were made over such a long period of time, later examples serve as guides to early forms.

Stoneware, made of finer clay than redware and fired at a much higher temperature, was more durable and needed "no other glazing . . . than what is produced by a little common salt strewed over the ware" while it was in the kiln. It was not made in New England until the late eighteenth century, but it was being produced in New York and Pennsylvania before 1700.

A third type of pottery was made in America in the seventeenth century, though only for a short while. Its production was

*Jug, redware; American.*
Smithsonian Institution.

*Delft gourd bottle,*
*shape copied from Chinese; Dutch.*
Phelps Warren.

the result of the interest and initiative of Dr. Daniel Coxe, a prominent London physician who owned a good deal of land in New Jersey. Dr. Coxe proposed to make "white and painted earthenware and pottery vessells" (delftware), and although he never came to this country himself, his agents operated a pottery at Burlington, New Jersey, from 1688 to 1692.

These simple earthenwares and stonewares were the early settlers' only native ceramics. Although clay abounded and the

*Blue-dash charger, delft, polychrome center, sponged background; Bristol, England.* Metropolitan Museum of Art.

men to fashion it were among the first Englishmen to arrive in the New World, Colonists apparently preferred from the beginning to procure their best ceramics from Europe.

One of the leading European ceramic types was tin-enameled earthenware. An earthenware body was completely covered by an opaque-white tin glaze and often, in these early days, decorated with designs in blue, to imitate Oriental porcelain. The type was made throughout Europe, as well as in England. It is variously named: Delft identifies the Dutch and English product (spelled with a lower-case "d" for the English), while faïence refers to the French, and majolica to the Italian. It was made in Holland from

*Plate, slipware, by Thomas Toft; Staffordshire, England.* Nelson Gallery–Atkins Museum, Burnap Collection.

*Mug, delft, decorated in blue in the Chinese manner; English.* Nelson Gallery–Atkins Museum, Burnap Collection.

the sixteenth century, but in the city of Delft itself only after 1600. England produced delft in Aldgate from 1571 and in Southwark probably from 1620–25. Bristol, nearby Brislington, and Lambeth began production after 1650. Faïence was made in France at Nevers and Rouen before 1650 and after 1675 at Moustiers.

English delft forms include posset pots with covers, in which posset, a spicy hot-ale drink, was served; globular wine bottles with the name of the wine and the date inscribed in blue; blue-dash chargers, round dishes with a border of bold blue dashes and a center painting in polychrome of a wide range of subjects—from Biblical scenes to royal portraits; and "Merryman" plates, made in

*Tyg, slipware*
*with applied stamped ornament;*
*Wrotham, Kent, England.*
Nelson Gallery–Atkins Museum,
Burnap Collection.

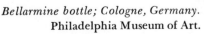

*Bellarmine bottle; Cologne, Germany.*
Philadelphia Museum of Art.

series of six, each bearing a different line of rhymed verse. Barrel-shape mugs, tygs (cylindrical beakers with from one to 12 handles), fuddling cups (three, five, six, or more attached cups that were connected on the inside), barber's bowls and tablewares were among the other forms made. A variation was provided by the delft sponged wares, which employed a crude, peasant-style decoration of freehand painting and sponge-dabbed designs. Their "bright, fancy character" made them popular for export—especially in the succeeding period.

Also very characteristic of English ceramics of the seventeenth century is slipware, or redware decorated with trailed slip, and some of it is very decorative indeed—much more so than American products of the time. Staffordshire was the center of the manufacture of such wares, and Thomas Toft of that district is particularly noted for his lively and original pottery. So-called Toft wares were distinguished by skillfully trailed designs, white dots for emphasis, and the use of light slip on dark grounds and vice versa.

Stoneware was another seventeenth-century type of English pottery. In 1671 John Dwight of Fulham received a patent for the "mistery of transparent earthenware, commonly knowne by the names of porcelaine or china, and of stoneware, vulgarly called Cologne ware." Dwight turned out salt-glazed stoneware busts and figures, as well as more useful wares. His finest things are semitranslucent and well made—the first superior English stonewares. Cologne ware was a durable gray and brown mottled stoneware made into such forms as bottles, pots and mugs that were imported from Germany. Dwight was able to imitate Cologne ware successfully. Metal molds used to stamp decoration on stoneware bottles have been recovered on the site of his pottery.

In 1693 the Elers brothers, believed to have come from Amsterdam, settled in Staffordshire. They produced a high grade of stoneware and have been credited with advancing the craft of ceramics in Staffordshire to the point where relatively crude—though expressive and lively—forms such as tygs and posset pots

were replaced by more sophisticated products. The Elerses are known particularly for their thinly potted red stoneware teapots that were the antecedents of Wedgwood's *rosso antico*.

In France Louis Poterat of Rouen applied for a patent to manufacture soft-paste porcelain in 1673. An earlier patent had been granted to Claude and François Révérend of St. Cloud in 1664, and these were among the first steps in the European quest

Plate, delft.

*Slipware jug, English.*

for its own true porcelain, up to this time obtainable only from the Far East. Soft-paste porcelain was made from a mixture of clay and glass to give it hardness, and covered with a lead glaze to give it a glassy look; but although it came closer than any other product to true, or hard-paste, porcelain, it did not achieve the hardness and close fusion of body and glaze that distinguished Chinese porcelain.

*Wine bottles, delft.*

*Elers red stoneware teapot, English.*

*Posset pot with cover, delft.*

*Octagonal plate, delft.*

# Glass

Jamestown's first settlers established a glasshouse in 1608, about a year after their arrival. Although little is known about this first American glassmaking venture, it is probably safe to assume that it failed because the struggle for existence so debilitated the surviving settlers that they were left with neither the time nor the ability to engage in any except essential activities.

There was another attempt at glassmaking in the Virginia colony in the early 1620s, but it, too, failed. The sites of these early factories have been excavated, and a reconstructed version now operates at Jamestown. But because hardly any seventeenth-century American glass survives, and because the fragments found at Jamestown were not large enough to make it possible to tell which objects were made there, we can only guess at what the settlers hoped to manufacture. Probably they planned to make bottles and window glass, for these headed the list of essential glass items.

Of other glasshouses in seventeenth-century America, there is record of one operating in 1641 in Salem, Massachusetts, which is said to have been active on and off for 20 years; one in 1683 in Philadelphia; and two in New Amsterdam, operated by Johannes Smedes and Evert Duyckinck from about 1650 to 1674. All were eventually unsuccessful, and as there are no authenticated examples of their wares, we conjecture that they, too, made window glass, bottles and possibly drinking glasses and other everyday forms.

The art of glassmaking did not really flourish in England until toward the end of the century, so there was little glass of any sort in the Colonies until the 1680s. But the history of the craft in England, and later in the Colonies, begins with its development on the Continent, so it is to Italy that we turn first to look at the evolution of techniques and forms.

Glassmaking is among the most ancient of the arts. It was practiced by the Egyptians at least 1,500 years before the birth of Christ, and their knowledge and skill were such that many of the techniques in use today were known to them. The craft was passed on to peoples around the Mediterranean and eventually to the Romans. It reached a high point in their wares and again in the delicate, fanciful creations of the Venetians, supreme in the manufacture of glass from the 1400s to the mid-1600s. A contemporary Englishman gives us an idea of just how valued Venetian glass was by his countrymen: "It is a world to see in these our daies, wherein gold and silver most aboundeth, how that our gentilitie as lothing those mettals (because of the plentie), do now generallie choose rather the Venice glasses, both for our wine and beere. . . ."

Colored and occasionally opaque-white glass was often used for early Venetian objects. Clear glass eventually became more popular, possibly because it lent itself so well to the numerous decorative techniques the Venetians practiced with such skill.

A prominent stem ornament was that of a knop decorated with molded lion masks or other motifs. Gilt and enamel decoration, sometimes in the form of "jeweling," or small dots of colored enamel applied to look like a jeweled design, are characteristic. Applied glass devices such as threading and prunts (drops of glass

worked into various shapes) were also used. One of the most spectacular was the latticinio technique, in which swirled, festooned or lacy patterns were created within the metal itself through the addition of colored or opaque-white "canes" of glass. Diamond-point engraving was also practiced, but because the glass of Venice was very fragile, even this delicate method was risky.

Venetian glassblowers took great pleasure in creating fantastically shaped stems and bowls: they produced glasses in the forms of animals, ships, monsters; elaborate stems with wings and tails and goblet bowls with wavy edges; as well as simpler objects with more conventional knop and pillar stems. All of these forms, plain or fancy, were very thin and brittle and the number that have survived is an indication not of their durability, but of the quantities in which they were made.

For many years other European countries, envious of Italian

Façon de Venise *goblet,*
*"wings" on stem,*
*diamond-point engraving;*
*Italy or the Low Countries.*
Ruth Bryan Strauss
Memorial Foundation.

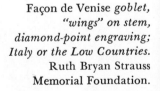

*Venetian cup with "jeweled"*
*ornament in gold and colored enamels.*
Cleveland Museum of Art.

artistry and technical skill and desirous of producing their own glass, had been luring Italian glassblowers from their native land. The mysteries of the craft were thus gradually spread throughout western Europe, whose glassmakers could always count on a ready market for wares in the *façon de Venise*. By about the middle of the seventeenth century Venice had lost its place as the world's foremost glass producer.

Chief among the raiders of Italian glass factories were the various states that made up the Austrian Empire, and German and Bohemian glass became a major influence in the development of our own glass. During the seventeenth century, much of Ger-

*German* Waldglas *beaker with prunts.*
Leopold Blumka.

many's most successful and inventive glass fell into the category of
forest glass, or *Waldglas,* a relatively crude type with thick green-
ish or brownish walls.

Among typical German forms were beakers, barrel-shaped or
cylindrical, and stemmed glasses. The *Humpen* was a cylindrical
beaker that ranged in size from quite small to very large; often it
was virtually covered with elaborate enameling. The *Römer* was a
distinctive stemmed glass with a spreading foot and a wide bowl
whose bottom half appeared to be a short, thick stem ornamented
with prunts. The *Römer* became popular in seventeenth-century
England "for Rhenish wine, for Sack, claret, Beer."

*Bun-footed beaker with
ruins painted
in enamel, Nuremberg.*
Ruth Bryan Strauss
Memorial Foundation.

*German* Humpen *of green glass with
enameled hunting scene.*
Los Angeles County Museum.

Nuremberg was the center of a tradition of which sophisticated enameling and wheel-engraved decoration were outstanding features. The difference between the wheel and diamond-point techniques is that the former employed small copper wheels rotated in a lathe, while the latter was done with a diamond-pointed hand tool. Early diamond-point engraving was light and delicate; wheel engraving offered greater surface variation and enhanced the light-reflecting quality of the glass.

The first known of a school of talented German wheel engravers was Caspar Lehmann, who dated a beaker at Prague in 1605. After Lehmann came the Schwanhardts, father and children, who were engraving glass at Nuremberg from 1622. There were others, and such work continued to be done with great skill well into the eighteenth century. Tall, multiknopped, multicollared goblets with relatively thin walls, as well as thicker tumblers and bun-footed beakers are among the forms associated with the Nuremberg glassmakers.

Colored glass was another important aspect of the craft in Germany. Johann Kunckel, working in Potsdam in the late 1670s, is credited with an important development in this direction. He worked out a method of producing gold-ruby glass on a commer-

*French candlestick.*
Victoria and Albert Museum.

*Colored-glass figures of a goddess and Hercules, possibly Nevers, France.*
Art Institute of Chicago.

cial scale—a technique that was then lost until the nineteenth
century.

French glassmakers, on the whole, turned out very few fine
domestic items in this period, but they did create a distinctive
group of figures decorated with colored-glass details in red, blue,
white and yellow. Such "grotesque figures for the decoration of
cabinets and chimney pieces" were made in several French towns,
but they are generally labeled *verre de Nevers,* because of that
city's long history of producing them.

Early English landmarks were Sir Jerome Bowes' acquisition of Verzelini's 1575 patent for the manufacture of "Venetian" glass with its Venice-inspired shapes, thin walls and diamond-point decoration; and the revolution in the type of fuel used in glass-making, which occurred during the period associated with Sir Robert Mansell, Bowes' successor. This involved the substitution of coal for the enormous quantities of wood that had previously been consumed. In 1623 Mansell's company was granted a patent for the manufacture of "all manner of drinking glasses, broad glasses [large sheets], window glasses, looking glasses and all other kinds of glasses, bugles, bottles, vials or vessels whatsoever"—in short, a monopoly. Mansell was followed by the Duke of Buckingham, who controlled several patents in the 1660s; from 1663 he monopolized the manufacture of mirror plate, produced in his Vauxhall factory.

Very important in the development of glassmaking in England was the charter of the Glass Sellers' Company in 1635, followed by the charter of the Glaziers and Painters of Glass in 1638. The Glass Sellers' Company, especially after the restoration of the monarchy in 1660, was a powerful force in supporting and guiding the industry until the end of the century; it dictated what glassmakers made and guaranteed a market for their products.

Around 1670, John Greene, an influential member of the Glass Sellers' Company, arranged to send his own designs to Italy for manufacture there and shipment back to England, for English glassmakers were apparently unable to meet the demands of an expanding glass-buying public. Greene's designs (over 400 in all) have been preserved, and some of his correspondence with Alessio Morelli of Murano also survives. From these valuable documents we learn that Morelli's performance was not satisfactory and this and a growing tendency in England toward self-sufficiency explain why the development of a new formula for English glass began to seem imperative.

One aid to the production of fine native glass had been the translation in 1662 of the standard Italian work on glass manufac-

*Verzelini goblet
with molded stem ornament,
English.*
Photo Sotheby & Co.

ture, Antonio Neri's *L'Arte Vetraria,* first published in 1612.
Fortunately, too, George Ravenscroft was at hand: he was engaged
by the Glass Sellers' Company in 1673 and began experimenting
with the use of ground flints to produce a clear and durable native
glass. His researches culminated in one of the outstanding dis-
coveries in the history of glass: lead (also called flint) glass, which
was clearer and more brilliant than the soda glass of Venice.

Glass results when silica is fused with the aid of an alkaline
flux, and the nature of the glass will vary with the ingredients
used in its manufacture. According to W. B. Honey (*Glass: A*

*Handbook*), lead glass "was totally different from the thin, rather horny Venetian glass. It had an oil-like brilliance, as well as a peculiar darkness in the shadows; and above all it had a light-dispersing character that gave it a remarkable interior fire."

Unfortunately Ravenscroft's first glass crizzled, or decomposed, so that it was covered by a network of cracks. By 1676 he felt that he had solved the crizzling problem through the addition of oxide of lead, and adopted the "raven's head" seal to distinguish the new formula from the old. Sealed glasses, bearing the maker's mark or seal, became a popular type of the period, but the Ravenscroft seal was later dropped because of continued crizzling. (Ordinary bottles often had seals which identified their owners. Most of the earliest bore the seals of taverns, but private individuals who maintained their own wine cellars also ordered sealed bottles, for use at home. Some seals simply showed the owner's initials, and some bore crests or other family emblems. Samuel Pepys recorded that on October 23, 1663, he "went to Mr. Rawlinson's and saw some of my new bottles, made with my crest upon them, filled with wine, about five or six dozen." See Ivor Noël-Hume's article in *Antiques* for September 1957.)

By 1682 Ravenscroft's successor, Hawley Bishop, had succeeded in modifying the formula so that heavy lead glass could be produced without crizzling, and "new flint glasses" went into full production. In the last years of the century "nearly a hundred glasshouses were making it [lead glass] in various parts of the country," according to Honey. It was exported, and Continental craftsmen began to engrave it, so that by 1685 England had succeeded to the mantle of Venice and Germany in the making of glass.

The new lead glass inspired the creation of forms that would display its "remarkable interior fire" to best advantage: finely proportioned baluster-stem wine glasses with round funnel or V-

*Covered lead-glass punch bowl,*
*probably London.*
Nottingham Museum and Art Gallery.

shape bowls were the earliest. Later, knops were added—the acorn, egg and mushroom shapes were typical, as well as knops containing a coin. *Verre églomisé*, or glass ornamented with reverse painting, was also new in late seventeenth-century England as a decoration for looking-glass frames.

Ravenscroft and his followers thus produced the first authentic English style in glass, not only in developing a metal of superior brilliance and lack of color, but also in choosing to fashion the perfected lead glass into simple, elegant designs.

*Goblet with waisted bo⟩ hollow knopped stem, English.*

*Goblet of* Römer *shape, raspberry prunts on stalk; English.*

*Nuremberg covered goblet.*

*Wine bottle, English.*

# Pewter
# and Other Metals

"The day the colonists landed at Jamestown (May 14, 1607) they began building a triangular fort, a 'setled streete of houses,' a church, a guardhouse, and a storehouse. All men familiar with tools and building practices must have been extremely busy during the first few weeks" (J. Paul Hudson, "Jamestown Artisans and Craftsmen," *Antiques*, January 1957). And therein lies the beginning of the tale of base metals in America, for of course iron tools were essential in creating shelter, chopping wood, making boats and other vital enterprises.

The first American ironworks built by Englishmen was located at Falling Creek, Virginia, not far from Jamestown. It was established in 1620–21 but in 1622 Indians attacked and wiped out both the ironworks and the ironworkers and their families. Evidence that some tools and a great many other iron objects were made there is provided by contemporary records.

Excavations on the site of Mathews Manor, a seventeenth-century Virginia plantation house, also turned up many metal objects of interest (described by Ivor Noël-Hume in *Antiques*,

December 1966). Among them were an iron skillet stand, long-handled frying pan, ice chopper and cooking pots. Garden implements, woodworking tools, nails and a variety of hardware were also recovered. Brass articles were found, and along with the fairly unsurprising skimmer, thimble and pins was a watering can which apparently has no parallel in America!

Early Massachusetts inventories indicate that ironwares were very much in evidence there, too. They are important not only to the student of domestic life in the seventeenth century, but also to those interested in design, as Ralph Edwards pointed out in his introduction to J. Seymour Lindsay's *Iron and Brass Implements:*

> Ruskin noted the mediaeval mason's prodigal expenditure of art on mouldings and spandrels too high to be seen: a similar principle guided the worker in iron who made skillets and pothangers beautiful for cooks and scullions. 'Put the porke on a *fayre* spete' directs a Cookery Book of about 1430; it meant only one clean and serviceable, but the phrase may stand as a symbol.

Among the "fayre" implements in and around the seventeenth-century fireplace were a crane, spit, pothooks, fire shovels, tongs, gridirons (for broiling), trivets, pots, skillets and ladles. Pots and kettles of copper and brass—and toward the end of the century brass trivets and plate warmers for those wealthy enough to indulge in them—brightened some fireplaces as well. Brass warming pans, mortars and possibly some gleaming candlesticks might also have been found in the "hall" or principal room of the early settler's house.

Pewter was there, too.

> "Here is good living for those who love good fires," wrote [the Reverend Francis] Higginson in his "New-Englands Plantation" [1630] and under the spell of the glowing flames, the bare, whitewashed walls, the brown timbers and floor boards of the ceiling, the dress of pewter, and the simple furnishings of the room, enriched by the shadows, became a place full of cheer—a place where privation and homesickness might be forgotten in the glow

of the bright firelight [George Francis Dow, *Domestic Life in New England in the Seventeenth Century*].

A pleasant picture indeed, and one which needs no elaboration except, perhaps, for the "dress" of pewter. This was the family's pewter collection displayed in the open-shelved cupboard then referred to as a dresser. The pewter mentioned above might have included candlesticks, saucers (small plates), porringers, spoons, plates, dishes, basins, beakers, mugs or pots, and even, perhaps, a tankard or two, for pewter was, among the moderately well-to-do, a necessity of everyday life. It was more durable than pottery—though not so durable as silver—and it lent itself well to attractive, serviceable forms.

Except for the now famous Chuckatuck spoon, made and dated 1675 by Joseph Copeland, working during the last quarter century in Chuckatuck and Jamestown, Virginia, there is no American pewter positively attributable to the seventeenth century. The pewterer Richard Graves is known to have been working in Salem from 1635, and Edmund of the pewtermaking Dolbeare family of Boston probably arrived from England about 1670. In all, fewer than ten men are known for sure to have pursued the craft in seventeenth-century America. Those who did make pewter usually engaged in some other trade as well, for a living could not be made by working in pewter alone. Some were general merchants, and some worked in other metals such as brass, copper or tin.

England held firmly to its policy of selling manufactured goods to its colonists in return for raw materials and regarded any Colonial manufacture as a serious offense. The making of pewter was specifically discouraged by the high duty on raw tin (the principal ingredients of pewter are tin and copper and there were no tin mines in the Colonies), and an absence of duty on finished pewter wares. Much American pewter, therefore, was made of old or damaged pieces melted down and recast. Pewter was made in molds of brass or bronze and these were expensive, so American pewterers turned out only a few basic forms; the molds were passed from one generation to the next. Since pewter, which commonly received hard use, was easily bent and could be mis-shapen by close contact with heat, there was a considerable amount of recasting to be done, but even so it was not a full-time occupation.

For variety in form and style, it was necessary to buy the imported pewter. Flatware, or sadware—articles for the service of food that were fashioned in one piece, such as plates, dishes, basins and so on—were shipped to the Colonies in the greatest numbers. According to pewter collector and authority Ledlie Laughlin

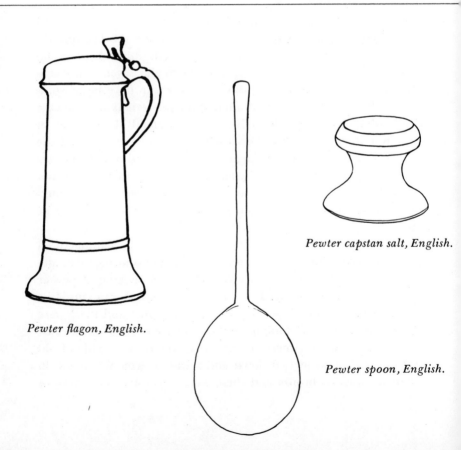

*Pewter capstan salt, English.*

*Pewter flagon, English.*

*Pewter spoon, English.*

(*Pewter in America*), such forms, since they could be stacked up inside one another, took up the least space in packing, and it was therefore more profitable to send a shipment of flatware than one of bulky hollow ware.

In discussing pewter, it is customary to refer to a "plate" when speaking of an example which has a diameter of nine inches or less; "dish" is the proper term for the same form with a greater diameter. Among early English types are those with a wide, smooth rim and a narrow reed just under the edge. From 1650 a very narrow-rimmed type was made, and a triple-reeded rim appeared about 1675.

It should be noted that forms made in both pewter and silver ordinarily followed, in shape though not in decoration, the silver styles of the day. Flagons are typical, and the earliest were tall and tapering with a squat, domed cover; about 1625 cylindrical flagons with finial and spreading foot came into fashion. Early candlesticks were of the heavy bell-base type (having a high, gracefully curving domed foot) with a mid-drip pan. About 1650 the bell-base stick was superseded by one with a square-pillar stem; and about 1675 the round-pillar variety came into fashion. As the century went along the mid-drip pan became a less prominent feature.

The tankard was the "aristocrat among drinking vessels in seventeenth-century England and America," as Laughlin puts it. The earliest examples are very simple, of plain cylindrical shape tapering slightly toward the top. In the closing years of the century, base moldings became more prominent, and there was a molding sometimes around the midsection of the body. This later period, too, saw the appearance of "wriggle work," incised designs produced by rocking a gouge from side to side. The effect of wriggle work, while not so sophisticated as that of engraving, was particularly suitable to pewter. Patterns were usually bold and had the same appealing freedom and individual quality as needlework of the period. Tankard handles were of an S-curve shape, with ornamental terminals; covers were flat with protruding rims that were sometimes crenelated. Toward the end of the century covers were domed or double-domed and the crenelated lip began to disappear. Mugs, or pots, followed the shapes of tankards in these years, as in succeeding ones. Liquid measures were a very characteristic pewter form. The most widely made was the baluster measure, varied by means of different thumbpieces on lidded examples.

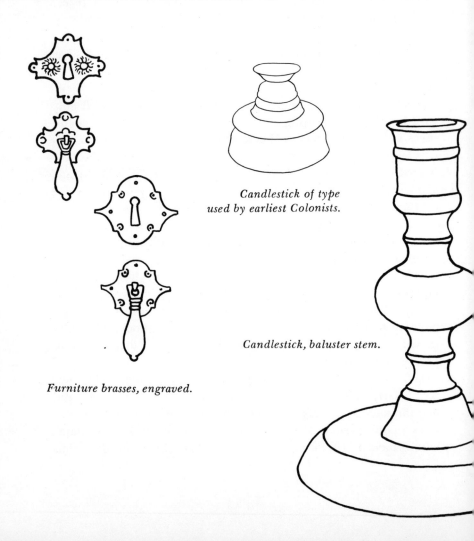

*Candlestick of type used by earliest Colonists.*

*Candlestick, baluster stem.*

*Furniture brasses, engraved.*

Porringers were an important item of household pewter in the seventeenth century, and Mr. Laughlin suggests that our earliest pewterers made them. English types of the period had pierced handles. In the last quarter of the century a fashionable item was the capstan salt, a spool-shape receptacle.

We come to spoons last, but they were probably the most ubiquitous pewter form of all. It is thought that the earliest

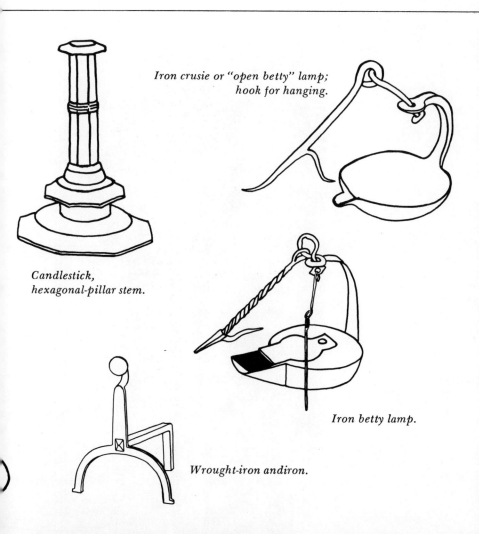

*Iron crusie or "open betty" lamp; hook for hanging.*

*Candlestick, hexagonal-pillar stem.*

*Iron betty lamp.*

*Wrought-iron andiron.*

settlers brought spoon molds with them so that they could melt damaged or broken specimens and recast them as it became necessary. When the seventeenth century began, the dominant pewter spoon shape was the slip end, or "slipped in the stalk," with a fig-shape handle. About 1650 the oval-bowled, trifid-end spoon came in, and the Chuckatuck spoon is a variant of this form.

Prominent among English brasswares is the lantern clock,

*Brass lantern clock.*

developed early in the century. A round brass dial was mounted on a framework composed of four pillars, from which rose additional pieces that intersected and were sometimes topped by a finial. The whole thing resembled a lantern in shape. It was very decorative as well as useful, for the clock face was engraved and often surmounted by an ornamental pierced crest. The next and extremely important development was that of the pendulum clock.

*Bracket clock by Joseph Knibb,*
*English.*
Photo Sotheby & Co.

*Splint or rushlight holder,*
*iron with wood base.*
Henry Ford Museum.

It was introduced into England by Ahasuerus Fromanteel, who, in 1658, advertised "clocks that go exact and keep equaller time than any now made without this regulator . . . and are not subject to alter by change of weather, as others are, and may be made to go a week, or a month or a year, with one winding up." Fromanteel made the short pendulum, which was used in decorative bracket or table clocks. They were very elegant, with cases of rare wood, and an outstanding feature was the ornately engraved brass backplate which could be seen through the glazed door of the back of the case. Brass mounts, appliqués, and other ornaments, sometimes gilded, added to the splendor of these clocks.

In a similar vein were the furniture brasses of the period. Seventeenth-century furniture called for relatively conservative handles and key escutcheons. Drop handles hung from simply shaped plates, often engraved; key escutcheons frequently echoed this shape but were more elaborately ornamented.

On a quite different scale were the chandeliers of the period. The earliest had globular bases, from which rose a series of smaller globes surmounted by a finial or hook for hanging. These had one or more tiers of graceful S-curve arms. Later, a baluster shaft copied from the Dutch chandeliers of the period superseded the earlier ball. Dutch influence was widely apparent in many brass objects, for the Dutch industry flourished in this period, and brass was imported from Holland into England from an early date, and later into the Colonies.

English andirons of the last quarter of the century exhibit Dutch influence in the baluster shaft topped by an urn or flame finial. These, when not made of brass, were of steel, but they were always mounted on an iron base.

Early seventeenth-century candlesticks of brass, as of pewter, had a high-rising base, prominent drip pan and simple shaft. The domed base lowered as the century went along, the stem became a baluster and the drip pan became less conspicuous. In the 1690s the process of brass casting was improved and candlesticks, instead of being solid, were cast in two halves so that the resulting form was hollow.

Latten, a brasslike alloy composed of copper and zinc and generally made in thin sheets, was used in the early years of the century for many of the same forms as brass and pewter (spoons of latten were fairly common in early Colonial houses, for example). It was then largely imported from Flanders, but during the third quarter of the century, the importation of latten was prohibited. Another brass alloy, "Prince's metal," was made to resemble gold and was used, in the last quarter, for ornamental castings.

Many of the foregoing forms for use around the fireplace and for lighting were also made in iron. Wrought-iron candlestands made attractive and practical lights. They were composed of a straight rod supported on a tripod base and had an adjustable arm equipped with one or more brass candle sockets.

Firebacks, used against the back wall of the fireplace to protect it and to reflect heat, were made exclusively of iron. Early examples were cast with armorial designs, but about the middle of the century pictorial designs commemorating people and events of contemporary interest appeared, as well as allegorical and mythological subjects. Here, again, there was strong Dutch influence, and in fact so many Dutch firebacks were used in England that it is now very difficult to distinguish English from import.

Kitchen equipment of all sorts, hardware including decorative hinges and latches, simple andirons, simple lamps and rushlight or splint holders, were made of iron in England and shipped to the Colonies. The production of Colonial ironwork increased when bog iron, found at the edges of spring-fed ponds, was discovered. An ironworks was begun at Saugus, Massachusetts, in 1644, and its products were found by one of the company's agents to be "as good as any worke England doth afoarde." Pots, mortars, skillets and even cast stoves were manufactured at Saugus. Nevertheless, iron hardware was one of England's principal exports up to and beyond the time of the Revolutionary War, so Colonial production was necessarily somewhat limited.

Since relatively little is left to us of the ordinary household implements of the seventeenth century, it is necessary to piece together a picture from such contemporary sources as diaries, letters and inventories. What emerges is remarkable: by the end of the century, the Colonies could provide excellent opportunities for a man with wit and willingness to work. And in his house he could, if he had succeeded, eat from pewter plates, cut his meat with a steel knife from Sheffield (England), drink from a pewter tankard and doze beside a fire supported on brass andirons. Brass, copper, pewter and iron not only made his life comfortable, they provided rich accents and satisfying shapes, at once reminding him of his homeland and giving him cause to feel pride in his success in the New World.

*1700-1725*

*The*

*William and Mary*

*Style*

SAMUEL SEWALL,
*whose diary describes events and*
*attitudes of this period,*
*by John Smibert.*
Museum of Fine Arts, Boston.

# Historical Background

With the new century came the founding of Detroit and New Orleans by the French, whose North American holdings then formed an arc from Quebec in the northeast to the Mississippi Delta in the south.

The struggle for ascendancy in the New World naturally led to hostility between the French and the English. Queen Anne's War, part of the Wars of the Spanish Succession fought among the powers of Europe over issues of commerce and sea power, was fought on North American soil by France and England. It lasted from 1702 until 1713 and affected American Colonists in New York, South Carolina and New England. A surprise attack by Frenchmen and Indians in 1704 resulted in one of the worst episodes of the war, the Deerfield Massacre. Men, women and children were either killed or captured, and from the account written by a captive in later years, it is difficult to know which was preferable. Stephen Williams, ten years old at the time of the assault, recalled, "They traveled [on their way back to Canada] as if they designed to kill us all . . . thirty-five or forty miles a day."

By the terms of the Peace of Utrecht in 1713, France ceded Nova Scotia (Acadia) and Newfoundland to Great Britain, and recognized British sovereignty in the Hudson's Bay Territory. Many other important concessions were made to the British, who emerged as a world power.

England's increasing wealth and growing interest in Continental society and culture encouraged well-heeled young Englishmen to embark on the Grand Tour. This included, according to Richard Lessels, the "Gent. who Travelled through *Italy* Five times, as Tutor to several of the English Nobility and Gentry," a visit to Italy for *"gentile conversation"* and "the sweet exercises of *musick, painting, architecture, and mathematicks."* Then on to France, where "he must learne of the *French,* to become any clothes well; but he must not follow them in all their Phantastical and fanfaron clothings" (Lessels, *The Voyage of Italy . . .,* 1670). This practice of acquiring polish and, in some cases, culture, through travel on the Continent was taken up by wealthy Americans in the second half of the eighteenth century.

Addison and Steele's famous publication, *The Spectator,* began early in the century. Its purpose was "to enliven morality with wit, and to temper wit with morality." Comment on the current London scene, with emphasis on manners, morals and literature, was offered by "Mr. Spectator" himself.

In France the period following the Peace of Utrecht found many citizens looking for a profitable investment. The Mississippi Company had, among other apparent assets, a monopoly of trade with Louisiana and seemed a very good prospect for quick riches. But in 1720 the rush to buy stock suddenly took an opposite turn, and many life savings and ancestral estates were lost when the "Mississippi Bubble" burst.

Significant developments in the Colonies include the beginning of the whaling industry. From cod, mackerel and whales washed up on shore, the fishermen of Gloucester and other New England towns moved on to a new occupation which proved to be tremendously important in their economy: offshore whaling.

On shore Yale University was founded in New Haven, challenging Harvard's supremacy in the realm of education. Current events were being described in *The Boston News-Letter* and in Philadelphia's *American Weekly Mercurie*. And in 1704 Madame Sarah Knight set forth on an extraordinary journey from Boston to New York. Her journal, containing an entertaining and enlightening account of life in the rugged country between towns, was first printed in 1825. Taking the shore route, she accomplished the rough trip on horseback with periodic transfers to small boats; these were not always reassuringly balanced, and on one occasion she feared "a wry thought would have oversett our wherey." Fortunately none did, and Madame Knight returned safely to Boston, where she started a school whose pupils included a future American hero, Benjamin Franklin.

# Development of the Style

The modern notion that beauty and comfort are of as much importance in the decorative arts as practicality took root in the period that began with the 1660 restoration of the "merry monarch," Charles II. Many Englishmen, only too happy to put the enforced asceticism of the Cromwell period behind them, welcomed the new ideas and luxuries introduced by Charles and his Portuguese bride, Catherine of Braganza. With them came influences from the Continent and the Orient that added gaiety and color to English life.

Twenty-five years later, another event of importance to the development of English decorative arts occurred. The revocation of the Edict of Nantes caused many talented Protestant craftsmen to leave France in search of homes where they could practice their religion in peace and safety. Both England and America profited from this event in gaining fine artisans who introduced fresh techniques and styles as they helped supply the domestic needs of their adopted countrymen. The accession of William and his wife, Mary, to the throne of England brought more Continental arts

*New England furnishings on display with European accessories.*
Bayou Bend Collection, Museum of Fine Arts of Houston.

and encouraged new directions in design. The style that resulted from all these diverse influences has come to be called "William and Mary," for it was during their reign that it became dominant.

One salient feature of the style was a great interest in color, pattern and texture. There was also an impressive increase in variety of forms, indicating that people were diverting themselves in ways that required objects with new functions. The Flemish scroll (a boldly arching curve), high-relief ornament consisting of naturalistic motifs, and the use of lighter forms and lighter materials in general are other elements of the style.

Oriental lacquer, cane, porcelain and chintz had been trickling into the West from a very early date, but by the end of the seventeenth century the flow had increased to sizable proportions. Not only had the genuine articles become more plentiful, but Western imitations were being made—with varying results. Chinoiserie, a decorative vocabulary which expressed the European idea of the Oriental scene, came into being as a result of the increasingly prosperous China trade. A charming and influential publication whose purpose was to instruct Englishmen in the art of imitating Oriental lacquer (or japanning, as it was called) was Stalker and Parker's 1688 *Treatise of Japaning and Varnishing*. Speaking of their chinoiserie designs, the authors asserted that they had "exactly imitated their [Chinese] Buildings, Towers, and Steeples, Figures, Rocks, and the like." And, they added, "Perhaps we have helpt them a little in their proportions, where they were lame or defective, and made them more pleasant yet altogether as Antick."

Little by little the new trends appeared in the Colonies, and by the beginning of the eighteenth century the American William and Mary period was in full swing.

# Furniture

In this first quarter of the eighteenth century walnut and maple succeeded oak, implying an interest in lighter, less ponderous furniture. Plain surfaces replaced heavily carved ones, while veneers and marquetry—though always more popular in England than in the Colonies—indicate a new sophistication and the means to indulge it. Painting and japanning were yet other variations, and the scenic and floral chinoiserie decorations on William and Mary furniture are imaginative and humorous, conveying a feeling of freedom of expression not present in earlier, more arduous times. Caned furniture was another innovation, bringing increased lightness and a more resilient seat.

Rigid geometric and naturalistic ornaments were replaced by arches and scrolls. The Flemish scroll, trumpet turnings, boldly shaped skirts and stretchers, ram's-horn arm terminals and the Spanish foot were some of the new decorative elements.

Tables were made in a wide range of sizes and shapes, and for a number of new specific uses. The gateleg was made in many sizes, one of which was the dining table with vase-and-ring or the

71

less frequent ball-and-ring turnings. Butterfly tables continued to be very popular. The beginnings of the more comfortable and self-indulgent way of life that characterized the eighteenth century are apparent in the small tables for writing, reading, gaming, drinking tea and so on, which began to appear in this period. A small side table now often called a "mixing table," with set-in slate or marble top, is one of the characteristic William and Mary types.

Chairs became more comfortable as well as more numerous.

*Slate-top table, trumpet-turned legs,*
*shaped cross stretchers;*
*walnut frame from New England,*
*marquetry and slate top imported.*
Photo Parke–Bernet Galleries, Inc.

*Caned side chair,*
*arched crest rail and front stretcher.*
*Privately owned.*

The easy chair, now often called the "wing chair," was a new form that grew increasingly popular. And the very decorative caned chairs with arched and carved crest rails, exported from England to the Colonies and sometimes copied here by our own chair-makers, were a characteristic type. They are related to banister-back chairs, also light in weight but not so elegant as the caned ones; the banister back is more frequently found in American work. Some contemporary inventories mention a "Boston chair,"

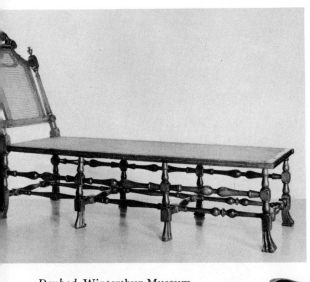

*Daybed*. Winterthur Museum.

*Boston chair,*
*Spanish feet; maple*
*with leather upholstery.*
Photo Parke–Bernet.

which was popular not only in New England, but also in the middle colonies, to which it was exported. This handsome chair had leather upholstery and, very often, a spooned back anticipating the Queen Anne chair. Daybeds, often caned, were another typical form of the period and could serve as extra beds in crowded houses.

New kinds of case pieces began to appear in the last quarter of the seventeenth century. The high chest, or highboy, replaced

*Highboy, maple
and pine japanned;
"steps" added separately
for the display of
English and Dutch delft.*
Metropolitan Museum of Art.

court and press cupboards in importance. It sometimes had a matching lowboy, or dressing table, with drawers on either side of an arched skirt, making a comfortable arrangement for the sitter. Desks became much more frequent, the desk on frame being the typical William and Mary form, though it was to be superseded by the slant-top desk with a full case of drawers beneath the writing surface, and the desk and bookcase, or secretary (this form was rare in America until the next period).

*Slant-top desk, bun feet;*
*burl-walnut veneer banded with walnut.*
Henry Ford Museum.

Looking glasses were in use in early Colonial homes, but few have survived. Throughout the eighteenth century, American examples are often impossible to distinguish from imported ones. It is, however, possible to say that American-made looking glasses of this period were very plain.

Few cabinetmakers of the William and Mary period are known by name, though many skillful craftsmen must have been at work in the Colonies. Nehemiah Partridge and William Randle, japanners, were among the Boston craftsmen who met the

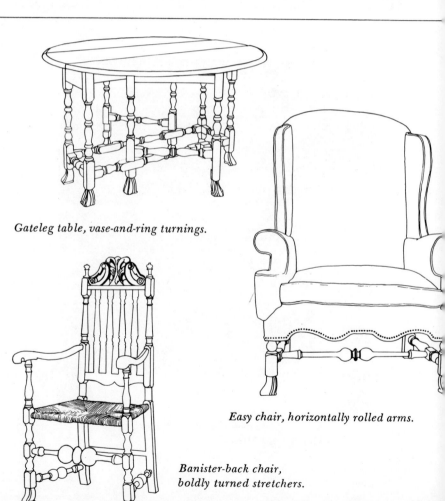

*Gateleg table, vase-and-ring turnings.*

*Easy chair, horizontally rolled arms.*

*Banister-back chair,*
*boldly turned stretchers.*

increasing demand for furniture, and in Portsmouth, New Hampshire, John Gaines was turning out the distinctive chairs that now bear his name.

England had by this time passed on to the Queen Anne and (about 1715) early Georgian styles. In Georgian pieces chair backs were lowered and splats pierced, the cabriole leg acquired a claw-and-ball foot, and carving became important. The duty on mahogany was repealed in 1721, enabling craftsmen to work increasingly in this beautiful and durable wood.

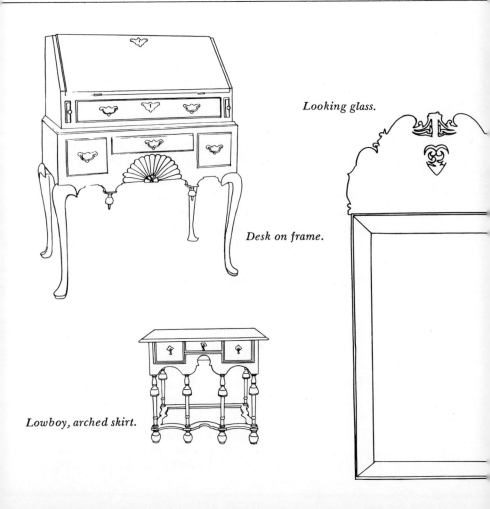

*Looking glass.*

*Desk on frame.*

*Lowboy, arched skirt.*

# *Silver*

Though the reign of William and Mary had ended in 1694, silver in the William and Mary style continued to be made in America until 1715. It was characterized, as were all the decorative arts of this period, by boldness in size and by richly decorated surfaces, especially those in which contrasting areas of ornamented and unornamented silver created the pattern. Gadrooning, fluting, embossing and casting were among the ways the desired effect was achieved.

Engraving continued to be important in the decoration of silver, often in the form of heraldic devices. The bold gadrooning of this period required equally assertive heraldic motifs, and silversmiths, especially in New York, met the challenge by enlarging their plume or acanthus mantling and producing increasingly imposing baroque surroundings for coats of arms. The traditional mantling of feathery foliage was joined in this period by an oval mantling based on baroque architectural motifs. All through the

*Tankard with cut-card ornament*
*on cover, by Jeremiah Dummer, Boston.*
Historic Deerfield, Inc.

period Guillim's *Display of Heraldry,* the standard English work on the coats of arms of that country, was available to Colonial smiths in search of up-to-date heraldic designs.

William and Mary silver reflects the degree of sophistication achieved in the Colonies by the beginning of the eighteenth century. Far-ranging merchants and ship captains in cities up and down the eastern coast were familiarizing Colonists with goods and customs from around the world. Tea, coffee, chocolate and punch were soon as widely enjoyed among well-to-do Colonists as they were in England; and other luxuries, such as sugar, were finding expanding markets. There was a growing number of estab-

*Tankard with engraved coat of arms,*
*applied leaf border, by Benjamin Wynkoop, New York.*
New-York Historical Society.

lished families who were only too happy to add to their comfort and consequence by commissioning a new silver tankard or teapot. Wills and inventories of the period indicate that the wealthiest Colonists possessed a surprisingly wide assortment of such plate.

Spoons were among their store of silver, with a wavy end instead of the earlier trifid. The bowl was oval with a rattail extending from the back of the handle onto the bowl. New York spoons with cast caryatid handles were also made.

Tankards were similar to their seventeenth-century predecessors, but in New England the cover often had a gadrooned band and sometimes cut-card decoration. In New York finer

*Standing cup with gadrooned bands*
*by Dummer, Boston.*
First Parish Church, Dorchester, Mass.

moldings and thumbpieces distinguished William and Mary tankards. Beakers, too, remained relatively unchanged, although the inverted bell shape is occasionally found instead of the straightsided or flared body.

Specifically designed for ecclesiastical use were the flagon, a tall, plain form, and the chalice with paten cover.

Caudle cups persisted in New England, though they were now made in a bell shape and ornamented with gadrooning. Spout cups with straight necks were also typical, of globular shape with handle usually at a right angle to the spout.

In New York the distinctive two-handled punch bowl was still

*Porringer by Dummer, Boston.*
Albany Institute of History and Art.

being made. And porringers had begun to catch on there. New York examples boasted ornate handles very much in keeping with the lively baroque spirit of the period. In Boston and Philadelphia handle designs were cast in more restrained geometrical molds.

This period saw the beginning of the eighteenth-century trend toward a greater variety of specific objects for specific functions; in silver casters and dredgers for sugar, pepper and other spices, and pots for mustard we have several examples. Casters were cylindrical with flaring bases and pierced covers often topped by a finial. Spice dredgers were smaller, about four inches high, with a scroll handle and a domed top that was flatter and less

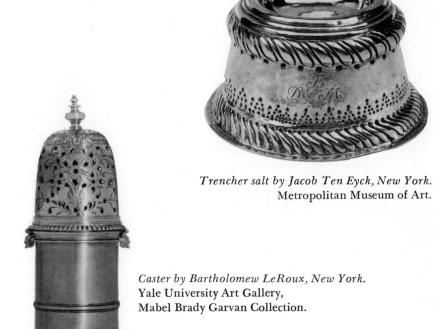

*Trencher salt by Jacob Ten Eyck, New York.*
Metropolitan Museum of Art.

*Caster by Bartholomew LeRoux, New York.*
Yale University Art Gallery,
Mabel Brady Garvan Collection.

elaborately pierced than caster tops. The standing salt, of spool shape with prongs on top to keep a protective napkin or plate from lying directly on the salt, continued to be made in this period— though it was joined by the simpler round trencher salt.

Among the most ambitious productions were two-handled covered cups, monteiths with notched rims for the suspension of wine glasses, and sugar boxes. This last form, of which fewer than

*Embossed sugar box by John Coney, Boston.*
Museum of Fine Arts, Boston.

a dozen examples—all from New England—survive, were very elaborately embossed and otherwise ornamented oval boxes with hinged lids and four little feet.

Another important group is that of pots for chocolate, tea and coffee. These vessels showed Oriental influence in their shapes—a trend which was to increase greatly during the next period. Chocolate pots were often of a somewhat stiff pear shape with curved

*Chocolate pot by Edward Winslow, Boston.*
Metropolitan Museum.

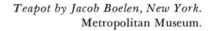

*Teapot by Jacob Boelen, New York.*
Metropolitan Museum.

spout and removable finial to facilitate the stirring of the beverage while it was in the pot. Teapots were modeled on Chinese hot-water pots of globular shape with straight spouts.

Salvers retained the trumpet foot of the seventeenth century and were frequently decorated on rim and foot with gadrooned bands. Also similar to their seventeenth-century predecessors were candlesticks, showing architectural influence in their columnar stems and square or octagonal bases. Since so very few silver candlesticks have survived from the Colonial period, candlesticks are illustrated here more often in the brass and pewter section than with the silver.

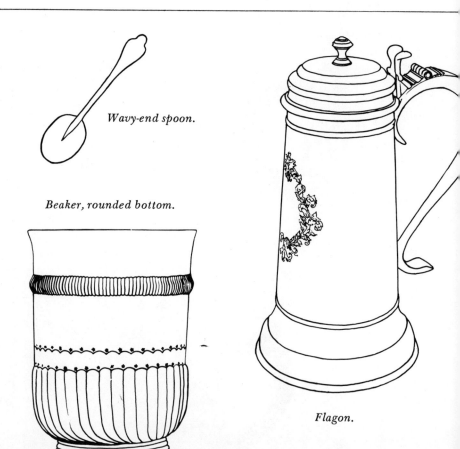

*Wavy-end spoon.*

*Beaker, rounded bottom.*

*Flagon.*

By 1715 the Queen Anne style had superseded the William and Mary, and the pear shape became a favorite. Some of the forms included here show Queen Anne influence, but a full discussion of the style and more complete illustrations may be found in the following section. American silversmiths of the 1700–1725 period include John Allen, John Burt, William Cowell, John Edwards and John Noyes of Boston; Cornelius Kierstede, Charles LeRoux, Bartholomew Schaats, Simeon Soumain, Peter van Dyck and Benjamin Wynkoop of New York; Samuel Vernon of Newport; and Johannis Nys, Francis Richardson and Philip Syng, Sr., of Philadelphia.

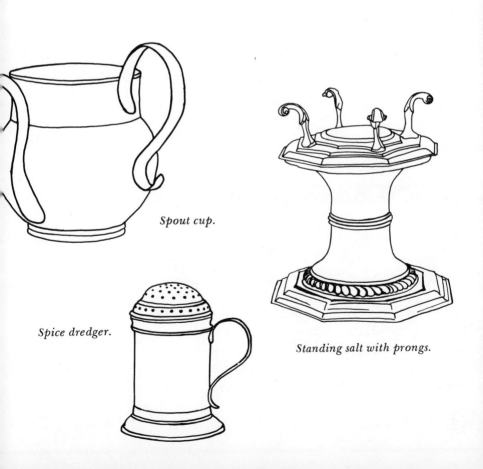

*Spout cup.*

*Spice dredger.*

*Standing salt with prongs.*

English silversmiths of the time were working in the Queen Anne style, but their products were much more elaborately ornamented than those of Colonial smiths. Sophisticated forms were being developed to accommodate the affluent Englishman at teatime, over the punch bowl and at the dinner table.

Paul de Lamerie recorded his first mark in London in 1712. He is probably the most famous of the Huguenots who exerted such a lasting influence on English silver design, but the following list includes several other prominent smiths of Huguenot stock: Augustine Courtauld, Louis Cugny, Peter Harrache, Lewis Mettayer, Anthony Nelme, Simon Pantin, Humphrey Payne, Pierre Platel, Benjamin Pyne and David Willaume.

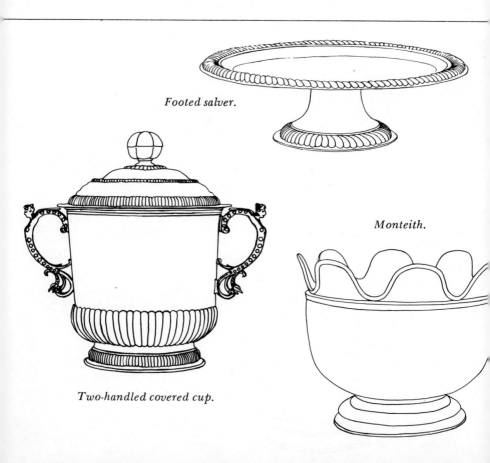

*Footed salver.*

*Monteith.*

*Two-handled covered cup.*

# Ceramics

"Every one Incourages the Growth and manufactures of this Country and not one person but discourages the Trade from home, and says 'tis pitty any goods should be brought from England," said one Bostonian in 1718. Despite the Colonists' convictions or intentions, however, they continued to use imported ceramics except for kitchen, dairy and other traditional utilitarian wares, instead of encouraging native potters to experiment with more sophisticated materials and forms.

Very appropriate to the interest in surface variation characteristic of these years was the use of Dutch tiles to decorate fireplaces. "Square Dutch tiles to be set in chimneys" were advertised in a Colonial newspaper as early as 1716.

Blue and white no longer dominated delftware. Other bright colors began to appear on English delft, adding reds, greens, purples and yellows to the formerly restricted palette of the potter. This was due to increased exposure to Chinese porcelains, whose varied color schemes, shapes and decorative motifs were imitated with enthusiasm if not strict accuracy by English makers of delftware. The use of *trek,* a dark blue-green outline filled in with lighter colors, was borrowed from the Dutch around the turn of the century, and is found on wares of the following ten or 20 years.

Plates and dishes of round, octagonal and scalloped or wavy-edged shape are the most common delft forms of the period. Although they are now rare, pots for tea, coffee and chocolate, as well as the cups for these beverages, sugar bowls, creamers, tea cad-

*Jug, delft, polychrome
decoration; Bristol, England.*
Colonial Williamsburg Foundation.

*Posset pot, slipware
with applied molded ornament,
mottled glaze; Staffordshire, England.*
Nelson Gallery–Atkins Museum,
Burnap Collection.

dies, sauceboats, tureens and other drinking and dining accessories were made in delft. Punch bowls (which succeeded posset pots) with ladles, and monteiths were made, as were labels to be hung round the necks of wine bottles. Bricks, puzzle jugs and straight-sided mugs continued to be produced.

In 1710 Liverpool joined the major delftware potteries of Lambeth and Bristol, and the newcomer soon replaced Lambeth as Bristol's chief rival.

*Dish, combed ware, Staffordshire.*
Victoria and Albert Museum.

*Jug, salt-glazed stoneware
with double walls; outer wall
pierced and sgraffito-decorated;
Nottingham, England.*
Nelson Gallery–Atkins Museum,
Burnap Collection.

*Mug, brown salt-glazed stoneware, by
John Dwight of Fulham; English.*
Nelson Gallery–Atkins Museum,
Burnap Collection.

Lead-glazed earthenwares were still in demand for practical forms, and those with trailed slip decoration made in Staffordshire continued outstanding. The Toft wares of the previous century changed character slightly about 1700. Tulips and formal flowers became popular motifs along with impressed geometrical patterns. A new process involved working semiliquid clays of different colors into a pattern with a brush or stick to create feathered and combed designs. Posset pots, jugs, cups or mugs, jugs in the form of

*Tea set, hard-paste porcelain,*
*chinoiserie decoration by J. G. Herold, Meissen.*
Ralph Wark.

an owl, and dishes are some of the main forms on which combing can be found.

Charming Staffordshire *sgraffito* wares, decorated with animals and foliage, were one of the earthenware types of this period. Mugs, dishes and posset pots were common forms of this genre.

Also produced in Staffordshire at the time were brown and white salt-glazed stonewares. White stonewares, when carefully and thinly potted, were highly regarded, and served as a substitute

*Plate. China Trade porcelain,*
*armorial design.*
Ex coll. William Martin-Hurst.

for porcelain. The "white" stoneware was really buff color with a strong, thin, somewhat pebbly glaze. Some examples are sprigged, or ornamented with designs in relief formed by applying wet stamped clay decorations to the surface of the piece.

Nottingham was a center for a distinctive type of stoneware which was finely made of various shades of brown and often decorated with incised inscriptions and flower designs. Stamped patterns were also used and, more rarely, molded and applied designs. Among the Nottingham forms is an unusual group of jugs in the form of a bear with a shaggy coat of applied bits of clay.

In France the search for the secret of true porcelain con-

*Delft bowl with chinoiserie; Liverpool, England.*

*White salt-glazed posset pot, Staffordshire.*

tinued. The factory at St. Cloud, the first important French porcelain works, was granted a patent for soft paste in 1702. The soft paste of St. Cloud is of an unusual ivory color, often decorated with applied molded fruit, flower and leaf motifs. Faïence was made at St. Cloud, too, as it was at Marseilles where factories flourished from 1700, and at Strasbourg, an important center after 1720.

An event of great importance in the development of Western ceramics in general, though it had no immediate bearing on ceramics in the Colonies, was Johann Friedrich Böttger's creation of the first European hard-paste porcelain. Though Böttger's

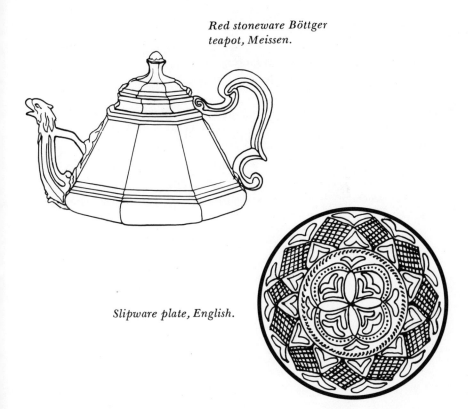

*Red stoneware Böttger teapot, Meissen.*

*Slipware plate, English.*

original formula was somewhat different, true, or hard-paste, porcelain is made of china clay (kaolin) and china stone (petuntse). When glazed and fired at a high temperature, these elements take on a hard, vitreous, translucent appearance. Böttger perfected his ware in the first decade of the eighteenth century, and it was manufactured at the Meissen factory, founded by 1710 specifically to produce hard-paste porcelain. About the same time Böttger also developed his famous red stoneware, an extremely hard material that took a very high polish and was sometimes engraved by lapidaries and glass engravers. Applied molded decoration was also employed.

Böttger was placed at the head of the Meissen factory, and he encountered many problems—related both to technique and to personnel. Among them was the defection of two workers to Vienna, where by 1719 they had initiated Claude Innocent du Paquier into the mysteries of porcelain making and assisted him in the founding of a porcelain factory. That same year, 1719, Böttger died and the gifted artist Johann Gregor Herold succeeded him as director of the Meissen factory. Herold introduced a new range of enamel colors as well as many new decorative styles and motifs, and it was during his directorship that Meissen porcelain achieved much of its fame.

Porcelain from China was still coveted by Europeans and continued to be imported by the East India companies. Some of these wares, including those decorated with the then popular armorial designs, found their way to the Colonies.

# Glass

There is no record of glasshouses in America in this period, but it is very likely that window glasses and bottles were being made at factories established earlier. Other forms were probably also made, but there are no datable artifacts to tell us what they would have been.

Fine glasswares were imported, mainly from England. There glassmakers were working the new lead glass into shapes that owed very little to contemporary European fashions in glass. Wineglasses were the commonest form, although the monteith, punch bowl, cordial glass, dram glass and decanter were also then made in glass as well as in ceramics and silver.

Shapes were often, in fact, similar to those in silver, and their simple, rather massive lines were complementary to the heavy, dark, "oily"-appearing lead glass. The usual wineglass or goblet shape was that with a conical, rounded or waisted (incurved) bowl, and a solid baluster or knopped stem. The combinations in which balusters (a symmetrical carrot shape) and knops were used in the stems of "heavy baluster" glasses, as the characteristic form of this period is called, were innumerable, so that while the same few elements were always present, one glass can easily be differentiated from another. Feet were plain, folded (these had their edges turned under), domed, or folded and domed.

A unique English contribution was that of enclosing air bubbles or "tears" in baluster stems. The single tear was earliest, but as the century went on several tears were often enclosed within one stem.

*Wineglass, domed and folded foot, stem with acorn knop, conical bowl, English.*

*Wineglass, tear-drop stem, waisted bowl, English.*

*Beaker, wheel engraved, Bohemian.*
Photo Robert M. Vetter.

Whereas English glass was distinguished by the combination of a beautiful metal (glass substance) and shapes whose proportions were simple and eminently suited to their material and function, German glass was almost always embellished with enameled or engraved ornament. Neither technique was widely practiced in England until, with the Treaty of Utrecht (1713) and the accession of George I (1714), the German art of engraving and cutting began to spread slowly in England. The most effective

*Bowl echoing silver and delftware shapes, diamond-point engraving; English.* London Museum.

*Bottles with enamel painting,*
*type made for modest citizens of*
*eighteenth-century Germany.*
Photo Gustav Pazaurek.

English engraving seems to have been simple flowers, fruit or border scrolls, rather than the elaborate scenes and designs found on the finest German glass.

Toward the end of the seventeenth century Bohemia had taken the lead in the production of a finer metal than had previously been made on the Continent. It was similar to the English glass of lead, but "the German metal, which was made without lead, had none of the sensuous beauty of the English" (W. B. Honey, *Glass: A Handbook*). Even so, it was of excellent quality and lent itself especially well to engraving. Wheel-engraved designs employing flowers, foliage and strapwork were skillfully executed by artists—mostly anonymous—in Bavaria, Brandenburg and Silesia particularly. In Nuremburg, Georg Friedrich Killinger carried on the Lehmann-Schwanhardt tradition of beautifully

*Goblet, wheel-engraved, Bohemian.*
Photo Robert M. Vetter.

engraved scenes and landscapes. Less sophisticated ornament, such as the flowers and figures engraved on Bohemian glass for sale at country markets and for export, was also produced.

Enameling, too, appeared in simple and sophisticated versions. Intricate scenes, views and armorial designs decorated the finest pieces, while floral and wildlife subjects sketched in blues, reds, yellows and greens brightened unpretentious tumblers and bottles. These simple but decorative items were the prototypes of wares made later in this country.

*1725-1750*

*The*

*Queen Anne Style*

*Boston had a busy,*
*prosperous air in the early eighteenth century.*
Whaling Museum, New Bedford, Mass.

# Historical Background

With the hardships of survival and adjustment to a new world a century behind them, the Colonists continued in the second quarter of the eighteenth century to expand into unsettled territory. Adventurous Europeans as well as pioneering Americans formed new settlements and developed new institutions in ever greater numbers, gradually colonizing and civilizing the eastern seaboard of the new continent. James Oglethorpe's establishment of the first permanent settlement in Georgia, 1733, was followed by the founding of two new communities in Pennsylvania: a religious settlement at Ephrata (where a paper mill and printing press were shortly set up) and a group of Moravians at Bethlehem. As older communities developed and flourished, several new kinds of services became available: the first stagecoach was put into operation between Boston and New York, and in Philadelphia Benjamin Franklin founded a circulating subscription library and a fire company. Among literary landmarks were Franklin's *Poor Richard's Almanack* (1732) and Dr. Alexander Hamilton's *Itinerarium* (1744), describing his trip from Annapolis to New England

and New York (Dr. Hamilton was no relation to the first Secretary of the United States Treasury). Contemplative Philadelphians found congenial companionship at the American Philosophic Society, another brainchild of Ben Franklin.

Peaceful progress was interrupted in some areas by a series of wars among Spain, France and England, involving the Colonies and the West Indies, but by and large this was a period of continuing cultural and material achievement. From Boston to Charleston, a wealthy upper class boasted houses, furnishings, food and drink rivaling the amenities of their European counterparts. Just below them in the social structure, a numerous middle class of sturdy, self-reliant men were steadily improving their condition. And in the background, frontiersmen moved warily into the interior, anticipating the post-Revolution wave of westward-bound settlers.

In contrast to all this forward-looking New World activity, excavation of the ruins at Herculaneum and Pompeii was stimulating the revival of classical art in Europe and England. Under the spell of the nearly 2,000-year-old ruins, artistic Europeans began turning from the present to re-create the splendors of ancient Greece and Rome.

# Development of the Style

The style that had grown up in England during the reign of Queen Anne (1702–1714) did not really take hold in the Colonies until roughly 1725. Then it continued dominant until about 1750, and even for years thereafter the simpler Queen Anne remained popular in small towns and among those who did not try to be first in fashion.

While many William and Mary forms were carried over into the Queen Anne period, they were transformed from relatively large-scale, ornate pieces into lighter, curvier ones. Surface ornament gave way to plain surfaces sparingly ornamented, the impact now deriving from gracefully curving outlines rather than ornament. The S curve, the main theme of the Queen Anne period, can be traced through all the decorative arts; it is seen in vase-shape splats of chair backs, in cabriole legs, in the pear form so popular for ceramic and silver vessels and in the undulating scallops ornamenting trays and tabletops—to mention just a few examples. Probably the most popular decorative motif was the scallop shell, which, in its classic elegance and simplicity, sums up the Queen Anne period.

*Decorative objects of the Queen Anne period
arranged in a contemporary setting.*
Bayou Bend Collection, Museum of Fine Arts of Houston.

The Oriental influences that appeared in the William and Mary period increased, and chinoiserie decoration is typical of Queen Anne art as well. The tea-drinking public was expanding, and as coffee, chocolate and punch were also favorite beverages, equipment for preparing and serving them was in great demand. Chinese prototypes provided models for pots and other vessels.

The simple though sophisticated outlines of decorative arts of the Queen Anne era have charmed collectors for decades. The combination of skilled craftsmanship with uncomplicated shapes and ornaments seems to represent for many the spirit of America.

# Furniture

Cabinetmakers of the William and Mary period had begun to move away from the ages-old concept of furniture as architectural in structure and appearance, and strictly practical in function. Queen Anne cabinetmakers completed the move by combining utility, comfort and grace with outstanding success.

There were not a great many new forms in the Queen Anne period, but the ones that had appeared in the previous quarter century were transformed by the new style, and many acquired the look they would retain throughout the Chippendale period. General characteristics of American Queen Anne furniture were the use of native woods such as walnut, maple, cherry and bilsted (gumwood), for mahogany had not yet come into wide use; the substitution of carving, painting and japanning for extensive veneering; and the use of the cabriole leg and the pad foot (or variations such as the slipper and trifid foot). There was also, as in every period, a good deal of transitional furniture; in the early years William and Mary characteristics were sometimes combined with Queen Anne, and in the closing years Chippendale features began to appear.

Typical forms, which helped to create for the affluent Colonist surroundings as luxurious (if not so ornate) as those of his European contemporary, included pieces of varying functions. The tea table was one of the most important, for, like Dr. Samuel Johnson, many a Colonist "with tea amuses the evening, with tea solaces the midnight, and with tea welcomes the morning." Tea tables were made mainly in two shapes: the rectangular dished- or tray-top variety, with a molded rim to prevent teacups from slipping; and the round table with tripod base, sometimes with a bird-cage attachment which permitted the top to be revolved and tilted to a

*Rectangular tea table
with dished top, New England.*

*Tripod tea table
with bird-cage attachment,
New York.*

vertical position. This latter style was to achieve even greater popularity in the Chippendale period. Gateleg tables, those admirable space savers, were replaced in the Queen Anne period by tidy drop-leaf tables, often large enough to be used for dining. The card table with folding top was an innovation in the Queen Anne period, reflecting another popular new pastime, but it, too, was more frequently made in the succeeding period. Other types were marble-topped center and side tables; the smaller "handkerchief" table, a variant of the drop leaf usually used as a breakfast table; and such small occasional tables as the candlestand.

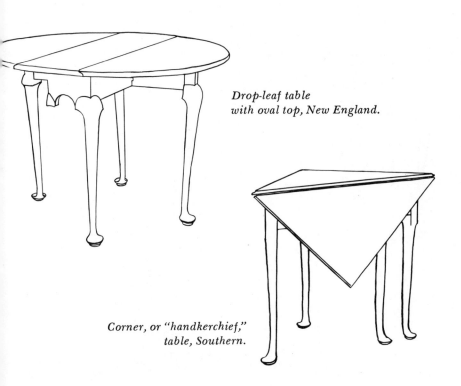

*Drop-leaf table
with oval top, New England.*

*Corner, or "handkerchief,"
table, Southern.*

It was in the Queen Anne period that the high chest of drawers, or highboy, took on the characteristics by which we now recognize it as a typical American form, with its scrolled pediment and carved shells on upper and lower center drawers. Lowboys, or dressing tables, also took the form that they retained until the end of the Chippendale period. The secretary, or desk and bookcase, replaced its flat William and Mary top with a pediment of broken scrolls—becoming another form that endured throughout the next period. The slant-top desk gradually succeeded the desk on frame, and it, too, persisted during the Chippendale epoch.

*Dressing table, or lowboy, Philadelphia.*

*Slant-top desk on frame with boldly scalloped skirt, Connecticut.*

Seventeenth-century chests and cupboards were superseded by corner cupboards, either built in or free standing. Such cupboards not only were attractive architectural adjuncts, but also served the important purpose of providing a showcase for imported ceramics. The shell cupboard, with brightly colored shell top and three or four shaped shelves, is typical of the Queen Anne era. Other variants were dressers and china cupboards—less elegant than shell cupboards, but equally serviceable—and the *kas,* a Dutch wardrobe made in New York and New Jersey from the seventeenth century.

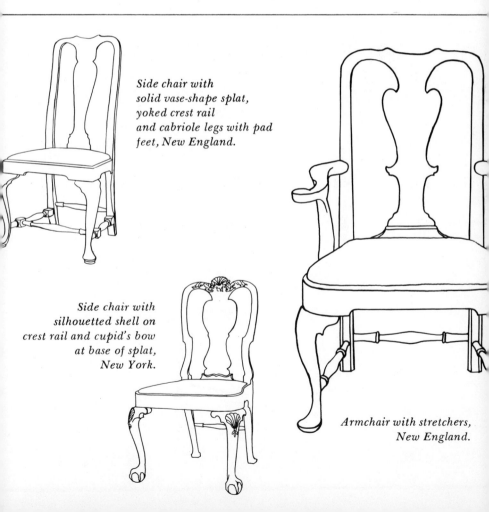

*Side chair with solid vase-shape splat, yoked crest rail and cabriole legs with pad feet, New England.*

*Side chair with silhouetted shell on crest rail and cupid's bow at base of splat, New York.*

*Armchair with stretchers, New England.*

A typical Queen Anne looking glass was the pier glass made to hang on a pier, the wall space between two windows. Because of their height, and because large sheets of glass were not available until later, pier glasses were made with two pieces of glass, one above the other. Silvered glass was imported from Europe throughout the eighteenth century, as were many frames, which are often impossible to distinguish from those made in America.

The chair is perhaps the form in which all the attributes of the Queen Anne style are most readily apparent: the recurving

*Side chair with hooped back and paneled trifid feet, Philadelphia.*

*Corner, or "roundabout," chair Philadelphia.*

*Armchair with fiddle-back splat, Philadelphia.*

line that typifies the style can be seen in the entire outline with its spooned back, seat gracefully blending into front legs and back uprights, and hooped or gently rounded rectangular back. These curves are repeated in the vase-shape splat (copied from Chinese vases), cabriole legs and crest rail. The chair is also the form in which it is easiest to perceive regional differences, which began to show themselves now, though not so markedly as they would in the Chippendale period. New England examples were slender with graceful outlines and very little ornament. Those of New York were well-proportioned and worldly, combining structural

*Secretary with carving very like that of seventeenth-century Connecticut Valley chests, cherry; Connecticut.* Henry Ford Musuem.

*Highboy with characteristic scrolled pediment and carved shells, mahogany, New England.* Privately owned.

elements borrowed from New England to the north and from Philadelphia to the south, so that they were neither so severe as those of New England nor so generously scrolled as those of Philadelphia. The silhouetted shell on crest rail and the cupid's bow at base of splat were other New York characteristics. Philadelphia chairs were richly curved and carved, often with shells, scrolls and volutes that repeated and refined the recurving lines of splat and legs. The paneled trifid foot was typical of Philadelphia, as was the elaborate fiddle-back splat. In Newport, a busy seaport which had not yet reached the height of its prominence as a regional

Kas, *cherry, New York or New Jersey.* Dey House, Wayne, N.J.

*Painted corner cupboard with shell top, filled with ceramics of the period.* Henry Ford Museum.

center, the chair might show the early use of the claw-and-ball foot or have a silhouetted shell on crest rail. Shells repeated on the knee were another favorite Newport device.

Besides armchairs and side chairs, others popular in this period were the corner chair, convenient to draw up to desk or secretary; and the easy, or wing, chair. Daybeds remained popular in the Queen Anne era, their backs and legs resembling those of contemporary chairs.

In the South in this period many plantation owners imported their best furniture from England, so that surviving examples that

*Pier glass with japanned chinoiserie decoration, New York.*
Winterthur Museum.

*Pier glass of a type often found in New England, walnut veneer and gilded gesso.*
Henry Ford Museum.

were locally made were of a very unpretentious nature. Some of the best-known furniture makers of other regions were John Pimm of Boston, Job Townsend of Newport, William Savery of Philadelphia, and John Gaines of Portsmouth, New Hampshire. Clockmakers included Benjamin Bagnall of Boston, William and Thomas Claggett of Newport, and Peter and Thomas Stretch of Philadelphia.

Toward the beginning of this period English cabinetmakers were working in the early Georgian style, with William Kent setting the trend for architectural outlines and motifs. By 1730, in

*Side chair with silhouetted shell on crest rail and early use of claw-and-ball foot, mahogany, Newport.*
Museum of Fine Arts, Boston.

*Side chair with transitional features, maple, attributed to John Gaines of New Hampshire.*
Metropolitan Museum of Art.

the mid-Georgian era, mahogany had supplanted walnut. Typical forms were the commode (chest of drawers), bureau (desk), and console table—pieces that lent themselves well to the use of claw-and-ball, paw, and ogee-bracket feet, and bold ornaments in the shapes of masks and shells. Gilt gesso and parcel (partial) gilding supplemented carving in imparting an architectural look. In 1740 Matthias Lock's *New Drawing Book* illustrated rococo details, foreshadowing the style that was to dominate English furniture for the next few decades—the style that we have come to call "Chippendale."

*Tall clock, Philadelphia.*
Mrs. Thomas D. Thacher.

*Easy, or wing,*
*chair with stretchers,*
*New England.*
Henry Ford Museum.

# *Silver*

With silver, as with furniture, "Queen Anne" is a stylistic rather than a historical designation, for the style did not become dominant in America until after the death of Queen Anne. The new fashion in silver did precede that in furniture by a full ten years, however, possibly because it was easier to carry a piece or two of currently fashionable plate from England to America than a desk or chair. A more compelling reason is that last year's plate could always be melted and reworked in this year's style, while furniture was not so amenable.

The switch from the highly ornamented silver of the William and Mary period to the simplicity of the Queen Anne is said to be partly due to the requirement, in effect in England from 1697 to 1720, that silver plate meet the Britannia standard. This meant that the alloy used in the manufacture of plate had to have a higher percentage of pure silver than formerly and that the metal was therefore softer. So the elaborate embossing of the previous period was no longer practical, and ornament became subservient to form.

Generally speaking, the pear shape was the favorite, sometimes in combination with the same cabriole leg that graced furniture of the period. Chinese teapot and teacup shapes were extremely well liked, too, and served as models for a variety of forms. Objects of the period were often octagonal, especially in New York, where Dutch prototypes had made the shape familiar and welcome.

Engraved ornament was perfectly suited to chaste Queen Anne forms, and the silversmiths and engravers of the period achieved an extraordinary degree of proficiency in this art. Heraldic devices continued to appear on silver for identification as well as decoration, but their designs owed more to the ingenuity of the engraver and less to traditional patterns than formerly. Another popular motif for engraving was the cipher, or monogram and its reverse worked into an intricate design. Sympson's *New Book of Cyphers,* published in England in 1732, provided British and Colonial smiths and engravers with a useful source. Cut-card work, in which ornaments were stamped or cut from sheets of flat silver and applied to the surface of the object they were made to decorate, was another technique of the period, though it is not frequently seen on American silver. There was an increased use of cast elements in Queen Anne silver, too; such things as handles and spouts and candlesticks could much more easily be cast in molds than worked by hand.

New forms were not so important in this period as new shapes, most of the necessary pieces having evolved in the William and Mary period. The commonest piece of flatware was still the spoon, which now had a rounded end with pronounced center ridge on the front and a rattail on the back. About 1730 the rattail was replaced by a double drop or shell just below the back of the bowl. The strainer spoon, or mote spoon, made its appearance in this period; it had a pierced bowl so that it could be used to skim leaves from the surface of tea.

Tea was not the only exotic item that became more common as the eighteenth century progressed: salt, too, grew less scarce, and the ceremonial standing salt of the seventeenth century was replaced by a smaller, less pretentious receptacle called the "trencher salt." One was meant to be placed near the trencher, or plate, of each diner.

The two-handled covered cup was the most imposing form of the period and was often commissioned as a presentation piece. Because of their value and importance, cups like these were fre-

*Octagonal bowl, decorated with engraved cipher, by Joseph Richardson, Philadelphia.* Privately owned.

*Great spoon with rounded, ridged handle and double drop on back.* Privately owned.

*Can, or mug, with rounded bottom an cast double-scroll handle, by Myer Myers, New York.* Ex coll. John D. Kernan, Jr.

quently presented or bequeathed to churches and have thus been preserved. The characteristic form was a bell-shape body with two strap handles and a molded foot.

Porringers, developed early and made by generations of silversmiths, were gaining in popularity throughout the Colonies. They were used for porridge and similar food, and by 1725 the familiar keyhole type (so called because of the shape of the scroll at the

*Cream jug with pear-shape body and cast legs and handle, by Adrian Bancker, New York.* Mrs. Arthur Lenssen; photo Museum of the City of New York.

*Sauceboat with cabriole legs, by William Swan, Worcester, Massachusetts.* Worcester Art Museum.

*Chafing dish with pierced decoration, by Jacob Hurd, Boston.* Mrs. John Wells Farley.

handle end) was made everywhere, though an earlier three-hole type continued to be made in New York. Useful in the feeding of infants or invalids was the spout cup, which adapted itself very well to the pear shape. The caster, too, in sets of three for the serving of pepper, dry mustard and sugar, was made in pear form.

Cans (or mugs) and tankards must have been made in large quantities, for many have survived. Tankards reflect especially well the regional differences that also began to assert themselves in furniture in this period. The New England example can be recognized by its marked verticality, flattened-dome lid, flame or bell

*Tray, or salver, with scrolled rim and engraved heraldic device, by Jacob Hurd, Boston.* Museum of Fine Arts, Boston.

finial, and horizontal rib just below the middle of the body. Generosity of proportion characterized New York crafts of all sorts, but nothing illustrates this better than the tankard. Its lines are broad, its girth ample and its appearance solidly handsome. The flat top, corkscrew thumbpiece and applied leaf border are other characteristic features. Philadelphia tankards are closest in appearance to London examples, having a domed lid topping a tapering body, no finial and occasionally a middle band. By 1730 the base of the Philadelphia tankard was rounded and its handle had become a double scroll, foreshadowing the rococo.

*Small box, Boston.*
Photo Parke–Bernet Galleries, Inc.

*Tea caddy, one of a pair*
*by Thauvet Besley, New York.*
Museum of the City of New York.

The lantern shape was well liked for coffee and chocolate pots, though chocolate was apparently losing favor as a beverage. Chocolate pots frequently had spout and handle at right angles to each other, an arrangement also occasionally found on coffeepots.

One of the loveliest contemporary forms was the chafing dish, which had been introduced in the preceding period. Made apparently mainly in Boston in the first half of the eighteenth century, this form is a fine example of the proficiency of America's best silversmiths, with its beautifully pierced pan and gracefully curving frame section. It was used to keep dishes and teapots hot. Another attractive serving piece was the sauceboat, new in this period. Like the chafing dish, it reflects a growing refinement in dining accessories.

*Ladle with turned wooden handle.*

*Two-handled covered cup
with bell-shape body.*

In addition to all these items, the Queen Anne smith had the fashioning of all sorts of paraphernalia for tea to keep him busy. New York continued to prefer the sturdy pear-shape pot throughout the period, but this was superseded in Boston by the globular pot based on ceramic examples from China. This type might have a single scroll handle, S-curve spout, low molded foot and set-in cover. Other necessities were the cream jug and sugar dish, the first usually pyriform, or pear shape, and the second modeled on the China tea bowl, or cup. The cream jug was at first set on a low molded foot but later mounted on jaunty cabriole legs. The sugar dish rose from a narrow band or foot to a very delicately flared rim. The teakettle, for hot water, was made in the same shapes as the teapot, but it is a great rarity in American silver. The tea

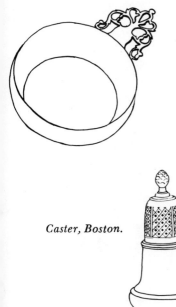

*Porringer with keyhole-design handle.*

*Caster, Boston.*

*Tankard with domed lid, flame finial and rib just below mid-body, Massachusetts.*

caddy, which came in a set of three—two for tea and one for sugar—was another elegant appurtenance, though complete sets are also extremely rare in American work. Spoons and such utensils as sugar tongs completed the Queen Anne tea service.

The tray, or salver, used on the tea table and elsewhere, too, evolved in this period from the footed variety of the William and Mary period to the elegant scroll-edge type that is related to the piecrust table of the Chippendale era.

Silversmiths produced many objects besides those intended for domestic use, including such personal items as knee and shoe buckles, rings, buttons, lockets, thimbles and small boxes for snuff and tobacco. Sword hilts also offered a challenge to the silversmith's ingenuity.

*Tankard with flat top, corkscrew thumbpiece and applied leaf border, New York.*

*Teapot with wooden scroll handle and cast polygonal spout, New York.*

Most of the silver illustrated here is simple in outline and ornament, but as midcentury approached, silverwork took on many characteristics of the rococo. This increased embellishment coincided with a general growth in prosperity: articles of silver became available to a larger segment of the Colonial population, and craftsmen began to appear in smaller towns and cities, making it unnecessary to send to Boston or New York for well-wrought plate. In Albany, for example, were Jacob and Barent Ten Eyck; in Connecticut, Cornelius Kierstede and John Potwine, who migrated from New York and Boston respectively. Naturally, the leading seaport cities continued to produce the majority of fine silversmiths: Boston was the home of Jacob Hurd, Knight Leverett, John Potwine (until he moved to Connecticut) and Paul

*Teapot with globular body and flat set-in top, Boston.*

*Two ciphers from S. Sympson's* A NEW BOOK OF CYPHERS, *1732.* New York Public Library.

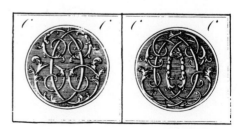

Revere, Sr.; while in New York Adrian Bancker, Henricus Boelen, Peter Quintard and Peter Vergereau were at work. Philadelphia, founded only in the last quarter of the seventeenth century, had grown rapidly and could boast excellent craftsmen almost from the beginning. From 1725 to 1750 Elias Boudinot, Philip Syng, Jr., and William Vilant were leading silversmiths there.

England in this period was moving ahead to new styles in silver, as in the other decorative arts. The Queen Anne style was succeeded about 1730 by the simple early Georgian, which lasted only ten years, giving way about 1740 to the rococo. Scrolls, dolphins, scallop shells, embossed chinoiserie and mythical figures relieved silver of its previous simplicity and set it to dancing on tea and dining tables. Huguenots continued to exert the dominant influence, and Paul de Lamerie still led London silversmiths, among whom were also Courtauld, Pantin, Peter Archambo and William Fawdery. In Sheffield in 1743 Thomas Boulsover discovered that copper and silver could be fused, rolled into sheets and worked like solid silver to create the material we know as Sheffield plate.

# Ceramics

At their best Queen Anne silver and furniture reflect the artistry and taste of Colonial craftsmen, but there was no similar development in the field of ceramics until much later. American Colonists ordered their best china from England and relied on native potters for everyday wares only. Tea, which had inspired an abundance of new forms in silver and furniture, gave even greater impetus to potters and porcelain makers, who adopted Chinese shapes and produced charming chinoiserie decoration. The work of English potters increased greatly in variety at this time, ranging from ordinary plates and dishes to fancifully molded teapots and ornamental groups.

English delft forms characteristic of the period include tea wares, punch bowls and "bricks" (rectangular flower holders). Another popular item was the puzzle jug, in whose neck holes were cut to give rise to such challenges as, "Here, gentlemen, come try your skill/I'll hold a wager if you will,/That you drink not this liquor all,/Without you spill or let some fall." The solution was to plug all the holes except the one to be drunk from. Delft ornament was now sometimes painted on a powder ground—that is, a ground with a speckled appearance obtained by blowing colored powder onto an oiled surface. The established makers of delftware were joined in this period by a pottery at Wincanton, Somerset, which produced delft from 1737.

Among the earthenwares of Staffordshire were two similar types known as "variegated wares," because of their mottled surfaces. In one type, called "agateware," this effect was achieved

*Salt-glazed stoneware teapot, scratch-blue decoration, English.*

*Stoneware pot and redware jug, New England.*

*Redware pot with incised decoration, New England.*
Smithsonian Institution.

with the use of mixed clays of different colors under a clear glaze; the name of potter John Astbury is often associated with agateware. In the other type the streaked or mottled look was due to the use of a variety of colored glazes over clay of a single color. Both types were used in the making of tablewares, both are found with sprigged ornament, and both were often fashioned into "image toys": figures of characters indigenous to the English countryside, such as musicians and soldiers. Thomas Whieldon, an extremely

*Redware plate with slip decoration, probably southeastern Massachusetts.* Smithsonian Institution.

*Delft puzzle jug, white with blue decoration; Bristol, England.* Museum of Fine Arts, Boston.

*Salt-glazed stoneware jug, gray with blue decoration and molded stamp, Germany.* Privately owned.

successful and influential potter of the time, founded his own factory at Fenton Low in Staffordshire in 1740, turning out a great variety of wares and introducing many technical improvements. Among his best-known productions before 1750 were tortoise shell (so called because of the colors and effect of the glazes used) and agateware.

Salt-glazed stoneware, also important in this period, was often molded into unusual shapes and polychromed, to make a wealth

*Delft plate with powder-blue ground on rim, Bristol.*
Photo D. M. & P. Manheim.

of imaginative articles of either a useful or a purely decorative nature. Besides tablewares and tea wares, there were, for example, the pew groups and so-called arbor groups of Staffordshire, stiff little seated figures with a naïve appeal. They are related to the previously mentioned image toys also made in Staffordshire as decorations, indicating the trend away from the strictly practical that had dominated the seventeenth century.

Soft-paste porcelain, found in the Colonies less often than

*Delft dish, chinoiserie decoration in polychrome, Bristol.*
Colonial Williamsburg Foundation.

earthenware and stoneware, was made in Chelsea from 1745 and in Bristol from 1748.

In addition to these English ceramics, German salt-glazed stoneware and Dutch Delft, the latter usually in the form of tiles, were imported for Colonial use. The stoneware, gray with blue decoration and molded ornament, was made in Germany for export to the English market and was apparently in daily use in the Colonies. The tiles, decorated in blue, purple or polychrome, were occasionally used for tabletops, but most often they were set into fireplaces, where they contrasted attractively with the painted or polished wood of the mantel.

*Delft punch bowl, polychrome decoration, England.* Colonial Williamsburg.

*Delft brick, red and white, England.* Photo D. M. & P. Manheim.

*Pottery, principally Englis delft, displayed in a corner cupboar* Colonial Williamsbur

New England, New York, New Jersey and Pennsylvania all supported potters during this period. Their products were intended for use in the kitchen or dairy and were made in simple, pleasing shapes ornamented with bands of incised straight or wavy lines, or with trailed slip. Such pieces saw hard use, and as they were as easily broken as they were replaced, relatively few have survived to the present day. William Crolius and John Remmey I were makers of stoneware in New York; Adam Staats was making

*Salt-glazed stoneware pew group, Staffordshire, England.*
Nelson Gallery–Atkins Museum, Burnap Collection.

*Salt-glazed stoneware teapot,*
*Staffordshire.*
Cleveland Museum of Art.

redware in New Jersey; and in Pennsylvania the German settlers were producing *sgraffito* wares. New England continued as a center for the production of simple redware. In an entirely different direction, both geographically and stylistically, was Andrew Duché's venture in hard-paste porcelain making: he worked in Georgia around 1738–43, but apparently never developed a ware fine enough to market.

Although few examples reached the American Colonies, beau-

*Salt-glazed stoneware teapot with sprigged decoration, Staffordshire.* Nelson Gallery– Atkins Museum, Burnap Collection.

*Tortoise-shell-glazed cream jug, Staffordshire.* Art Institute of Chicago.

*Agateware plate, Staffordshire.* Nelson Gallery–Atkins Museum, Burnap Collection.

tiful ceramics were being produced in Europe during these years. In France charming objects were made in soft-paste porcelain at Chantilly from 1725, at Mennecy-Villeroy from 1732 and at Vincennes from 1745. Germany continued supreme in the manufacture of hard-paste (or true) porcelain: at Höchst from 1746 and at Nymphenburg from 1747. Meissen, where it had all begun, acquired the services of Johann Joachim Kändler, a talented sculp-

*Tortoise-shell-glazed image toys (bagpipers), Staffordshire.*
Nelson Gallery–Atkins Museum, Burnap Collection.

tor, in 1731. Outside these official production centers was the *Hausmaler* tradition, in which freelance artists decorated and sold articles cast off because of slight imperfections by the major factories; it continued to be important in German ceramics until 1760. Italy had a porcelain factory at Capo di Monte, where soft paste was produced from 1743.

Along with the rich output of European factories was the

*Soft-paste porcelain plate with painted decoration, Chelsea.* Photo W. B. Honey.

*Soft-paste porcelain coffeepot, Chelsea, England.* Photo D. M. & P. Manheim.

constant flow of ceramics from the East. This China trade porcelain arrived in the Colonies by way of England, for it was not until after the Revolutionary War that there was direct commerce between America and the Far East.

*China Trade teapot with painted decoration.*
Historic Deerfield, Inc.

*Delft tiles, Holland.*
Privately owned.

# *Glass*

Fine glasswares, when they appeared on Colonial tables of the Queen Anne period, were almost certain to be imported from England. American glass of the period is extremely rare, for what was produced commercially was still limited to bottles and window glass.

Although it is recorded that a glasshouse was operating in New York in 1732, the first glass factory of the eighteenth century to be a commercial success was begun by Caspar Wistar in southern New Jersey in 1739. From Wistar's establishment came not only bottles and windowpanes but also some offhand-blown tablewares, the first of what has come to be known as the "South Jersey type." These were useful items such as bowls, jars and pitchers in simple, pleasing shapes. They were made by the glassblowers on their own time, for their own families and neighbors, and since Wistar's workmen were imported from the Low Countries and western Germany, their products reflect German glassblowing traditions.

Characteristic of South Jersey wares is the use of relatively coarse bottle and window glass in greens and ambers for decorating as well as for making the body of the piece. The South Jersey type was made in several parts of the country throughout the eighteenth century and into the nineteenth, and is treated in greater detail in the 1800–1825 and 1825–1850 sections.

Most of the glass the English exported to the Colonies consisted of drinking vessels and decanters. English forms of the period, some of which were probably not exported, included a wide variety of glasses for spirituous beverages. Among the most

*Bowl, amber, South Jersey type.*
Privately owned.

*Wine or spirits bottles,*
*dark olive-green (black); example*
*at left is onion shape,*
*that at right bears the seal of*
*its original owner.*
Ex coll. George S. McKearin.

*Pitcher, yellow-green with*
*applied threading on neck and*
*crimping at base*
*of handle, South Jersey type.*
Ex coll. George S. McKearin.

*Covered sugar bowl,*
*deep green, South Jersey type,*
*possibly Wistar.*
Corning Museum of Glass.

popular were ratafia, a fruit-and-nut cordial served in a glass with a long stem and a narrow, tapering bowl, and syllabub, a type of milk-and-wine punch which in this period was often served in small jelly or syllabub glasses whose bowls rested on a knopped or collared foot; sometimes such glasses have one or two handles, and these may be referred to as "posset glasses." There were also sweet-meat glasses, occasionally called "champagne glasses," which were carefully made and ornamented footed bowls for serving desserts. Another fashionable way to end the meal was to serve dessert in a footed plate holding a sweetmeat glass surrounded by smaller jelly

*Sweetmeat glass, cut bowl and Silesian stem, polygonal with twisted ribs and bosses, English.* Victoria and Albert Museum.

or syllabub glasses; or a pyramid of footed plates of graduated sizes holding small dishes of various kinds of sweetmeats.

There was a good deal of variation in wineglass bowls, stems and decoration. Stems in the style often called "Silesian" achieved popularity upon the accession of George I in 1714; these were quite different from other stems because they were molded, the earliest into four-sided shapes. Later, the polygonal stem, sometimes twisted and vertically ribbed or reeded, became fashionable. Stems were either drawn out from the bowl or applied separately, and were sometimes decorated with spirals formed within the stem by

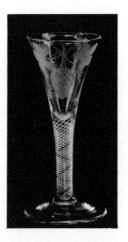

*"Flower'd" ale glass,*
*wheel-engraved hops-and-barley*
*motif and air-twist*
*stem, English.* Privately owned.

*Jacobite wineglass,*
*wheel-engraved carnation and roses,*
*knopped air-twist stem, English.*
Victoria and Albert Museum.

*Jacobite wineglass, wheel-engrav*
*portrait of Prince Charles Edwa*
*knopped air-twist stem, Engli*
Corning Museu

threads of air or of white or colored glass. These were called "air-," "cotton-," or "enamel-twist" stems.

With the accession of the Hanoverians and the reign of George I came the German decorative techniques of wheel engraving, cutting and diamond-point engraving. Diamond-point engraving was practiced with great skill by Frans Greenwood, working at this time in Holland. He is credited with inventing a process of stippling with diamond point which, according to W. B. Honey (*Glass: A Handbook*), can produce a result that "seems to rest like a scarcely perceptible film breathed upon the glass."

*Amen glass,*
*diamond-point engraving, English.*
Photo Arthur Churchill, Ltd.

Wineglasses with wheel-engraved grape-and-vine motifs and ale glasses with hops-and-barley motifs belong to a group called "flower'd glasses." Another popular engraved type was the Jacobite glass, decorated with one of many Jacobite symbols, such as a portrait of the Young Pretender, Prince Charles Edward; a Jacobite flower, such as the rose or carnation; or verses from the Jacobite hymn, ending always in the word "Amen," giving rise to the popular designation "Amen glasses."

Newcastle glasses, made at Newcastle-upon-Tyne, were another characteristic type of the period. They had rounded funnel-

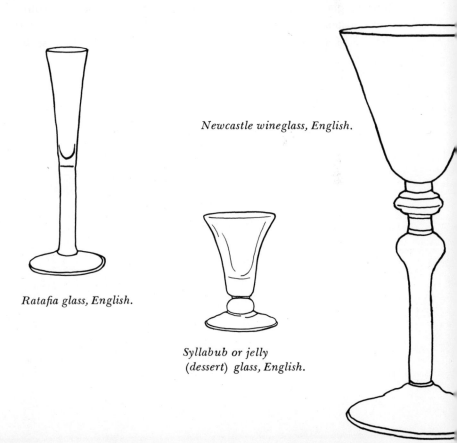

*Newcastle wineglass, English.*

*Ratafia glass, English.*

*Syllabub or jelly (dessert) glass, English.*

shape bowls and delicate baluster stems, often elaborately knopped.

Typical decanters were onion-shaped, like bottles, with squat bodies tapering to a narrow neck.

One of the most successful and charming uses for glass was in the making of sconces, candelabra and chandeliers based on brass examples of the time. The interplay between soft candle flames and the faceted glass of these devices creates a romantic—almost magic—atmosphere.

Though it would, of course, have been altered eventually by the growing popularity of the rococo style, the direction of English glassmaking was abruptly changed in 1745 with the passage of the Glass Excise Tax. This was a tax levied according to weight, forcing glassmakers to make their glass thinner and to concentrate instead on ornament. Thus the following period saw the demise of the simple, relatively heavy shapes, and the rise of a lighter, more richly decorated type of glass.

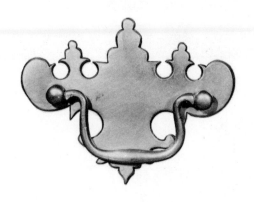

*1750-1775*
# The
# Chippendale Style

**THE BLOODY MASSACRE** *of March 5th 1770*
*"Engrav'd Printed & Sold"* by Paul Revere.
Historic Deerfield, Inc.

# Historical Background

England continued to expand her holdings in America—at the price of long and bitter conflict. The Seven Years' War in Europe spread to the New World as the French and Indian War (1754–1763), in which American Indians sided with the French against the British and their Colonists. Bloody battles were fought in many places along the frontier; one of the strategic points was at the forks of the Ohio River, where Pittsburgh now stands. The French were first to occupy the site, then called Fort Duquesne, from which they launched expeditions that defeated Washington at Great Meadows in 1754 and ambushed General Braddock's forces in 1755, fatally wounding the general. After 1758 British forces controlled the region from Fort Pitt, established near the site of Fort Duquesne. Finally, when Quebec fell to General Wolfe in 1759, the British gained Canada and the Midwest.

That war over, the alliance between Colonists and British grew weaker as the thriving Colonies chafed under increased trade restrictions and taxes such as the Stamp Act imposed by the Crown. Fierce opposition to taxation without representation led to the formation of Sons of Liberty groups and, in October 1765, to the Stamp Act Congress. Pressure from the Colonies finally forced repeal of the Stamp Act, but tensions persisted. The Boston Massacre and Tea Party expressed further hostility, which culminated in the First Continental Congress, held in Philadelphia in 1775.

As revolution brewed in the East, Daniel Boone was exploring Kentucky, and the Mason-Dixon Line was drawn between North and South. In 1752, a new (Gregorian) calendar was adopted in Britain and the Colonies. That same year Benjamin Franklin experimented with electricity; later he began his well-known autobiography (1771–1789).

Many institutions came into being in this period of expansion and growth: the Royal Academy was founded in London; a theater was established in New York City; Princeton, Dartmouth, Columbia, Brown, the University of Pennsylvania, and the Philadelphia Medical School were founded. And Shakers settled in New York State.

# Development of the Style

In spite of increasing political unrest, the Colonies prospered as the century progressed. Great houses were built, demanding the creation of appropriately elegant furnishings, and artisans both here and abroad were only too happy to comply. As in all periods, the new styles of the Chippendale era caught on first in the cities and among citizens wealthy enough to buy the up-to-date.

Forms of the first half of the century continued to be popular, but in general the simplicity of the Queen Anne period gave way to greater richness in materials and ornament. Ornament itself was still valued as an enhancement of the basic form, but it was much less restrained.

Though different mediums always require different treatments, common themes can be discerned in all the decorative arts at this time: the S curve is dominant and everything curves more, often curls and spirals; the shell and other naturalistic motifs abound; and colors—glowing reds, blues, yellows, greens—unite floors, walls and furnishings in a deeply satisfying whole.

Relationships were not always confined to line and decorative

*A variety of forms furnish this Chippendale parlor.*
Historic Deerfield, Inc.

motif. Teapots of silver, ceramics and pewter might be made in
the same pear or reverse-pear shape; or the lovely curving rococo
outline of a late Queen Anne silver tray might be echoed in the
piecrust edge of a Chippendale tilt-top table.

The Chinese influence continued strong in the Chippendale
period. Tea was as popular as ever and served as an excellent
excuse for social gatherings. This meant that new forms in furniture, silver, ceramics and other materials were developed to supply
the tea-drinking public. Chinese shapes were popular in ceramics

and silver, especially, and chinoiserie decoration was used on all types of objects. A certain amount of furniture in the style known as Chinese Chippendale was produced in America during this period. Furniture brasses, too, were sometimes created in the Chinese style, making decorative additions to case pieces.

The elegance and gaiety of the rococo at its height are best exemplified in this period by the decorative arts of France, where the style originated. In England the spirit of the rococo was expressed differently but it was always stronger there than in America, and high-style English decorative arts of the Chippendale period are very imposing and often much more elaborate than those of the Colonies.

In the late Georgian period (beginning in 1765) Robert Adam, inspired by the ancient ruins at Herculaneum and Pompeii and by later Italian art and architecture, was leading the neoclassical revolution in England. The naturalistic shells and scrolls of the rococo were transformed into fine, languid lines, and shapes and decorative patterns came to be governed by geometry.

# Furniture

The furniture style that gave its name to a period of great richness and individuality in all the decorative arts was not developed by one man alone, as the name suggests. It had evolved in England from earlier Georgian styles, with shapes and motifs borrowed from Gothic, Chinese and French rococo sources, and it has come to be called after the cabinetmaker Thomas Chippendale, whose design book set forth pieces in the contemporary taste. As the style evolved in America, it remained relatively simple, retaining more Queen Anne and Georgian characteristics and showing fewer of the borrowed influences than its English counterpart. Among the most sophisticated pieces of American Chippendale furniture are those in the "Chinese Chippendale" style. This was distinguished by lacy frets, key motifs and various other Oriental details used in combination with geometrical shapes similar to those of actual Chinese pieces. The Marlborough leg, square in section and often with a block foot, reveals Chinese inspiration; it is found on Chippendale pieces of the highest quality, many of them from Philadelphia.

High-style furniture is given precedence here because it best exemplifies the trends under discussion, but much furniture of a plain and practical nature was made, too, and some of these unpretentious pieces are illustrated.

With the construction of larger houses and the attendant necessity for a wide variety of types of furniture, several new forms and many variations of old ones appeared. There was great diversity among tables, for example, some of the fashionable ones being small, such as kettle, basin and candle stands; some a little larger, such as the Pembroke table, a contemporary term for a drop-leaf breakfast table with a wide center section and narrow leaves; card tables; and round tea tables with piecrust edges. China tables, another new form, developed from the rectangular Queen Anne tea table. They had a gallery to prevent china from sliding off, and were described by Thomas Chippendale as suitable "for holding each a Set of China, and may be used as tea tables." For the dining rooms of the Chippendale period, tables of the drop-leaf sort that had appeared in the Queen Anne period were still popular. The form showed few changes, except that the claw-and-ball replaced the pad foot and some examples substituted a square top for the earlier oval. Well-appointed dining rooms were also likely to contain a serving table, or side table, which was the forerunner of the sideboard.

Related to the tripod-base tables that were popular as candle stands, tea tables and similar occasional pieces is the pole screen. This consisted of a fire screen, usually of needlework, that could be moved up and down on a pole supported on a tripod base.

The types of chairs made in the Queen Anne period were continued in the succeeding period, but Chippendale examples were more richly decorated and more commodious than earlier ones. Windsor chairs, though they had been made here in earlier years, survive in greater numbers from the Chippendale period and still later. They belong not to the craft of the cabinetmaker, as do most of the things illustrated, but rather to that of the less sophisticated turner. There are many variations on the Windsor form, of which Wallace Nutting, in his *American Windsors,* says,

"Though its lines are so simple, it is at its best very dignified, attractive, and decorative." To determine whether it *is* at its best, it is necessary to examine the shape and rake of the legs; the shapes of the seat, arms, crest rail and ears; and the number of spindles. Throughout the eighteenth century it was customary to paint Windsors—adding color to the rooms they occupied and concealing the several different woods used in their construction (a practice adopted to ensure that each part was made of the wood best suited to it).

Daybeds had gone out of style with the Queen Anne period,

*Side table, cherry with marble top, Connecticut.* Winterthur Museum.

*Kettle stand possibly by John Townsend of Newport, mahogany.* Winterthur Museum.

but a very attractive sofa with a serpentine back rail, sometimes called a "camel-back sofa," had evolved from the Queen Anne settee. Easy chairs were much in favor, too, and reflected in their flowing curves the luxury of this quarter century.

Many kinds of case pieces were made, most of them Chippendale versions of Queen Anne forms. The highboy and lowboy—as we usually call them today, although they were generally known in their own day as high chest of drawers or high chest, and low chest or dressing table—are among the most distinctively American pieces made in the Chippendale style. The form is basically Queen

*China table, mahogany, New York.*
Winterthur Museum.

*Pole screen with needlepoint panel,*
*mahogany, owned by Paul Revere.*
Museum of Fine Arts, Boston.

Anne with Chippendale trappings in the way of rich carving, elaborate brasses and claw-and-ball feet. These two pieces were frequently made as a pair and were meant for use in the bedroom. It was in Philadelphia that the most sophisticated Chippendale furniture was made, and it was there that the highboy attained its greatest glory, though it was made in most other regions as well (one important exception is New York, where flat-top chests-on-chest were favored). Other popular case pieces were the desk and bookcase, or secretary, the slant-top desk, the chest-on-chest, or double chest of drawers, and the chest of drawers. A new form was

*Chippendale carving.*

*Chippendale brass.*

the kneehole desk or chest of drawers, sometimes used, too, as a dressing table.

One of the highest expressions of the rococo in America occurred in looking-glass frames. Though they usually retained a basic geometrical shape, leaves and scrolls, flowers and rockwork motifs were wound in and out of the frame to give it a gay rococo look. The architectural mirror, usually associated with Philadelphia because many examples have been found there, was also popular; its design was based on a Georgian door frame or chimney breast. Looking-glass frames were widely imported, and it

*Side chair, mahogany, New York.*
Metropolitan Museum of Art.

*Armchair, mahogany, Philadelphia.*
Philadelphia Museum of Art.

*Side chair, mahogany, Massachusetts.*
Metropolitan Museum.

is often impossible to be sure whether a given example is native or foreign.

Distinct regional traits grew more pronounced in this period, and the number of areas producing recognizable styles increased. Some of the most thoroughly studied regional centers, where the most sophisticated work was done, were Boston, Newport, Connecticut, New York, Philadelphia and Charleston (South Carolina), but there were others as well. Each of these regions interpreted the Chippendale style somewhat differently, although several of its basic features were common almost everywhere it was

*Dressing table, or lowboy, mahogany, Philadelphia.* Art Institute of Chicago.

*High chest of drawers, or highboy, mahogany, by Thomas Tufft of Philadelphia.* Privately owned.

made. The Queen Anne pad foot, for example, had given way to the claw-and-ball; and case pieces often displayed ogee bracket feet. Furniture of all kinds was more elaborately decorated than formerly—most often with carving, but also with parcel gilding and veneering. Woods commonly used in American Chippendale furniture include mahogany, maple and cherry.

A very brief catalogue of some of the distinguishing features of the regions follows: in Newport there was an unmistakable combination of blocking with graceful and distinctive carved shells (variant types of blockfront construction appear in Con-

*Highboy, curly maple,*
*by the Dunlap family of New Hampshire.*
Winterthur Museum.

*Secretary, bombé base,*
*mahogany, Massachusetts.*
Historic Deerfield, Inc.

necticut and Massachusetts, but rarely elsewhere); an S scroll on the insides of bracket feet; and a claw-and-ball foot of oval shape, sometimes with undercut talons. The Townsend and Goddard cabinetmakers have long been associated with the elegant furniture produced in Newport, and in the Chippendale period Job and John Townsend and John Goddard represented these related families of craftsmen. In Massachusetts the slender verticality of New England chairs of the Queen Anne period was replaced by a more complicated, though still delicate, balance; the cabriole legs of Massachusetts chairs often were reinforced by stretchers, which were considered anachronistic in most other sections by this pe-

*Kneehole desk, or chest of drawers, mahogany, Newport. Museum of Fine Arts, Boston, Karolik Collection.*

*Chest-on-chest, mahogany, attributed to Thomas Elfe of Charleston; the Elfe fret decorates frieze and corners of upper section. Charleston Museum.*

riod. The claw-and-ball foot with sharply bent side claw is a typical Massachusetts feature, and the bombé, or kettle-base, form distinguishes a limited number of sophisticated case pieces. Among the Boston cabinetmakers who are known to have produced Chippendale furniture are John Cogswell and Benjamin Frothingham. Connecticut furniture is frequently made of cherry, often with exuberant and naïve carving of such stylized motifs as the pinwheel. There is still much reliance on line and proportion for effect, as there had been in the Queen Anne period. Benjamin Burnham and Eliphalet Chapin were among those plying the cabinetmaker's trade in Connecticut, and because both men had

*Looking glass, carved nd gilded wood, labeled by John Elliott of Philadelphia. Privately owned.*

*Tall clock, walnut; works by Daniel Rose and case by John Bachman of Pennsylvania.* Photo Parke-Bernet Galleries, Inc.

*Looking glass, walnut with parcel gilding, probably Philadelphia.* Ex coll. Mrs. Francis P. Garvan.

worked in Philadelphia, their work often combines features of that city with those of Connecticut. New Hampshire, though not classed among our main style centers, produced some notable furniture. Probably the most famous craftsmen working there were the Dunlaps of Chester and Salisbury; they have become well known for producing furniture in a unique family idiom which combined fat **S** scrolls, incised sunburst and shell carving and unusual basketwork cornices. New York Chippendale work gains its own particular regional flavor from the lingering influence of the solid Dutchmen who founded the city. It would be hard to find a true rococo spirit in the thick gadrooning, square claw-and-ball feet, stringy acanthus-leaf ornament or popular tassel-and-

*Chest, painted in the Pennsylvania German tradition.*
Ex coll. George Burford Lorimer.

*Two-part walnut corner cupboard*
*with pine secondary wood;*
*Spartanburg County, South Carolina.*
Walnut Grove Plantation.

ruffle motif seen on New York pieces. Gilbert Ask, Thomas Burling, Joseph Cox and Samuel Prince are New York cabinet-makers whose names we recognize today. A love of richness, expressed most often in carving, was characteristic of eighteenth-century Philadelphians, and that is undoubtedly why the work produced there comes closer to English Chippendale than the furniture of any other American region except Charleston. Nowhere in America was the Philadelphia cabinetmaker surpassed in artistry and skill, and in a Philadelphia highboy of quality, proportion and carving are united to produce a peculiarly American masterpiece. Philadelphia chairbacks, too, were the most intri-

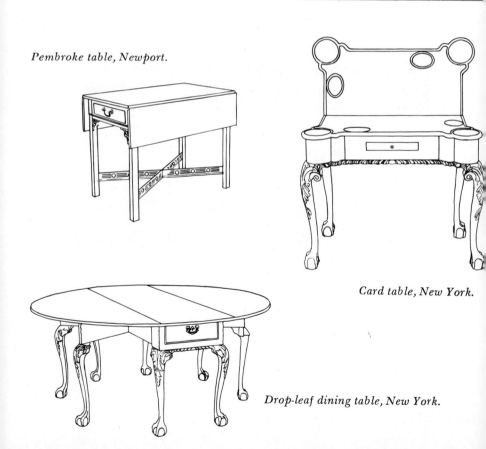

*Pembroke table, Newport.*

*Card table, New York.*

*Drop-leaf dining table, New York.*

cately carved in the Colonies, and the wing or easy chair there took an elegant and distinctive shape. The front legs faced forward instead of being set at an angle, and the horizontal roll of the arms is graceful as well as inviting. Among Philadelphia cabinetmakers of note were Thomas Affleck, Edward Duffield (clocks), John Elliott (mirrors), James Gillingham, Jonathan Gostelowe, Benjamin Randolph, William Savery and Thomas Tufft. In nearby Lancaster County, John Bachman II was creating furniture in a very personal style. The furniture of the South has been widely scattered and much of it has been destroyed, but it is known that Charleston, particularly, supported a flourishing cabi-

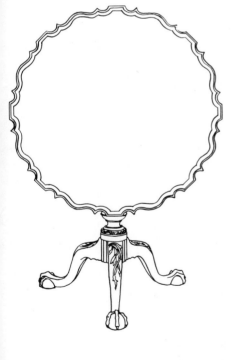

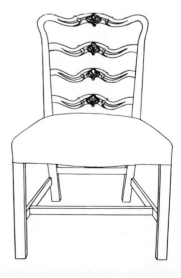

*Piecrust tea table, Philadelphia.*

*Side chair, Maryland.*

netmaking industry. Thomas Elfe is the most famous Charleston maker, and as one of his account books has been preserved, it has been possible to learn a good deal about the tastes of his customers. They were obviously sophisticated, and it is apparent from furniture that has survived that Charlestonians didn't have to send north or across the ocean for fine Chippendale furniture. A distinguishing mark of Charleston pieces is a design for borders known as the "Elfe fret," whose main feature is a pattern of horizontal figure eights.

Although Colonial styles mainly reflect English ones, settlers from other European countries brought their native styles with

*Commode chair, Philadelphia.*

*Windsor armchair, New Englan*

*Side chair, Connecticut.*

them to their new homes, too, and for that reason there were national styles existing within the broader framework of almost every major style period. This phenomenon occurred from the earliest days onward, into the nineteenth century. Two good examples—though there are many others—are the crafts of the Pennsylvania Germans, which reached their peak in the Chippendale period, and the crafts of the Moravians who settled in Pennsylvania and North Carolina.

English cabinetmakers of this period were producing ornate furnishings in the Chippendale style for the magnificent establishments of the wealthy, along with less pretentious pieces for the

*Windsor armchair.*

*Camel-back sofa.*

lower orders of society. China, library and Pembroke tables; "ribband-back" chairs; and breakfronts were among the fashionable forms made for the well-to-do. The cabriole leg was still an important element of the style, but in English pieces it frequently terminates in a scroll toe (a feature very occasionally found in Philadelphia). Gadrooning and fret carving were popular decorative techniques. Cabinetmakers William Vile and John Cobb were dominant from 1755 to 1765, a decade during which many other craftsmen compiled their designs for publication: Lock and Copland, *New Book of Ornaments,* 1752; Edwards and Darly, *New . . . Chinese Designs,* 1754; Chippendale, *The Cabinet-*

*Easy chairs, Philadelphia.*

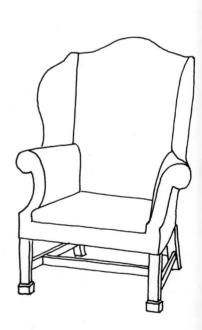

*Makers Director,* 1754, 1755 and 1762; Johnson, *New Designs,* 1756–1758; R. Dossie, *Handmaid to the Arts,* 1758; Ince and Mayhew, *Universal System,* 1759–1763; Manwaring, *Cabinet and Chair-Makers' . . . Companion,* 1765.

About 1765, with Robert Adam and the neoclassical age, came furniture on which inlay, restrained carving and painting influenced by the neoclassical artists Angelica Kauffman and Pergolesi replaced the motifs of the Chippendale era. Matthias Lock's *Pier Frames* and *Foliage* (1769), illustrating classic details, reinforced Adam's work, and by the last quarter of the century calm classicism had supplanted the rococo in fashionable salons.

*Chest of drawers, Massachusetts.*

*Highboy, Newport.*

# Silver

Many American silversmiths who worked in the Queen Anne style had adopted the rococo by 1750. Forms of the first half of the century continued to be popular, but the more infectious curves of the rococo added a touch of playfulness to their simplicity. Pear and inverted-pear shapes were often used along with domed covers, double-scroll handles, C scrolls, and cast shells and other naturalistic forms. Engraving, flat chasing, casting and piercing were employed to complete the decoration.

The flatware form produced in greatest quantity was, of course, the spoon, which was made in a variety of shapes and sizes. Tea, table, soup and salt spoons continued to be made in the Queen Anne shape with rounded upturned handle end; the Queen Anne shell on bowl backs was replaced by a more ornate rococo shell. About 1770 the handle end turned down and the handle was given feather-edge decoration; the back of the bowl might now have stamped floral ornament or a bird singing "I Love Liberty" from the top of his open cage. In New York and Philadelphia an English pattern in which the handle was an Ionic volute was sometimes used for large spoons and ladles; the ladles frequently had fluted bowls. Forks, which were made in spoon patterns, were still not common; and knives, which were generally imported, were pistol handled.

Two implements which lent themselves beautifully to rococo treatment were sugar tongs and strainers. The former, used in the service of tea, were made in the curving Queen Anne scissors shape with shell grips. The strainer, used for adding fresh lemon juice to punch, had two scroll handles and a shallow pierced bowl.

Tankards were still in demand, expressing the rococo spirit in

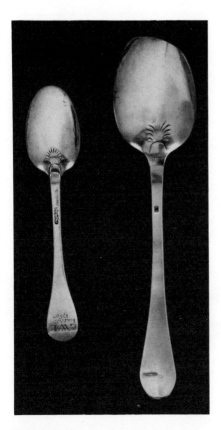

*Table- and teaspoons with shell on bowl back.*
Ex coll. Charles E. Batchelder.

*Sugar tongs with engraved cipher, by Charles Oliver Bruff, New York.*
Winterthur Museum.

a variety of ways: pear-shape bodies, high domed covers, double-scroll handles with florid terminals, and pierced thumbpieces. The body of the Boston tankard tapered a little more and frequently had a mid-band and a flame finial. The flat-top tankard (like the flat-top high chest) continued to be made in New York, sometimes with the addition of a pierced thumbpiece which resembled a contemporary chair splat in design.

Wine and punch were still widely enjoyed and the monteith and punch bowl remained in demand. The Boston punch bowl was plain with an everted rim and molded splayed foot, while the

*Liberty bowl, the original*
*Revere bowl, by Paul Revere, 1768, Boston.*
Museum of Fine Arts, Boston.

New York type was footed and had a broad, curved body embellished with heraldic engraving or flat-chased decoration.

Ecclesiastical plate resembled that of the Queen Anne period, except that the emphasis was on curved lines with asymmetrical engraved lambrequins setting off the arms of donors.

The keyhole porringer had become popular throughout the Colonies by this period, although there was an additional type made in New York in which an interlacing design with central lozenge was prominent for handles.

Sauceboats retained the boat shape, with serrated or beaded

*Advertisement in the* PENNSYLVANIA GAZETTE *for March 28, 1765.*

*Round salt, one of a set of four with spoons by Thomas Hammersley, New York.*
Historic Deerfield, Inc.

rims, but were slenderer than their Queen Anne counterparts. Cast shells and acanthus leaves were characteristic ornaments on legs, feet and handles. Circular salts supported on shell and claw feet were the typical form. Casters appeared in both pear and inverted-pear shapes, set on a molded foot and topped by a high, pierced dome with flame finial.

Teapots were naturally an important form in the Chippendale period, when a foreign observer noted, "One of the principal pleasures of the dwellers in these cities consists of parties in the country with their family or some friends. Tea is the basis of these, especially those which take place after dinner." The early rococo

*Teakettle and stand, a rare form in American work,*
*by Joseph Richardson, Sr., Philadelphia.*
Yale University Art Gallery, Mabel Brady Garvan Collection.

form was the bullet shape evolved from the Queen Anne globular pot, but it was succeeded by the inverted pear shape with domed cover, cast finial and wooden scroll handle. Boston and Philadelphia examples are usually quite plain, perhaps with the owner's arms or monogram engraved on them; New York examples are almost always more elaborately ornamented with flat chasing.

Cream pots were often of inverted-pear shape. Sugar bowls made in Boston followed teapot shapes, those made in New York were generous inverted pears, and those of Philadelphia had flame finials and everted basin rims with gadrooned or feathered edges.

An elegant vessel for dispensing hot water at tea parties was

*Tea set by Pieter de Riemer, New York.* Photo Museum of the City of New York.

*Teapot, inverted-pear shape, by Samuel Casey, Rhode Island.* Ex coll. Edward E. Minor.

*Salver with scrolled, shell-decorated rim, by Myer Myers, New York.* Henry Ford Museum.

the teakettle-on-stand, but surviving American examples are very rare. Luxury items such as this were frequently more lavishly ornamented than ordinary forms. Another in which the silversmith expressed the rococo with less restraint than usual was the cruet stand; examples are also rare in American silver.

Coffeepots were either pear shape with low, splayed foot, molded domed cover with cast finial, cast shell-ornamented spout, and scroll handle; or inverted-pear shape. Later examples are more ornate, sometimes with gadrooning and flame finials.

Salvers continued to resemble piecrust table tops, somewhat more uninhibitedly scrolled and engraved than Queen Anne examples. They sat on cast shell, claw or claw-and-ball feet.

Smiths working in Boston included Zachariah Brigden, Benjamin Burt, John Coburn, Daniel Henchman, Benjamin Hurd, Samuel Minott and Paul Revere (whose "Sons of Liberty" bowl of 1768 was the original Revere bowl); in New York Cary Dunn, Daniel Christian Fueter, William Gilbert, Thomas Hammersley, John Heath, Myer Myers, Elias Pelletreau and Pieter de Riemer;

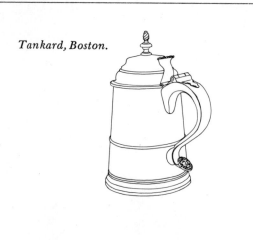

*Tankard, Boston.*

*Tankard, Philadelphia.*

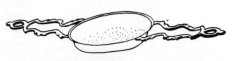

*Strainer.*

in Philadelphia Daniel Dupuy, William Hollingshead, Edmund Milne, Joseph Richardson, Sr., and Thomas Shields; in Rhode Island Samuel Casey.

The rococo persisted in England, too, until 1770, when Robert Adam's neoclassic influence prevailed in silver as well as in other areas. The pear was replaced by the urn as a favorite shape, and swags, husks and oval shields were characteristic motifs. Bright-cut engraving, which gave the decoration a sharper, more sparkly look, superseded traditional engraving on silver. John Cafe, William Cripps, William Grundy, Richard Gurney, Nicholas Sprimont and Edward Wakelin were some of the leading London silversmiths.

Things were happening outside London, too: in the 1760s Joseph Hancock of Sheffield and Matthew Boulton and John Fothergill of Birmingham had found that Sheffield plate could be used to make large objects hitherto made only of solid silver, such as tea- and coffeepots, and they began to expand the working of the fused metal into a separate industry.

*Porringer.*

*Coffeepot.*

*Caster.*

# Ceramics

While European factories were producing increasingly sophisticated porcelains and other ceramics, American wares of the mid-eighteenth century remained largely utilitarian. In New England Daniel Bayley and his sons operated a pottery in Newburyport from about 1764 to 1795. Its site has been located, and shards found there indicate that painted and trailed slip decoration was a prominent feature of their redware. Mugs, tea bowls, plates and platters with slip decoration were turned up, as well as pitchers and various cooking utensils.

Moravians who migrated from Bethlehem, Pennsylvania, to Wachovia, North Carolina, had a pottery in operation from 1756, with Brother Gottfried Aust in charge. Redwares were produced there until 1768, when the pottery was transferred to Salem, North Carolina.

For a brief period finer ceramics were attempted by Bonnin & Morris of Philadelphia. In 1769 they first advertised "good porcelain as any heretofore manufactured at the famous factory in Bow near London," and indeed the few examples which have so far come to light are of soft-paste porcelain. Bonnin & Morris produced objects of a more elevated nature than their contemporaries; rococo sauceboats and openwork bonbon and sweetmeat dishes, most of them decorated in blue and white, represent their sophisticated forms.

English earthenwares continued to increase in variety. England was the innovator in an important area of ceramic decoration: transfer printing, a process in which a design engraved on a copperplate is inked with enamel color and transferred to the ceramic surface by means of a thin paper. The Liverpool firm of Sadler & Green may have discovered the process, but whether they did or not, their prosperous factory printed many Staffordshire and Liverpool wares from 1756 on. Widely exported to the Colonies were delft tiles with transfer-printed decoration.

Also produced at Liverpool was a kind of delftware called "Fazackerly," characterized by bold polychrome flower decoration. Delft with *bianco sopra bianco* decoration was another characteristic earthenware type in which an opaque white pattern was applied to a pale blue or gray ground. At Jackfield in Shropshire a black-glazed red earthenware was produced from about 1750 to 1775. It was decorated with oil gilding and unfired painting—both of which have been worn away on most surviving examples—and commonly bore Jacobite inscriptions and symbols. Similar wares with applied relief decoration were made in Staffordshire and are often mistakenly attributed to Jackfield.

Among the Staffordshire pottery commonly classed with Whieldon wares is a type made in cauliflower and pineapple forms with bright glazes. Josiah Wedgwood, probably the outstanding figure in the history of Staffordshire ceramics, was in partnership with Whieldon from 1754 to 1759, and during those years he perfected the green and yellow glazes typical of cauliflower and pineapple forms—usually teapots and similar pieces.

Toby jugs and figures of earthenware with colored glazes or enamel decoration are another well-known Staffordshire type of the period. Ralph Wood I, Ralph Wood II, Aaron Wood and possibly the talented modeler John Voyez made figures of cream-ware covered with colored glazes or, later in the century, enameled. Toby jugs, usually modeled in the form of a seated man holding a mug and a pipe, sometimes with a hat made separately to form a cup, were first made by the Ralph Woods, and their popularity caused them to be copied in potteries throughout England.

In 1759, when he ended his partnership with Whieldon, Josiah Wedgwood set up his own factory at Burslem. There he began making the glazed earthenwares and salt-glazed stonewares for which Staffordshire is famous. At the same time he was devot-

*Restored pieces from the pottery
of Daniel Bayley, Newburyport, Massachusetts.*
Smithsonian Institution.

ing considerable effort to improving creamware, which W. B. Honey has called "virtually the creation of Josiah Wedgwood." He was so successful that by 1765 he had obtained the patronage of Queen Charlotte, and after that his creamware was called "queen's ware." Creamware was manufactured at many other English potteries and subsequently on the Continent and in the Colonies as well. It became the accepted ware for everyday use, though there was probably little creamware on Colonial tables until well into the Chippendale period.

Much of Wedgwood's creamware was sent to Sadler & Green for transfer-printed decoration. Other pieces were decorated by

*Sauceboat by Bonnin & Morris, Philadelphia.*
Brooklyn Museum.

hand or bore molded decoration, but in any case simple neoclassical motifs were favored. Pierced decoration was also employed, in imitation of that of contemporary silver. A great variety of forms were made of creamware—wall tiles, and table, dairy and kitchen dishes, to mention a few. Slip- or glaze-covered creamware made to look like agate or marble was another Wedgwood innovation.

Beautifully suited to the manufacture of decorative objects was the black basalt that Wedgwood began producing about 1767. This was fine stoneware hard enough to polish on a lapidary's wheel. It was much used for classical vases, busts, seals and plaques, but it was also made into teapots and other practical

*Transfer-printed tiles by Sadler & Green of Liverpool.*
Photo Edwin Jackson, Inc.

objects. The same forms were made in red and buff stoneware, called *rosso antico* and caneware, respectively.

Wedgwood's great interest in classical styles and motifs was fostered by his friend William Bentley, a Liverpool merchant. They became partners in 1768 and built a new factory, called Etruria, for the production of vases and ornamental wares in the neoclassical style.

Jasper, Wedgwood's most important decorative stoneware, went into production about 1774 or 1775. This was also very fine-grained and was first made in light blue and sea green with white molded decoration; later sage green, olive green, dark blue, lilac,

*Coffeepot, red earthenware
with black glaze,
molded decoration; of a type often
miscalled Jackfield; English.*
Henry Ford Museum.

*Delft plate with
bianco sopra bianco decoration;
Bristol, England.*
Concord Antiquarian Society.

yellow (rare) and black (different from black basalt) were used as well. An imaginative range of forms was made of jasper, from jewelry and opera glasses to many kinds of useful and ornamental wares.

Among other distinctive English ceramics of the period were a fine creamware from Leeds, Yorkshire, and creamware and stoneware equal to Wedgwood's from the Staffordshire pottery of John Turner.

"Turning from earthenware to porcelain," says W. B. Honey in *English Pottery and Porcelain*, "we enter a world of sheer amusement, where considerations of usefulness are irrelevant and seriousness an impertinence." Practical objects were also made in porcelain, of course, but the medium lent itself to the frivolous ornaments and forms which express the essential spirit of the rococo.

Porcelain making was a much more complicated process than pottery making. For one thing, the porcelain body, whether of soft or hard paste, was more difficult to mix and could be temperamental in the kiln. Porcelain was better suited to elaborate forms and decorations than pottery, too, and the skills of several different kinds of artisans, instead of just one, were required. A designer or modeler, often a sculptor of considerable talent, was needed to design the wares, and the molded or modeled pieces were then turned over to an artist for decoration. In the case of figures, a "repairer" was needed to assemble each figure after its parts came out of the several molds in which they were made. The skill of the repairer was an essential factor in the quality of the finished piece.

The Continent was the porcelain center of the Western world, providing inspiration for English makers of ceramics. At Meissen, where a hard-paste porcelain formula had been worked out almost half a century earlier, the useful and decorative wares of the early

*Figure of Saint George an*
*the Dragon, by Ralph Wood, Sr., earthenwar*
*with colored glazes, Englis*
Colonial Williamsburg Foundation

years of this period were still setting ceramic styles all over Europe. As time passed, however, Sèvres acquired the stylistic lead.

Meissen porcelain was made in almost every conceivable form for the table, as well as in decorative figures. Tureens were sometimes in the shapes of animals, birds, fruits and vegetables. Characteristic types of painted decoration in enamel colors included vignettes of gallants and ladies, grotesque Chinese figures (from the paintings of Watteau) and so on; *indianische Blumen*, flowers copied from those decorating Oriental porcelains; *deutsche Blumen*, naturalistic flowers, either single or in bouquets; and odd flowers and insects scattered at random over the piece, adding

*Chelsea group of an itinerant musician*
*with boy and dog, soft-paste porcelain, English.*
Cleveland Museum of Art.

charm and often at the same time disguising flaws in the glaze. Enamels, usually applied over the glaze, provided porcelain makers with a wider range of colors than was available for underglaze decoration. Underglaze colors had to be able to withstand the high temperatures required in firing porcelains, while enamels, applied after the glaze had been baked on, could be fired at a lower temperature.

Kändler was the great sculptor and modeler who contributed so much to Meissen's reputation, and his figures and groups were copied by all the other factories of Europe. At first figures were in the round for table decoration, but from about 1760 front-view-

*Worcester teapot, shape and decoration inspired by Chinese wares, soft-paste porcelain; English.* Historic Deerfield, Inc.

*Chelsea jug painted with fruits, butterflies, and insects in the manner of Meissen.* Photo Sotheby & Co.

only figures for display on mantels or in cabinets were made. These often had *bocage,* or leafy bowers which formed a background and setting for the central figure or group. Decoration was usually in enamel colors, sometimes enhanced by gilding.

Other fine German hard-paste porcelain was produced at Frankenthal from 1755 and at Ludwigsburg from 1756. The renowned modeler Bustelli was responsible for the outstanding figures of Italian comedy characters, cavaliers and ladies, and so on, produced at Nymphenburg from 1754 to 1763.

The major French porcelain factory had its beginning at Vincennes. There, after a period of trial and error, a superior soft

*Worcester leaf dish.* Photo D. M. & P. Manheim.

paste was evolved and molded into rococo forms with "a peculiarly French suavity and grace." Among them were dinner and decorative wares, figures and porcelain flowers. Biscuit porcelain was introduced sometime before 1753 and was soon much more popular for figures and groups than the glazed body. In 1756 the factory was moved to Sèvres, where for some time simple early forms coexisted with the large pretentious vases associated with later Sèvres. As the period advanced, however, more elaborate shapes and decorations became the rule. Large dishes and tureens, flower pots and vases replaced the smaller wares.

All Western porcelain showed strong Chinese influence in

*Worcester tureen and cover in the style of Sèvres.* Privately owned.

*"Fazackerly" bowl, English.*

decoration as well as in the body itself, but it was also influenced by the porcelain of Japan. The two main Japanese types available to Europeans were the so-called Kakiemon (a style in which undecorated areas were as important as decorated ones in creating a subtle asymmetrical balance) and Imari (a brocade-like pattern in red, blue and gold). Although these and Meissen styles and decorations provided inspiration for Sèvres artisans, they soon transformed borrowed motifs into a style of decoration peculiarly their own. Painted and gilded exotic birds, landscapes, sentimental scenes and the like are characteristic, as is the rich colored ground that was used increasingly throughout the 1750s. Blues,

*Whieldon-type cauliflower teapot, English.*

*Wedgwood's rosso antico teapot, Staffordshire.*

*Creamware plate with colored rim, Staffordshire.*

turquoise, daffodil yellow, greens and pink served as background for gilding and painting. By 1769 hard-paste porcelain was being made at Sèvres, while soft-paste wares continued to be made until the end of the century.

From 1763 the factory at Sceaux in France produced soft-paste porcelain of excellent quality, too, typically decorated with fruit and birds.

Soft-paste porcelain was made from 1751 at the Tournai factory in Belgium. Many Tournai wares, which were often decorated in blue and white, were intended for everyday use by middle-class customers. Decorative styles were frequently copied from

*Bow soft-paste porcelain cocks, English.*

*Bow figure of a bullfinch.*

*Toby jug, Staffordshire.*

Meissen and Sèvres, and they seemed to have wide appeal, for the output of the factory was very soon in great demand.

Catering not to the middle class but to the nobility was the soft-paste porcelain factory at Buen Retiro in Spain. This factory had been transferred from Capo di Monte when Charles III became king of Spain in 1759. Early wares were rococo, like those of Capo di Monte, while those made toward the middle of the period were neoclassical. Especially noteworthy were the groups of rustic figures in relaxed attitudes.

An abbreviated history of the development of porcelain on the Continent has been set forth here not because many Continental pieces ever reached American shores in the eighteenth century, but because European ceramics formed the base for the development of the ceramic art in England and eventually in the United States.

English porcelain making was progressing at a tremendous rate. Soft-paste porcelain was being made at a number of factories and a very high degree of technical competence and artistry is apparent. In 1768 William Cookworthy of Plymouth took out the first English patent for the manufacture of hard-paste porcelain, but throughout the 1750–1775 period most English porcelain was of soft paste.

A great many decorative objects were made, especially figures of mythological, pastoral and Italian comedy characters. Dinner and tea wares, vases, pitchers and similar pieces for use or display were also produced. Shapes and decorative motifs were largely derivative, drawing inspiration from silver forms, Chinese and Japanese porcelains, Meissen and Sèvres. Colors, too, were based on those of Continental and Far Eastern porcelains.

There is some uncertainty as to whether Bow or Chelsea was the first English soft-paste factory, but at present the experts seem to lean toward Chelsea. The existence of a group of "goat and bee" jugs, some of which are impressed with the date 1745, implies that the Chelsea factory was in operation before that. A series of marks used by the factory during the 1750s and 1760s serves as a guide to the progression of style and form there: the raised-anchor mark was used from 1750 to 1753; the red-anchor mark from about 1753 to 1758; and the gold anchor from about 1758 to 1770. Chelsea wares show the usual Meissen and Sèvres decorative motifs, including tureens in animal and leaf forms, rococo pieces with the solid-color ground characteristic of Sèvres, and figures with *bocage*. These figures are considered remarkably fine and represent a high point in English ceramics. "Toys," or small objects such as scent bottles, seals, etuis and patch boxes, are another charming and sought-after class of Chelsea wares.

Chelsea-Derby wares, manufactured 1770–1784, show considerable influence from Tournai and Sèvres, and the neoclassical style predominates. The Derby factory had been in operation from 1750 and was under the proprietorship of William Duesbury from 1756. Premerger Derby wares imitate those of Chelsea.

Longton Hall, producing soft-paste porcelain from 1750, is known for a characteristic ware in the form of delicately painted leaves with veins usually outlined in pink. That factory also produced a number of forms which follow salt-glazed prototypes. The figures produced at Longton Hall, at their best, approach the Chelsea standard and are very desirable.

Worcester, the factory with an unbroken record of production from the earliest days of English porcelain making to the present, has been in business since 1751. The first period of the factory, from its founding to 1783, is often referred to as the "Dr. Wall period," after Dr. John Wall, who was one of the factory's first and most enthusiastic supporters and later its director. Worcester porcelain has always been of high quality, with an emphasis on useful forms for everyday use. Many of the early wares were based on silver designs and Chinese porcelain forms, and many were decorated in underglaze blue in patterns reminiscent of Chinese ones. Jugs molded in the form of overlapping leaves, also made at Lowestoft and Caughley, were popular for many years, and some of the later examples have a mask molded on the lip. Dishes in leaf shapes were another well-liked form. Few figures were produced at

Worcester, probably because of the tradition of keeping to more practical forms. Transfer printing was adopted in 1757 and has been used extensively ever since. Mugs decorated with transfer-printed portraits of popular or eminent figures are characteristic of this period.

Evidence of another factory's interest in the manufacture of useful forms is provided by this contemporary (c. 1750) observation: "The chief endeavors at Bow have been towards making a more ordinary sort of ware for common uses." Meissen and Oriental porcelains served as models for most Bow forms, but the finished products escape being merely derivative through inventive and fresh use of the borrowed elements. Color was used with imagination, too, in the decoration of porcelain at the Bow factory.

Lowestoft was producing porcelain from 1757, much of it based on simple Chinese porcelain forms. Swansea began production in 1764. Caughley, whose blue-and-white porcelains resemble those of Worcester, went into production in 1772. Caughley porcelain is also sometimes impressed with the name "Salopian," which Honey (*European Ceramic Art*) explains is "from the ancient Roman name for the country." An enamel factory was in operation at Battersea from 1753 to 1756, and such work was done later at Bilston in south Staffordshire.

# *Glass*

Even though he died a pauper, Henry William Stiegel has come to be one of the most famous men in American glass history—and he was certainly the most flamboyant. Stiegel, who was sometimes called Baron though he actually had no claim to such a title, came to this country from Germany in 1750 and was successful enough in the cast-iron business to start three glasshouses. Stories—perhaps apocryphal—are told about Stiegel's lavish way of life: the one about his keeping a coach and *eight,* when four were considered very grand, and traveling with outriders who announced his approach gives an idea of his style. Such tales, true or not, add interest and romance to the figure who is credited with producing the first American glass tablewares equal to some of the European imports. He was so successful in imitating English and Continental wares, in fact, that today it is impossible to tell his glass from European specimens (or from similar products of other American factories). As a result of his extravagance and of overextending himself in his zeal to compete with the output of European factories, Stiegel lost everything in 1774 and went to debtor's prison.

Advertisements, Stiegel's personal documents such as letters and ledgers, and glass fragments found on factory sites provide us with some concrete knowledge of the first American-produced glass of a relatively sophisticated nature, although there are virtually no pieces definitely attributable to Stiegel's glasshouses. Because of the problem of differentiating his glass from European and other American-made wares, we refer to glass of the kinds Stiegel made as "Stiegel type." The characteristic wares, made for the most part at his third glass factory at Manheim, Pennsylvania, were of both lead and nonlead glass, colored and clear, free-blown and pattern-molded, and enameled or engraved in the folk-art tradition of Germany.

*Stiegel-type beaker with enameled decoration.* Privately owned.

*Stiegel-type pattern-molded sugar bowl and salt dish, sapphire blue.* Photo Parke–Bernet Galleries, Inc.

Most of the colored glass, in tones of blue, purple, amethyst and green, was of lead, pattern-molded in the English manner (patterned in a mold, then withdrawn and blown to full size). Ribs, flutes and the well-known diamond daisy were usual patterns. Various other diamond patterns, like the diamond in hexagon and checkered diamond, are also seen, though less often.

Engraved and enameled decorations are very much in the Central European folk-art tradition of designs composed of such naturalistic elements as flowers, leaves and birds. Wavy lines are characteristic for borders or to set off the central motif. Engraved designs include the tulip, flower basket and sunburst with birds; enameled wares are found with the floral design with dove, woman

*Sconce, cut glass with spires, drops, festoons and canopies, English or Irish.* Henry Ford Museum.

in boat and steepled building laid on in black, blue, red, yellow and white. Colored glass was occasionally enameled, but the majority of enameled pieces are clear.

Among forms associated with these three characteristic Stiegel types are salts, creamers, sugar bowls, flips (a modern collector's term for large tumblers), mugs, wines and decanters. Baron Stiegel himself was probably not making these things until 1769, when his third and last glasshouse was completed. His first two factories, one at Elizabeth Furnace, Pennsylvania (1763), and the second also at Manheim (1765), probably produced mainly bottles and window glass.

It has been suggested by students of early American glass that

*Wineglass with color-twist stem, English.*
Photo Arthur Churchill, Ltd.

*Decanter, white enamel decoration, En*
Privately owned.

*Cider glasses, faceted stem, English.*
Photo Arthur Churchill, Ltd.

the Philadelphia Glass Works, advertising in 1773 from an address in the Kensington district of Philadelphia, produced glass of the very same kinds as Stiegel and that probably "many specimens attributed to Stiegel were actually made at this glass works" (George S. and Helen McKearin, *American Glass*). No authenticated examples from the Kensington factory have yet turned up, but advertisements tell us that many different forms were made there.

Another possible source of glass of the Stiegel type is the Glass House Company of New York, moved to a new site and expanded from an earlier glasshouse in 1752. Information about this factory is scanty, and while there is no precise knowledge of what was

*Goblets with landscape painting*
*and armorial decanter by*
*the Beilbys of Newcastle-on-Tyne.*
Photo Delomosne, Ltd.

made there, we do know that imported workmen were turning out "Bottles . . . also a variety of other Glasswares too tedious to mention." There was apparently a branch of this factory in Ulster County, New York, in business from about 1752 until about 1785.

Very likely a number of other glassworks were in operation during this period, but so little concrete evidence is available that we mention only two: Caspar Wistar's enterprise in New Jersey, carried on after his death in 1752 by his son Richard; and the Quincy, Massachusetts, glasshouse operated by Joseph Palmer from 1752 until it burned in 1756. Case and snuff bottles and pickle and conserve jars were among its wares.

In spite of the efforts of American entrepreneurs, large quan-

*Blue cut-glass cruets, probably London or Bristol.*
Ex coll. Mrs. Applewhaite Abbott.

tities of glass were still imported from England and the Continent. The bulk of the imports were drinking glasses—various wines and water goblets—and decanters.

Beauty of line and proportion had been the hallmark of the heavy English lead glass of the first half of the century but now, in response to the demands of the new rococo style and as a result of the Glass Excise Tax of 1745–1746, which taxed glass by weight, the emphasis shifted to decoration.

The outstanding attribute of English glass in this period is therefore not the number of new forms, but a transformation of existing ones. Glasswares were lighter, not only in actual weight, but also in appearance. Chinoiserie was a dominant theme in all

*Opaque-white glass vase with enamel decoration attributed to Michael Edkins, Bristol.* Metropolitan Museum of Art.

the decorative arts of the rococo period, and in glass it is found in engraved and enameled ornament, and in the various elements of chandeliers—most obviously in the canopies that perch atop these increasingly fantastic creations. This was a form that appealed enormously to the skilled glasscutter, and in the words of one authority, "No art in the repertoire of the early cutter of glass is so aesthetically effective as the chandelier" (E. M. Elville, *The Collector's Dictionary of Glass*). Spires, pendent drops and notched arms contributed to the grandeur of the Chippendale chandelier, as well as that of candelabra. Candlesticks lost their knops and balusters and, like wineglasses, had straight stems, often with twist decoration.

*Group of opaque-white glass objects, Bristol.*
Victoria and Albert Museum.

Wineglass and goblet stems were no longer of the baluster type but were straight, often with air-twist or other twist decoration or with faceting. The plain funnel was the commonest bowl shape, though both ogee and straight-sided flat-bottomed bucket types were also made. Decanters were gracefully shaped, with sloping shoulders and long necks and stoppers.

Engraved "flower'd" and Jacobite glasses continued to be produced, and during the Seven Years' War glasses engraved with portraits of Frederick the Great and Britannia joined them.

Into the category of enameled glasses fall the well-known Beilby glasses made by William Beilby and his sister Mary of Newcastle-on-Tyne. They were at work in the 1760s and 1770s and

*Stiegel-type tumbler with engraved decoration.*

*Stiegel-type bottle in pattern-molded diamond-daisy design.*

*Deep cobalt-blue decanter with gilt and white enamel decoration, English.* Henry Ford Museum.

*Sealed bottle; full name on seal is very unusual.*

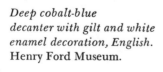

their output, "though sharing some of the motives of porcelain painting, as well as of glass engraving, was distinct in color and very highly original" (W. B. Honey, *Glass: A Handbook*). There is a group of polychrome heraldic designs probably by William, but better known are the hunting, fishing, shooting and similar scenes in a bluish-white monochrome on Newcastle wineglasses, which usually had enamel-twist stems. The Beilbys decorated other kinds of glasses and decanters with popular motifs of the day and occasionally with pastoral or Chinese scenes.

Bristol was probably best known in England in this period for its clear glass, but today's collector thinks of deep-blue and opaque-white glass as Bristol's most characteristic products. The opaque white was undoubtedly made in an effort to simulate Oriental porcelain, whose shapes it reproduces. Bottles and vases, tea caddies, mugs, cruets, plates, basins and candlesticks were decorated in enamel colors and sometimes with chinoiserie. Michael Edkins, a well-known painter of the opaque-white and blue glass of Bristol from 1762 to 1787, is credited with some chinoiserie-decorated tea caddies and vases. He is said to have been "exceedingly clever at ornamenting enamel and blue glassware, then very much in vogue, at which he had no equal."

Both the opaque-white and what is now called "Bristol blue" were made in that city, but also in other English glass centers. Decanters, toilet bottles, patch boxes, wine coolers and fingerbowls in the deep-blue glass were often decorated with gilding. It is known that Bristol opaque white was exported to America, though it is likely that plainer, less elegant types of wineglasses and decanters were landed at the wharves of New York, Philadelphia and Boston more often than novelties like "Bristol" glass.

*1775-1800*

*The*
*Early Federal Style*

*Detail of a Massachusetts bond, 1777,*
*said to have been engraved by Paul Revere.*
Whaling Museum, New Bedford, Mass.

# Historical Background

GEORGE III. LOUIS XVI; DIRECTOIRE, 1795–1799.

PRESIDENTS: WASHINGTON, 1789–1796; JOHN ADAMS, 1796–1800.

The events that led to the American Revolution, 1775–1783, occurred over a number of years. They had mainly to do with "taxation without representation" and with many instances in which the Americans, used to a certain amount of independence, felt their needs and wishes were ignored by the British. The war began, in fact, not as a struggle for independence but as a demand by Americans for more voice in their government, and it was not until a year later that the sentiments expressed in Tom Paine's *Common Sense* resulted in the Declaration of Independence. In 1778 Betsy Ross stitched together the first American flag, and four years after that, in 1782, the Great Seal was adopted.

With the end of the war in 1783, the former Colonists had gained independence and a new dignity for the common man, but there was a tremendous amount still to be done. There was no effective national government with the power to collect taxes, enforce laws and so on, and it soon became clear that without a unifying government such pressing problems as the stabilization of money, trade and commerce, to name only a few, would almost certainly remain unsolved. One constructive joint effort by the states before unification was the Northwest Ordinance, adopted in 1787, which opened the territory north of the Ohio River to orderly settlement by citizens of all 13 states. Aside from this, squabbling and ill feeling grew among the states until 1787, when all except Rhode Island elected delegates to the Constitutional Convention, out of which came the U.S. Constitution, ratified in 1788.

In the meantime various national organizations were springing up, and advances were being made on several domestic fronts. Robert Morris established the Bank of North America, first bank in the United States, in Philadelphia in 1781. The Society of the Cincinnati, comprising officers who had served in the Continental Army, was founded in 1783. In 1784 *The Pennsylvania Packet, and Daily Advertiser,* which had appeared periodically in Philadelphia since 1771, became our first successful daily newspaper. In 1785 the American China trade was launched with the round-trip voyage of the *Empress of China* from New York to the Orient. Two years later the famous Salem merchant Elias Hasket Derby welcomed his ship the *Grand Turk* home from a similar voyage. Mechanized industry made a beginning in the last years of this century of great craftsmanship: Samuel Slater began a spinning mill in Rhode Island in 1791 and Eli Whitney invented the cotton gin in 1793.

George Washington was unanimously elected President in 1789 and he was inaugurated in New York, the temporary capital, on April 30. In December of that year the capital was moved to Philadelphia, where it remained for ten years. As a result of Washington's strong leadership, the national government was being firmly established, but it wasn't long before trouble with England and France threatened again.

The Navy Department was founded in 1794, undoubtedly as a result of these new disturbances, and three frigates were ordered by Congress—the *United States,* the *Constellation* and the *Constitution* ("Old Ironsides") —all launched in 1797.

John Adams came into office in 1796. He resolved the international difficulties diplomatically but was a strong supporter of questionable domestic legislation, the Alien and Sedition Acts. A less controversial event of his administration was the establishment of the General Post Office in 1799.

George Washington, the "Father of Our Country," died on December 14, 1799, having lived entirely within the century of which he is one of the outstanding figures.

# Development of the Style

By the time the American Revolution was over, Americans found that a revolution of another sort had taken place in Europe. Rococo shells, scrolls and asymmetrical forms had been swept aside and replaced by classical and geometrical ones. Although Americans had freed themselves politically, they were by no means ready for artistic independence, and they turned to England as they had in the past for inspiration in expressing the new style.

Robert Adam had introduced his version of classicism in England in the 1760s, stressing refinement and restraint in contrast to the bold, assertive classicism of earlier generations. He concentrated on stylistic continuity to the extent of designing all the elements of a room—architecture, furnishings and fittings—but obviously this degree of perfection was neither desired by nor practical for many people. For this reason, and because of the war, Adam's work had little direct influence on American decorative arts. It had a strong indirect influence, however, via the more informal neoclassical designs of his followers in England, which served as models for Americans.

*Dining room furnished with early neoclassical pieces.*
Ex coll. Mrs. Giles Whiting.

Ovals, circles, squares and rectangles provided the basic plan for most items in the neoclassical taste. The linear quality of objects became dominant, and decoration in the form of bands of ornament was an excellent way of providing extra emphasis for classical outlines. All ornament was regular in shape, whatever its source. Urns, swags and husks were some of the popular motifs, and the eagle provided both classical and patriotic allusions—especially satisfying to American patrons.

Lightness was very important in achieving the effect of the new style. Movability had become a prerequisite of furniture, so it had not only to be light in spirit and appearance, but also in fact.

There was a period of transition in which classical decoration appeared on rococo forms. By the mid-1780s, however, the shapes, ornamental motifs and general air of delicacy characteristic of the neoclassical style prevailed in fashionable centers.

# *Furniture*

Many pre-Revolutionary cabinetmakers continued to work in the Chippendale style for some years after the end of the war. Chippendale pieces of the 1770s and 1780s are likely to have straight legs, and such geometrical forms as the pretzel-back chair were popular. Transitional pieces combined elements of both styles— often a Chippendale shape with classical decorative motifs. The simplified and modified Adam style that was to be illustrated in the very attractive and usable designs of Hepplewhite and Sheraton gained the ascendancy in furniture about 1785. The spirit of this new style was expressed with an understated richness and sophistication quite different from the obvious opulence of the best Chippendale pieces. Ornate carving, the glory of the Chippendale era, gave way to very controlled carved ornament, inlay, painting, reeding and veneering. Mahogany remained the favored wood, and although satinwood also made its appearance, its use in solid pieces was very rare.

Hepplewhite's designs, presented in *The Cabinet-Maker and Upholsterer's Guide* of 1788, were not so uncompromisingly classical as Adam's and included serpentine and other curved forms. Some of the motifs he favored were painted or carved swags, medallions, wheat ears and feathers. The square-sectioned, tapering leg, frequently ending in a spade foot, was an important aspect of his style, as were shield-shape, heart-shape and oval chair backs. The chair back was now separated from the seat rail and seemed to float between the stiles. The rear legs of such chairs curve inward slightly, and Hepplewhite case pieces stand on flaring bracket feet.

Sheraton's designs, published in *The Cabinet-Maker and*

*Card table with characteristic Baltimore bellflower pattern inlaid on legs.*
Ex coll. Mrs. Giles Whiting.

*Side chair with typical Rhode Island cylix in splat.*
Ex coll. H. Hoffman.

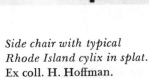

*Side chair with Salem urn-and-drapery motif in Hepplewhite shield-shape back; Samuel McIntire carved this for Elias Hasket Derby, and it shows the grapes and punchwork associated with his work.*
Bayou Bend Collection, Museum of Fine Arts of Houston.

*Upholsterer's Drawing Book* issued during the years 1791–1794, stressed square forms, verticality and legs round in section, often reeded. Both his designs and those of Hepplewhite, as well as those in Shearer's *Cabinet Maker's London Book of Prices*, 1788, were widely known and used in America. Cabinetmakers drew freely upon them, often mixing elements of more than one designer.

Cabinetmakers seem to have been inspired by the neoclassical style, for many new, practical and elegant forms made their appearance at this time. The worktable, small and beautifully

*Side chair with Sheraton square back enclosing New York urn-and-drapery motif surmounted by Prince of Wales feathers.*
Photo Parke-Bernet Galleries, Inc.

*Painted side chair with Hepplewhite oval back and tapering legs ending in spade feet, Philadelphia.*
Museum of Fine Arts, Boston.

*Open armchair with round, reeded Sheraton legs and back with Philadelphia looped urn-and-drapery splat.*
Art Institute of Chicago.

fitted to hold sewing supplies, was one newcomer. Another was the sectional dining table, composed of two or three parts that could be used separately or together; this form was rare in Chippendale times, but fairly common in the neoclassical period. Side tables with rounded ends, or of semicircular outline, and Pembroke tables, now with rounded leaves, were also popular.

Chairs include a round, or barrel-shape, easy chair, and an easy chair with more exaggerated serpentine wings.

The Martha Washington, or lolling, chair with upholstered

*Lady's desk with tambour closing, attributed to John Seymour of Boston.* Bayou Bend Collection.

*Secretary with inset* églomisé *ovals, cylinder closing, Baltimore.* Metropolitan Museum of Art.

seat and high back and carved wooden arms was another typical form. Lighter chests of drawers took the place of highboys and lowboys in the bedroom. The fitted dressing chest with hinged lid was another new (quite rare) form and is an example of the fascination that specialized and intricately made furniture had for many people in this period.

Although slant-top desks were still being produced, the tambour desk was an elegant new version, and secretaries were sometimes made with tambour closings, too. Tambour construction

*"Salem secretary" of satinwood by Edmund Johnson of Salem.*
Henry Ford Museum.

involved gluing narrow strips of wood to a sturdy fabric backing. This gave the appearance of a reeded surface, but could be rolled conveniently out of sight. From the Boston-Salem area came a new type of desk and bookcase sometimes called a "Salem secretary." This was an imposing form, frequently divided into three sections with a desk concealed behind the top drawer of the middle one.

The most important innovation of the period was the sideboard, an improvement on the side or serving table. The form was strongly influenced by Shearer's designs but American examples

*High-post bed with rice carving*
*on foot posts, Charleston.* Charleston Museum.

are usually classified as either Hepplewhite or Sheraton. The characteristic Hepplewhite type had square or concave ends, a recessed center and square, tapering legs; the Sheraton type had convex ends or a kidney shape and turned and reeded legs. Elements of both styles were frequently combined in American examples. A high, narrow sideboard called a "huntboard" was typical of Baltimore and the South.

Hepplewhite looking glasses probably embody the Adam spirit more than any other American form. They were pedimented and ornamented with delicate urns and floral sprays. Sheraton ones had flat tops with painted glass panels or molded, applied

*Hepplewhite looking glass with Adamesque urn and floral-spray ornament in wire and gilded composition.* Henry Ford Museum.

*Sheraton looking glass labeled by Edward Lothrop of Boston.* Henry Ford Museum.

composition ornament in classical motifs, under a cornice decorated with balls; such looking glasses were often gilded.

Regional characteristics were not so marked in this period as they had been formerly, owing to greater ease of communication among the states. The wide use of the design books mentioned above and the growth of specialization in the cabinetmaking trade are undoubtedly other important factors in the trend toward uniformity, but there were still enough variations and individual interpretations to lend a distinct character to the work of the different regions.

New England furniture retained the delicacy that had typi-

*Sectional dining table.*

*Worktable.*

*Pembroke table.*

fied it in the earlier years of the eighteenth century. Chairs, for example, still frequently carried stretchers to protect their fragile legs. Martha Washington chairs, Hepplewhite chairs with heart-shape back, bow-front chests of drawers and furniture in which light and dark woods were contrasted are also characteristic of New England. Salem work of this period has great distinction, and chairs from that city can be recognized by a shield back framing an urn draped with swags that extend to the outer edge of the shield. Rhode Island chairs are noteworthy for the cylix in the splat (a motif seen also in the silver of this time). Cabinetmakers at work in New England include Stephen Badlam, John and

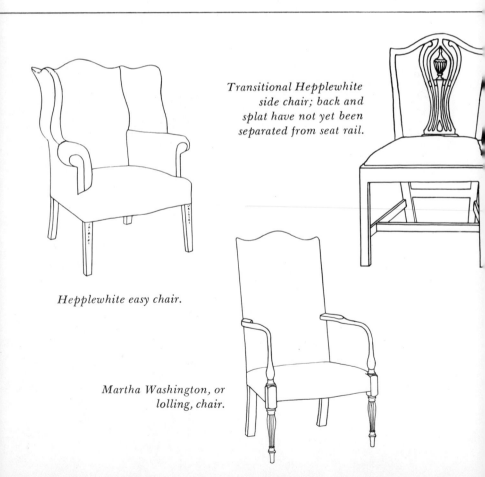

*Transitional Hepplewhite side chair; back and splat have not yet been separated from seat rail.*

*Hepplewhite easy chair.*

*Martha Washington, or lolling, chair.*

Thomas Seymour of Boston; Aaron and Eliphalet Chapin, Knee-
land & Adams of Connecticut; Samuel Dunlap II of New Hampshire; Edmund Townsend, Holmes Weaver of Newport; and
Edmund Johnson, William Lemon and Elijah Sanderson of
Salem. John and Simeon Skillin of Boston are renowned for their
carving. Among all these gifted craftsmen Samuel McIntire of
Salem stands out, though he was not a cabinetmaker. He was the
leading architect in the Boston-Salem-Newburyport vicinity,
where great fortunes were made in the shipping trade that grew
up after the Revolution. McIntire was also an expert carver and
his cornucopias, baskets of flowers, rosettes, waterleaves and

*Bow-front chest of drawers*
*with Hepplewhite flaring bracket feet.*

*Sideboard of the Hepplewhite type*
*with inset quarter fans*
*characteristic of New York.*

punchwork embellish some of the region's most outstanding pieces of furniture.

New York seemed to find chair backs with the drapery motif in combination with Prince of Wales feathers especially appealing; and New York sideboards were very frequently inlaid with quarter fans—although both motifs do appear elsewhere. Working in New York were Elbert Anderson, Duncan Phyfe and Mills & Deming. Philadelphia chairs were often square-backed with a looped urn-and-drapery motif, while sideboards made there were characterized by rounded ends. Well-known cabinetmakers of that city include John Folwell, Adam Hains and Daniel Trotter.

Baltimore became an enormously prosperous city in the years following the Revolution and supported a talented group of cabinetmakers. Among typical motifs are inlay of large ovals in mitered panels; light panels set into tapering legs and inlaid with a Baltimore bellflower pattern; and *églomisé,* or painted glass, panels ornamented with allegorical figures—a decorative technique characteristic of Baltimore work. Painted furniture from this area is also noteworthy.

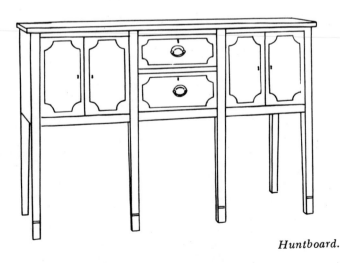

*Huntboard.*

Southern furniture, as we have mentioned before, has been widely scattered and destroyed, so it is difficult to draw firm conclusions about it. It is known, however, that a variety of elegant furniture was made in Charleston in the post-Revolutionary period, and one distinguishing feature is skillful carving in what is known as the "rice motif," sometimes found on the foot posts of high-post beds.

Among other cabinetmakers of the neoclassical period are John Shaw of Annapolis; Matthew Egerton, Sr., and Jr., of New Jersey; and Johannes Rank and Christian Selzer of Pennsylvania, chest makers and decorators in the Pennsylvania German tradition.

English neoclassical furniture was, as might be expected, more ornate than American, and exotic woods such as kingwood, harewood, tulipwood, Amboina, satinwood and rosewood were used. Decorative techniques there included turning, caning and japanning—revived after a long period of oblivion. England, even more than America, took inspiration from Sheraton, Hepplewhite and Shearer during the period.

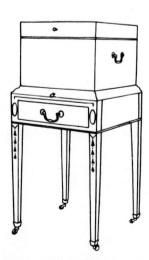

*Cellaret, a characteristic Southern form for the storage of wine or liquor bottles.*

# Silver

Rococo designs remained popular in America until after the Revolution. With the resumption of normal trade relations, however, Americans quickly caught up with British fashions and were soon ordering neoclassical silver from local smiths. The new style, which had taken hold in London 15 years earlier, about 1770, had replaced ebullient rococo lines with disciplined geometrical shapes and serene, unbroken curves. Simple ceramic shapes became popular in silver, in bowls and pitchers particularly. Although elements of the rococo style were sometimes combined with those of the neoclassical in this period, decoration was usually confined to reeded moldings, beading, fluted sides and bright-cutting. Parallel bands of ornament appeared on many objects, and urn finials were typical.

Engraved heraldic devices—so important in the decoration of earlier silver—did not lend themselves well to the delicate bright-cut technique, but monograms surrounded by elegant floral wreaths or swags were a particularly attractive feature of the new style.

Spoons of this period are found in all sizes. By 1785 the bowl had become pointed and the down-turned handle was sparingly decorated with, perhaps, the owner's monogram and a simple bright-cut border. Bowl backs were frequently decorated in relief in a variety of motifs, of which the eagle was one of the most popular. Another type had a handle which widened slightly where it joined the bowl. Sugar tongs, made all in one piece to create a bow shape, had oval or acorn grips.

The tankard was seldom made after 1800, and in its last incarnation it was cylindrical with a flat cover, decorated with bright-cut engraving or bands of horizontal reeding. Mugs were made in the same shape as tankards and decorated in a similar manner. Tumblers, too, were cylindrical with flat bottoms and sometimes with paneled sides; in this period they were made in sets. Goblets were oval with trumpet feet.

Among ecclesiastical pieces were the oval beaker and two-handled cup with trumpet foot, tall incurved cover and urn finial.

*Bill head of Alexander Gordon, dated 1796–97, New York.*

Punch bowls of the period show the influence of the Chinese bowl shape, with collet foot and smoothly curving sides. Porringers retained the earlier shape but their keyhole handles were more delicately fashioned. The pap boat, used to feed babies, was made in the streamlined shape of a Roman lamp. Sauceboats were also sleeker, set on an oval foot instead of three cabriole legs, with boat-shape bodies often decorated only with restrained gadrooning on the rim. The earliest neoclassical salts were ovals instead of circles, decorated in the same manner as earlier versions. Gradually their curving walls straightened and were pierced and they

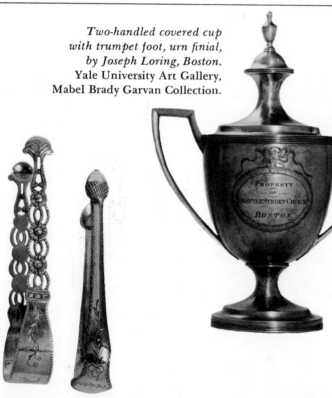

*Two-handled covered cup with trumpet foot, urn finial, by Joseph Loring, Boston.* Yale University Art Gallery, Mabel Brady Garvan Collection.

*Sugar tongs in bow shape.* Privately owned.

*Spoon with pointed bowl and handle end; dove bearing leafy spray decorates back of bowl.* Ex coll. H. E. Gillingham.

were lined with blue glass. The boat shape set on an oval foot became popular for salts toward the end of the period, as well as for sauceboats and cake baskets. For casters the urn shape seemed more suitable; it was topped by a flame finial and ornamented with bright-cut engraving.

Tea wares show regional variations more clearly than other forms. In Boston the teapot was elliptical with straight spout and sides. It was made from a rolled sheet of silver, saving the silversmith many long hours, for he could buy such sheets ready-made. His product was thinner than formerly, but the shallow bright-cut

*Teapot and stand by Paul Revere, Boston.*
Ex coll. Mrs. F. W. Wieder.

decoration of the period didn't cut deeply enough into the walls of the pots to weaken them. Occasionally teapot walls were shaped or fluted rather than straight. Tea sets came into vogue toward the end of the century, and the elliptical pot was often accompanied by a helmet-shape creamer and an urn- or boat-shape sugar bowl.

New York teapots were more richly decorated than Boston examples, though the shapes were much the same.

Philadelphia tea wares were distinguished by pierced galleries on the rims of teapots, sugar bowls and coffeepots. The urn was a popular shape there, trimmed with beading and urn or pineapple

*Teapot, cream pitcher and sugar bowl, by William Hollingshead, Philadelphia.* Philadelphia Museum of Art.

(symbol of hospitality) finial. The helmet creamer was also found, as was the elliptical, straight-sided teapot.

Curiously enough, the rococo inverted-pear shape was the standard coffeepot form in all silvermaking centers, though neo-classical ornament was used for decoration. The urn was a new form of the period, well liked for serving tea and coffee. Salvers continued to be made, small, circular ones set on claw-and-ball feet and large, oval flat-bottomed ones with handles for tea sets and tumblers.

Candlesticks were circular, oval or square in section, very

*…amer, helmet shape*
*h fluted sides,*
*Joseph Shoemaker,*
*iladelphia.*
*vately owned.*

*Coffeepot in inverted-pear*
*shape with delicate*
*bright-cut engraving, cast*
*spout, by Joseph Lownes,*
*Philadelphia.* Photo
Parke-Bernet Galleries, Inc.

*Miniature picture frame*
*encloses Charles Willson Peale's*
*portrait of Martha Washington.*
Mount Vernon.

chastely ornamented with beading or bright-cut engraving. They, too, were made of the thin rolled sheets and were therefore sometimes weighted. Many small personal items continued to be made, as in former periods.

A great deal of Indian trade and presentation silver was made during this period. The trade silver, consisting of such ornaments as brooches, earrings and crosses, was either bartered for furs or sold to Indians by traders. Presentation pieces, commissioned by the government and given to Indian chieftains as symbols of peace and friendship, included armbands, gorgets and medals.

Among smiths plying their trade in Boston were Coburn,

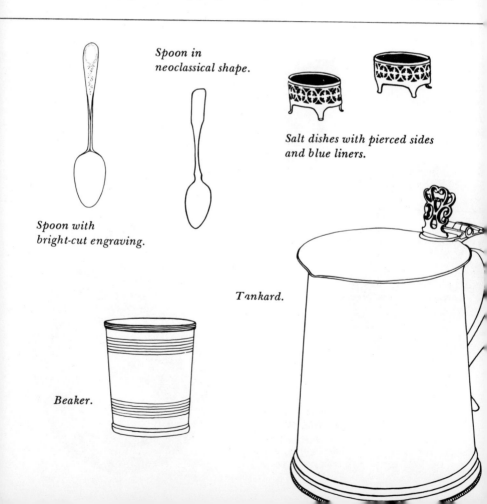

*Spoon in neoclassical shape.*

*Salt dishes with pierced sides and blue liners.*

*Spoon with bright-cut engraving.*

*Tankard.*

*Beaker.*

Minott, Revere, Benjamin Burt and Joseph Loring; in New York Ephraim Brasher, William G. Forbes, Lewis Fueter, Samuel Johnson, John Vernon and Hugh Wishart; in Philadelphia Joseph Anthony, Jr., Joseph Cooke, Abraham Dubois, Richard Humphreys, Joseph Lownes, Joseph and Nathaniel Richardson, and Joseph Richardson, Jr. (Indian medals).

The rage for the neoclassical persisted in England. George Baskerville, Hester Bateman, Jonathan, Peter and Ann Bateman, Henry and William Chawner, Robert Cruickshank and Paul Storr, whose first mark was recorded in 1793, were among London smiths working at this time.

*Sauceboat with cover.*

*Pap boat.*

*Reeded candlestick.*

*Tea or coffee urn.*

# Ceramics

The Revolutionary War interrupted the flow of ceramics from the Old World to the New, and by the time it was reestablished the neoclassical style was predominant in English and other European wares. American ceramics were as little affected by this shift as they had been by all the others of the eighteenth century: plain, practical household vessels continued to be the stock in trade of the American potter.

The cessation of trade with Europe had provided a strong incentive for the development of an American stoneware industry, for the sturdy mugs, jugs and jars of English and German stoneware were no longer available. Northern New Jersey and adjacent Staten Island contained the blue-clay pits from which clay suitable for making stoneware was drawn for an extensive period by the potters of New York, New Jersey and New England. Stoneware fragments marked 1775 and 1776 have been found at the pottery site of James Morgan at Cheesequake, New Jersey, and they indicate that jugs and jars, as well as mugs, flat-rimmed plates and cups were made there of stoneware frequently decorated with blue spirals. The name of Crolius is a familiar one in the history of New York pottery, so it is not surprising that one of the earliest dated stoneware survivals, a jug of 1775, comes down to us from the New York City factory of William Crolius II, "potbaker." At Bennington, Vermont, John Norton was turning out gray stoneware from 1793. The stoneware has been described as "good honest ware of its kind" but of "no special and distinctive excellence"—not up to the standard of the wares of the next century, for which Bennington was to become famous.

Earthenware which makes a "wide contrast to New England work, marked by a love of color, a play of ideas, an engaging humor," was being produced in this period by the Pennsylvania German potters in the area surrounding Philadelphia. Much of the ware is *sgraffito*, that is, scratched: it was made of slip-coated red earthenware with designs scratched through the slip to expose the red body beneath. Many forms were made, a number of them quite distinctive: flat fruit-pie dishes, apple-butter dishes, saucered flowerpots, fluted turk's-head cake molds, standing grease lamps, unusual banks and bird whistles. Plates, often of a very decorative nature, were produced in quantity, and the work of Georg Hübener stands out in this area. Such motifs as flowers, birds, human figures and inscriptions were combined in imaginative and original patterns.

Creamware, the smooth-surfaced, ivory-color earthenware that displaced delft and other types of pottery as the everyday tableware by 1780, was one of the commonest imports from England. Americans were anxious to cash in on the booming creamware market, and several Philadelphia potters attempted to manufacture a cream-color ware that would compete successfully with the English version. John Curtis was making creamware in 1791, and the next year the Pennsylvania Society for Encouragement of Manufactures and the Useful Arts offered 50 dollars for examples "approaching nearest to queen's ware."

In spite of these and other, now-forgotten ventures in pottery making, American potters were still not able to capture the

American ceramics market. Almost before the Revolution was officially over, English potters were planning wares to appeal especially to the former Colonists. Transfer printing had made it possible to decorate large matching sets with the same design, and the combination of this mass-production technique with the practical creamware made English tablewares available to a large new public at relatively low prices. Enameling and molded decoration were also employed, but less often. Wedgwood, of course, continued to produce queen's ware, but the type was made by many other English factories.

Herculaneum, a Liverpool factory founded in 1793, produced creamware transfer printed in blue or black, and other Staffordshire types. Neale & Company, Wedgwood's greatest competitor, also turned out blue-printed or lustered cream-color tablewares of

Salt-glazed stoneware crock

Sgraffito dish,
Pennsylvania German.

Salt-glazed stoneware mug from
Cheesequake, New Jersey.

excellent quality, as well as stoneware, earthenware figures and porcelain. The factory at Davenport manufactured an assortment of styles and forms in blue-printed creamware and porcelain from 1793. Castleford, established in 1790 by David Dunderdale, made creamware in the style of Leeds in this period.

Leeds, which is well known for its creamware, produced its most characteristic style from 1780 to 1820. It is of a slightly greenish-yellow tone with a brilliant, unblemished glaze, pierced decoration and twisted handles ending in blossoms or leaves. Skillfully and carefully produced, it was made in a wide variety of useful items and also in such decorative forms as elaborate centerpieces. Much of the output was unpainted, but transfer printing and enamel decoration were sometimes used.

A class which is now often referred to as "Anglo-American

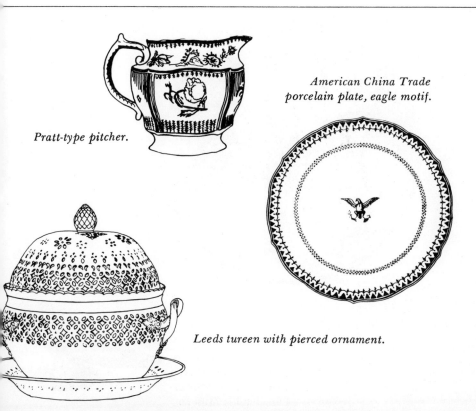

*Pratt-type pitcher.*

*American China Trade porcelain plate, eagle motif.*

*Leeds tureen with pierced ornament.*

ware" consisted largely of transfer-printed earthenware from Staffordshire and Liverpool. The earliest Anglo-American pieces were black-printed plates, bowls and barrel-shape jugs from Liverpool. At first Staffordshire potters sent their wares to Liverpool to be printed, but eventually they began to print their own, and the center shifted to Staffordshire. "Liverpool ware" has nevertheless remained a generic term for pottery of this type.

British potters were not the least bit reticent about using scenes and slogans in which the British suffered at the hands of the Americans. One transfer-printed scene showed *America triumphing over Britain,* and patriotic emblems such as the eagle appeared often. Other favorite motifs were portraits of American

*Sgraffito dish, Pennsylvania German.*
Philadelphia Museum of Art.

*Slip-decorated earthenware
peacock whistle,
Pennsylvania German.*
Philadelphia Museum.

heroes such as Washington, Jefferson and Franklin; American ships; armorials; and sentimental scenes. A Liverpool jug is dedicated to *The Crooked But interesting Town of Boston.*

Another English innovation was the technique of luster decoration. Lusterwares offered considerable novelty and variety, and became a very successful nineteenth-century export. The lusters were films of gold or platinum reduced from an oxide to produce a range of colors from gold, silver and copper to orange, rose and purple. The earliest was apparently silver luster (made from platinum) applied to the entire ceramic surface in imitation of true silver; this was sometimes called "poor man's silver."

So-called Prattwares, made from about 1780 to 1820, are white

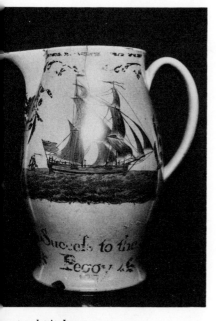

*...erpool pitcher,*
*...nsfer-printed design, English.*
*...body Museum of Salem, Mass.*

*Liverpool ale mug,*
*transfer-printed scene*
*obviously aimed at American market,*
*English. Philadelphia Museum.*

or cream-color earthenwares characterized by relief decoration of figures, fruits and so on in high-temperature oranges, blues and greens applied under the glaze. They were originally assumed to have been the work of Felix Pratt, but according to Griselda Lewis (*Antiques,* June 1967), they are "much more likely to be the work of William Pratt . . . mentioned in the Burslem directory of 1786 as a maker of 'cream coloured earthenware.'" Pratt's own work was seldom marked, and it is probable that other English potters were making this type of ware as well.

Josiah Wedgwood continued a major force in the ceramics world. The well-known sculptor John Flaxman did a good deal of modeling of groups, portrait busts and copies of antique statuary for Wedgwood from 1775 to 1787. These and the work of many

*Silver-luster teapot, made to resemble solid silver, English.* Art Institute of Chicago.

*Worcester porcelain fruit cooler, modeled on Sèvres, English.* Photo Lyman Huszagh.

other artists were either reproduced or adapted for use on seals, plaques and medallions in basalt, jasper or a similar ware. One of the outstanding decorative pieces of the period was Wedgwood's copy of the Portland Vase, the first edition of which was in production from 1786 to 1790. Pearlware, another Wedgwood innovation, was introduced about 1779. This was a fine pure-white or bluish-white body created as a result of the demand for a white earthenware that closely resembled porcelain; it contained a large proportion of china clay and china stone. Pearlware eventually superseded creamware and came to be used extensively for the transfer-printed Anglo-American wares.

Soft-paste porcelain continued to be an important part of the English ceramics scene, but it was never exported to America in

*Wedgwood jasper plaques, large ones modeled by Flaxman, English.*
Henry Ford Museum.

really large quantities. At Worcester, the "Flight period" of 1783 to 1791 was presided over by Thomas Flight, whose precise patterns in the neoclassical style lacked the warmth and subtlety of the Dr. Wall-period porcelains. In 1783 Robert Chamberlain established another factory at Worcester, and at first confined its activity to decoration; however, by 1792 a very good quality of porcelain was being produced. Much later, in 1840, the two factories merged. Thomas Minton's factory in Staffordshire produced porcelain of generally high quality from 1798 to 1811. And in 1799 Caughley merged with Coalport.

A group of five Staffordshire potters joined together in 1781 to buy the Bristol patent for hard paste, along with the right to sell china clay and china stone. The next year they established a factory at New Hall, where, among their other productions, they made porcelains in the Bristol "cottage style," a pattern of simple festoons and sprigs.

The successful commercial production of bone china, in which bone ash is an important ingredient, was an achievement of the second Josiah Spode, who took over his father's business in 1797. Bone china is a cross between porcelain and earthenware, and it became the standard English body for fine dinnerware, as it has remained.

The establishment of American independence made it possible for American merchants to enter directly into the lucrative China trade, and one of the effects of the new venture was to bring a variety of China trade porcelains to the American market. These were usually less elaborate and diversified than European China trade wares, but they added greatly to the variety available for order by American buyers.

The ware itself was smooth and white with a gray tinge. Forms, generally taken from European silver or ceramics, consisted of punch bowls, mugs, flagons, pitchers and so on; large dinner and tea services were also made. Purely decorative items, such as five-piece garnitures and pairs of covered urns, were rarer.

Decoration of American China trade porcelain was largely

confined to stock patterns, though special designs were occasionally ordered. Among the major stock patterns were the monogram, floral, ship, armorial, emblematic and underglaze decorations, two of which were often combined. The eagle, such a popular motif in American decoration, appeared in a good many different shapes and attitudes.

The underglaze patterns called Nanking, Canton and Fitzhugh found wide acceptance. Fitzhugh, with its wide border made up of pomegranates, butterflies and latticework and its center of four large medallions of flowers and emblems, was especially well liked by Americans. The Fitzhugh pattern was usually done in underglaze blue, though overglaze green, brown, orange and rose were occasionally used.

The Nanking and Canton patterns are very much alike, their overall decoration in underglaze blue consisting of an island scene or landscape surrounded by a wide latticework border. Nanking porcelain was the finer ware and is often gilded.

Of the excellent porcelains being made on the Continent in the neoclassical style, only a few made their way to the New World in this period. French porcelain was particularly popular, owing to the surge of friendship engendered by French support during our Revolution and sympathy for the French during their own revolution. Among the important late eighteenth-century productions of Sèvres was a group of large ornamental urns with elaborate decorations of flowers, landscapes or portraits of eminent people, painted in polychrome and gilded.

The enthusiasm for creamware had spread from England to the Continent, and it was produced in France at Creil from 1794 and in Magdeburg, Germany, from 1786. These wares were copied from the English, and those of Creil were transfer-printed in the English manner with black or blue scenes, landscapes and so on.

# *Glass*

It is quite apparent from newspaper advertisements and other documented evidences and from absolutely authenticated specimens of Amelung glasswares that the new Bremen Glassmanufactory during the period from about 1787 to 1794 was the outstanding glass works of that time in America, both in the extensiveness of the production, distribution of its products, and the quality of its wares" [*American Glass,* George S. and Helen McKearin].

And still, John Frederick Amelung was declared bankrupt about 1795.

The New Bremen glasshouse had been established by Amelung in 1784, when he arrived from Bremen, Germany, with the necessary money, workmen and tools. The glass subsequently produced at New Bremen was, in Amelung's words, "cheaper, and of a better quality, than a great deal of what is imported." This may have been true, but the difficulty students have in telling them apart suggests that Amelung was perhaps a little biased.

There is a small group of handsome engraved presentation pieces positively attributable to Amelung which, until recently, served as the only basis for attribution of other pieces. However, an "exploratory excavation on the supposed New Bremen site was undertaken by the Corning Museum, in association with the Smithsonian Institution and archaeological personnel provided by Colonial Williamsburg" in the early 1960s. The excavation un-covered "many pieces which can be safely claimed as products of the Amelung factory" (this and much of the following from Ivor Noël-Hume's account of the project published in *Antiques* for March 1964). Drawn-stem wineglasses, firing and dessert glasses, many sizes of tumblers, tumbler or goblet lids, decanter and bottle stoppers, sugar bowls with ornamental handles, mugs, utilitarian bowls and pans, bottles, flasks and window glass were among the forms represented.

Obviously Amelung's stock was varied. Like Stiegel before him, he chose to work in both the English and the German tradi-tions in order to appeal to the widest range of potential buyers. He made free-blown wares plain or with ornamental glass details such as unusual handles or bird finials, as well as expanded ribbed and pattern-molded wares. Fragments of such pieces were in a wide range of colors—from greens and amber to blue and amethyst.

Two fragments bearing engraved decoration of the type usu-ally attributed to Amelung were found. Borders of sprigs or leaves, stiff drapery caught up at regular intervals by hanging tassels, and stylized flowers and bows are among the simple neoclassical designs that decorated his ordinary output (as distinguished from the elaborate presentation pieces).

Items found in America with this type of engraving have often been referred to simply as "Amelung," though it has long been known that the New Bremen wares were very like European imports. Amelung did apparently make a great deal of glass, but at the same time enormous quantities were shipped from Europe for sale in America, and the difficulties of establishing exactly what Amelung and his European competitors made and sold render attribution on stylistic grounds alone extremely hazardous.

Also significant are two glasshouses whose trade was mainly in bottles and window glass. They both made some tablewares, however, and are of interest in studying the development of an American glass industry. The New Geneva (Pennsylvania) Glass Works was set up in 1797 by Albert Gallatin, prominent in Pennsylvania and later Secretary of the United States Treasury, in association with a number of skilled glassblowers who were seeking new opportunities after the failure of Amelung's factory. Foremost among these glassmen was Baltzer Kramer, who had worked for both Stiegel and Amelung. His name is usually joined with Gallatin's in connection with pitchers, covered sugar bowls, tumblers, goblets and bowls attributed to New Geneva. Gallatin-

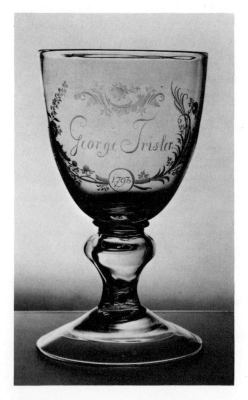

*Amelung goblet made as a presentation piece, cover missing.* Ex coll. Mrs. Christian M. Thomas.

*Checkered-diamond salt, pattern molded, attributed to Amelung's New Bremen Glassmanufactory.* Henry Ford Museum.

Kramer pieces were free-blown or pattern-molded, usually in green bottle glass. The names of many New Geneva workers recur in the history of nineteenth-century glass factories, in both the East and the Midwest.

The other noteworthy glasshouse was that of the Stanger brothers. One of them is known to have worked for Richard Wistar, and in 1780 or 1781 he and several brothers set up their own glassworks at Glassboro, New Jersey. Bottles were the Stangers' principal product, but offhand pieces in the South Jersey tradition are attributed to them, making it probable that their glassworks was the second link in the South Jersey chain that was to extend from southern New Jersey throughout New York

*Sugar bowl of Amelung type.* Mrs. Henry G. Smith.

and New England. The factory underwent several changes of management during its long history, which continued into the twentieth century.

In 1783 the Pitkin Glass Works was established near Hartford in East Manchester, Connecticut. Oval-bodied flasks with short necks and swirled or vertical ribbing made by the German half-post method, in which two gathers of glass were employed, are called "Pitkin flasks" by many collectors, though the type has been found on the sites of other glasshouses. They occur in various tones of amber and green.

The sturdy tablewares of New Geneva and Glassboro, Pitkin flasks and even Amelung's sophisticated glasswares seem plain in

*Small decanter and matching pitcher with engraved decoration in the style of Amelung.* Privately owned.

comparison with some European work of the period. In Amsterdam an artist named Zeuner produced fine *églomisé* decoration, while nearby in The Hague David Wolff was doing extremely skillful stippled diamond-point engraving on glass. There was a long Dutch tradition of fine engraving, and Wolff followed Frans Greenwood in practicing a demanding and specialized technique in which the design was produced by a series of tiny dots on the glass surface. Wolff did much of his work on English glasses from Newcastle, and known examples by him date between 1784 and 1795.

Another artist was J. J. Mildner of Austria. He altered the process used in mid-eighteenth-century Bohemia to produce

*Pitkin-type flask.*
Henry Ford Museum.

*Decanter decorated
by J. J. Mildner, German.*
Photo Corning Museum.

*Zwischengoldglas.* To make this rich decoration, engraved gold foil was applied to a glass which was then fitted into a very slightly larger glass so that the gold was enclosed between two glass surfaces. In Mildner's work the design usually consisted of an oval or circular glass medallion fitted into a corresponding cut-out portion of a plain beaker. Decoration—portraits (on parchment), coats of arms, the four seasons and floral designs—was engraved on gold or silver foil against a background of transparent red lacquer. Mildner signed and dated his work between 1787 and 1807, the year he died.

Well known in the field of French glass of the period are the colored *verre-de-Nevers*-style figures made by Charles François Hazard of Paris.

Across the English Channel many changes were taking place. This was the beginning of the cut-glass era, which lasted until the Great Exhibition of 1851. Though much was made in England, Ireland is often thought of as the cut-glass capital of the period. The second glass excise tax in England (1777) imposed such a financial hardship on glassmakers that many of them emigrated to Ireland. Several manufactories of fine glasswares were established there and when, in 1780, freedom of trade was granted to Ireland, they began to export large quantities of glass to the West Indies and America.

The Irish style, then, was not indigenous, but was a continuation of the English style. Classicism had begun to influence English glassmakers before the shift to Ireland, so the urn and other symmetrical classical shapes were favored, and forms in general took on an elongated appearance. Cut patterns, too, migrated from England; some of the popular ones were the plain diamond, strawberry diamond, hobnail diamond and sunbursts.

Because there was no excise on Irish glass, it could be made as thick and heavy as desired, so glass of the 1790s had brilliant, deeply cut patterns. Form and design became more closely related than before as a result of the practice of having cutters in the Irish glasshouses (instead of sending out blanks, or unornamented

*Pair of candelabra, deep blue canopies, pale amber drops, Irish.*
Corning Museum.

pieces, to a shop which specialized in free-lance cutting, as had previously been the system in England). Among well-known Irish glasshouses is Waterford, mentioned in newspaper advertisements as early as 1783 and noted even then for quality, originality and variety of form. All types of glass tablewares—decanters, jugs, glasses, salt cellars, bowls, dishes—were made at Waterford. Also first rate was Benjamin Edwards' glasshouse at Belfast, established in 1776 and first advertised in 1781. He, too, produced all sorts of

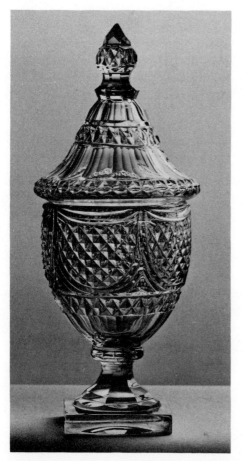

*Cut-glass vase of classical-urn form, Irish.* Victoria and Albert Museum.

*Waterford chandelier, urn-shape shaft.* Corporation of Waterford, Ireland.

lead-glass tablewares, including cut and plain decanters, punch glasses, cruets, salts and goblets.

Forms tended to be Anglo-Irish rather than strictly one or the other. Wineglasses had shorter stems, often faceted, and were frequently decorated with narrow horizontal bands of low-relief diamonds. Cylindrical tumblers are found with increasing frequency. And the "rummer," a long-bowled, very short-stemmed goblet which evolved from the old German *Römer,* became popu-

lar. The pleasing decanter shape with gradually sloping shoulders and a long neck was continued until, toward the close of the century, raised neck rings and mushroom stoppers reflected the trend toward more massive shapes.

Candlesticks, like almost all other forms, were elongated and their resemblance to classical columns increased. Square feet and urn-shape stems became popular in the latter part of the period. Chandeliers, the grandest production of glassmakers of any era, underwent a similar transformation. A Grecian urn replaced the globes of the shaft, and swags made of small pear-shape drops added to the already considerable glitter.

Thus the variety of elegant glasswares available to Americans with a taste for them was wide, but at the same time humbler wares of all sorts continued to be exported to America in quantity for those who may have had the taste but lacked the funds to indulge it.

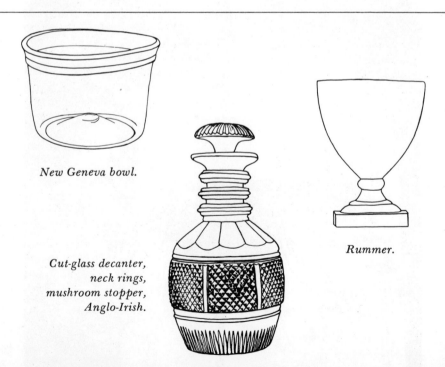

*New Geneva bowl.*

*Cut-glass decanter,
neck rings,
mushroom stopper,
Anglo-Irish.*

*Rummer.*

*1700-1800*
## Pewter
## and Other Metals

By the beginning of the eighteenth century many Colonists had fairly large houses and certain of the articles that had been the pride of the seventeenth-century hall lost prominence as others— for the bedroom and parlor—gained in importance. Iron and copper were now likely to be found mainly in the kitchen or around the fireplace, while brass and pewter were made in an increasingly wide variety of forms for every room in the house.

# PEWTER

Up until the time of the Revolutionary War pewter was imported from England in very large quantities. After the war, according to Ledlie Laughlin (*Pewter in America*), "the pewter trade in the larger cities declined precipitately, hastened to its end by the importation from England of china and other substitutes. . . . In country districts . . . the demand for pewter apparently kept up, perhaps increased; and, because the importation of pewter had dwindled, many country makers did a tremendous business." It was in this period, from late in the eighteenth century until about 1850, that the greatest number of surviving American pieces were made.

We know the names of several early eighteenth-century pewterers but very little American work of the first half of the century exists. Colonial craftsmen didn't try to equal the range of forms of European pewter, but produced instead necessities such as plates and basins, spoons and mugs. Some makers used the same molds in different combinations to achieve a greater variety of forms than would have otherwise been possible. The principal

*The Raleigh Tavern bar is equipped with pewter measures, mugs and tankards, and lighted by a tin chandelier.* Colonial Williamsburg Foundation.

*Pewter tablewares in a variety of forms and styles that were used in America.* Historic Deerfield, Inc.

influence was English, but other European styles were represented in the middle colonies by pewterers reproducing the forms and ornamental techniques of their native lands. The longer these men remained in America, of course, the more their work reflected prevailing English fashions.

The baluster was a popular English motif as the century opened, and in pewter it was represented by the pear-shape two-handled covered cup and the baluster measure with volute (scroll-like) thumbpiece. Also typical were the Scottish potbelly measure, whose name furnishes us with a description of the form; the acorn flagon, with a similarly descriptive name; and the tankard. Early eighteenth-century tankards were dome-topped tapering cylinders, sometimes with mid-band, but as the century progressed this basic shape was joined for a few years by the tulip shape with double-scroll handle. Plates were exported to the Colonies in quantity, for although European ceramics were available in increasing numbers throughout the 1700s, the average Colonial family continued to use pewter. Early in the century, English pewter plates had narrow rims, but within a few decades double or triple reeding, or a wavy edge, added a pleasing finishing touch.

An advertisement in the *Pennsylvania Gazette* for March 22, 1733, gives an idea of what pewter dealers had on their shelves: "to all lovers of decency neatness and Tea Table decorum. Just

*Pear-shape pewter teapot, English.* Old Sturbridge Village.

arrived from London, all sizes of the best white metal Pewter Tea
Pots, likewise Tea Stands, Cream Sauce Pans, Tea-Spoons, and
other Curiosities, all of which are of the newest fashion and so very
neat as not easily to be distinguished from Silver." Serving dishes
and a variety of other table items, lighting equipment, clock dials,
boxes, nursing bottles, chamber pots and buttons and buckles were
among the other wares offered to Colonial shoppers.

Silver shapes, where appropriate, were standard for pewter,
too, so tea wares and other fashionable forms were made in the
Queen Anne, Chippendale and neoclassical styles as they succeeded one another. But part of pewter's charm is its simplicity,
and the heights of rococo swirling and curling were usually left to
the silversmith.

American pewter of the period tends to show little stylistic
development because of the English reluctance to make molds and
raw materials available to Colonial pewterers. Early eighteenth-
century shapes were the ones that were used, generally speaking,
throughout the century, although after 1750 pewterers in the
larger cities began making such forms as teapots, creamers and
sugar bowls in rococo and neoclassical shapes.

Typical forms would include first of all those necessary for
dining: plates, dishes, mugs and tankards, beakers and spoons.
Plates were made during the whole century in a single-reeded
version and for a period during the middle years there was a
smooth-rimmed type as well. The cylindrical, tapering tankard
with mid-rib and domed or double-domed top was the usual
American form. As the 1800s approached, the mug superseded the
tankard, for by that time other materials (silver, Sheffield plate,
ceramics, glass) were filling the needs of the wealthy and pewter
was relegated to less affluent (or less fashion-conscious) homes.
Tulip-shape tankards and mugs never had much popularity
among American makers, although some do exist. Flaring pewter
beakers in a wide variety of sizes were standard throughout the
1700s.

Spoons were made in very large quantities in the Colonies,
the early ones being the slip end and trifid end. About the time of

the Revolution the oval-bowled, rounded-end form came into fashion. Long-handled serving spoons are considered rare, as are ladles.

In the second half of the century, when tea wares began to be made in America, they appeared in the Queen Anne shapes that had long since been outmoded in England; almost simultaneously, however, the round neoclassical teapot was introduced. Round and inverted-pear sugar bowls and footed pear-shape creamers were contemporary with these pots; today they are very rare.

Porringers were a widely made pewter form, and examples

*Pewter seal-top spoons*
*in pewter spoon rack, English.*
Colonial Williamsburg.

*Pewter plate with*
*single band of reeding, Boston.*
Dr. Robert Mallory.

vary considerably from region to region. They came into fashion in the Colonies about 1750, just as they were going out in England. Most extant American examples, in fact, were made after 1800. Several handle types were made (porringer bowls show little variation), among them the so-called crown handle, derived originally from the design of a viscount's coronet, in New York and New England; the flowered, or openwork handle—also English inspired—in New England; and the solid, or tab, handle in Pennsylvania, where its Continental origin was familiar and appreciated, and in Rhode Island, where the flourishing seaport town of Newport catered to buyers of both English and Continental extraction.

*Tankard, wriggle-work decoration, rare in America, by John Will, New York.* Ex coll. C. K. Davis.

*Sugar bowl, inverted-pear shape, Philadelphia.* Henry Ford Museum.

Ecclesiastical pewter is often treated as a separate category, but in fact many pieces used in the communion service were the same as those used at home. Flagons were frequently reserved for church use in the Colonies, but in less well-to-do communities a tankard was sometimes substituted. While European flagons were made in a variety of shapes, Colonial examples were usually conservative—tapering, cylindrical vessels resembling tankards but taller and more imposing. They also often had spouts. Lids were domed or double-domed, topped sometimes by a finial. Chalices are another form usually associated with ecclesiastical use in the Colonies, but here again, in modest churches cups or beakers took their place. Dishes, a basin or bowl for baptism, and plates or

*Pewter porringers with plain tab, crown and openwork handles, American.*
Henry Ford Museum.

patens (the articles used to hold communion bread) were the other pieces ordinarily set aside for communion service.

Pewterers working in the Colonies in the eighteenth century include, from 1700 to 1725 Francis Bassett I, John Bassett I and Joseph Leddel, Sr., of New York; and William Cox and Simon Edgell of Philadelphia. From 1725 to 1750 John Carnes, David Cutler and Thomas Simpkins of Boston; Thomas Danforth I of Connecticut; Peter Kirby and Joseph Leddel, Jr., of New York; and Thomas Byles of Philadelphia. From 1750 to 1775 John Danforth and Jacob Whitmore of Connecticut; Nathaniel Austin, Thomas Badger and John Skinner of Massachusetts; Richard Lee, Sr. and Jr., of New England (these men also worked in brass); Francis Bassett II, Frederick Bassett, Robert Boyle, Peter and William Kirby, and Henry and John Will of New York; Cornelius Bradford, Byles, Johann C. Heyne and William Will of Pennsylvania; and Samuel Hamlin and Gershom Jones of Rhode Island.

*Pewter flat-top tankard and mug.*

*Pewter measures in graduated sizes.*

From 1775 to 1800 Edward, John, Joseph, Samuel, Thomas II, Thomas III and William Danforth, Jacob Eggleston and Ebenezer Southmayd of Connecticut; Richard Austin, Badger, Samuel Green, Samuel Pierce and Skinner of Massachusetts; Francis and Frederick Bassett, George Coldwell, William Kirby, Henry Will and Peter Young of New York; Jacob Eggleston (from *c.* 1810) of North Carolina; William Billings, Parks Boyd, John Andrew Brunstrom, Thomas Danforth III and William Will of Pennsylvania; and William Billings, Hamlin, Jones and David Melville of Rhode Island.

In 1769 a metal rivaling pewter was introduced by John Vickers of Sheffield, England. This soft alloy of tin, called "white ware," was, to the casual observer, difficult to distinguish from silver. In the early 1790s a harder alloy, called "britannia," was evolved; it was so superior that it eventually superseded pewter in both England and America.

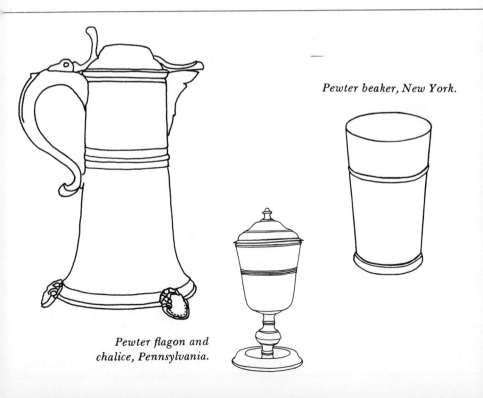

*Pewter beaker, New York.*

*Pewter flagon and chalice, Pennsylvania.*

# BRASS AND COPPER

The brass and copper articles which represented such an important and attractive part of the Colonial household are often impossible to pin down as to date and country of origin. A great deal of both was imported from the Continent and from England, and as was the case with pewter, old copper and brass pots, pans and kettles were melted down by American coppersmiths and brassfounders to obtain metal to make new pieces.

Saucepans, kettles, dippers and other utilitarian forms were made in the same style over long periods of time, which makes dating uncertain. And Colonial workers copied European styles, which makes attribution difficult. In addition, European examples were usually unmarked, as were many Colonial ones, so sorting out the various wares becomes even harder.

Unlike pewter, which required an ore not found in the Colonies, copper (from which both copper and brass objects are made) was available, but the unbending attitude of the British toward its use by Colonial craftsmen kept the production of native wares down. Copper was not an easy metal to deal with, so the

English welcomed improvements in refining and purifying it: in 1725 George Moore took out a patent for his improved process, and in 1728 the Hawksbee-Lund patent further improved existing methods. Also in 1728, John Cook patented a rolling machine for copper, brass and iron.

The Colonists who made vessels of brass and copper usually sold imports, too, and might have worked in one or more of several other metals—pewter, tin, iron or silver. Besides objects for household use, early metalworkers produced "all sorts of tools, construction materials for ships and houses, stills, and commercial equipment . . . cannon and firearms . . . tools for other crafts" (Dean Fales, "Notes on Early American Brass and Copper," *Antiques,* December 1958). One of the earliest-known American brassfounders was Caspar Wistar of glass fame, described in a contemporary document as a "Brass button maker of Philadelphia" (Wistar arrived in that city in 1717) .

*American copper teakettle.* Privately owned.

But it is the housewares that concern us here, and they are subject enough. Teakettles, one of the most attractive forms, were also the most frequently marked. There was quite a range in size, though not in form: a typical example would have a circular body curving up and out from the base to a gently rounded shoulder, an inset cover, an angular gooseneck spout and a flat handle which forms an arch over the body. Most of the signed examples are from Pennsylvania, but marked New York, New England and Virginia teakettles exist as well.

European teakettles differ in having covered spouts (Scandinavia), bulbous bodies (Holland) and cast handles (England), and they were not normally signed. (This and much of the following information is from Henry J. Kauffman's *American Copper and Brass*.)

Warming pans are another especially interesting form, partly because they are so decorative and partly because their function—

*European copper teakettle with covered spout.* Privately owned.

*Copper warming pan, engraved lid, oak handle, English or American.* Colonial Williamsburg.

warming the cold sheets just before retiring—evokes a nostalgic, maybe even envious, response in many of us. Although warming pans of silver, copper or marriages of brass and copper are known, they are most commonly found in brass. So highly regarded in the seventeenth century that they were mentioned specifically in wills, they continued to be lovingly made and used in succeeding periods. The pan itself was round and flat with a hinged top that lifted so that hot coals could be placed inside. Lids were chased, decorated with *repoussé* work, or engraved with flowers, animals or geometric patterns.

Kettles were made for all sorts of special uses: brewing, dyeing, cooking fish and making apple butter. Saucepans, scarce today, were widely advertised in the eighteenth century. They were flat-bottomed with slightly curving sides and were tinned inside. Stewpans, frying pans, coffeepots, chocolate pots, ladles and skimmers are other forms advertised in Colonial America.

*Brass fender showing Adam influence in pierced and engraved design, English.* Victoria and Albert Museum.

*Brass skimmer and ladle marked "R. Lee." Massachusetts.* Privately owned.

*Brass andirons found in Savannah, Georgia.* Museum of Early Southern Decorative Arts.

Brass, a durable metal that stood up well over the years, was perfect for objects that saw everyday use but were ornamental, too. It was, for example, eminently suitable for fireplace equipment for parlor and bedroom. Usually fire tools and andirons were made of a combination of iron and brass, but the most elegant ones, probably imported, were all brass. No early eighteenth-century andirons, in fact, are known to have been made in America, though it is possible that by the Queen Anne period Colonial examples were being produced. Characteristic of the first half of the century is the baluster form with cabriole legs and claw-and-ball, penny or snake feet. From 1760 classical column forms and urn finials were available. During the second half of the century short andirons came into fashion, some in the form of a steeple, and these remained popular into the nineteenth century.

*Eighteenth-century fireplace and lighting equipment in a contemporary setting.*
Historic Deerfield, Inc.

Brass and steel fenders, whose original purpose was to protect the room from flying sparks, appeared in England in the first quarter century. They served a decorative function, too, for they were often pierced and engraved. Early fenders had straight fronts and simple, curved corners; later ones were serpentine or had bowed fronts. As the neoclassical influence spread in the second half of the 1700s very delicate, intricate pierced patterns ornamented fenders. This concentration on detail, characteristic of the Adam style in England, extended to all finely made fire tools, which were wrought with great care, and to andirons, which were sometimes engraved.

Candlesticks are, of course, one of the most obvious brass forms. Many were imported, and they followed the general stylistic trends of the century. The baluster was common from the early

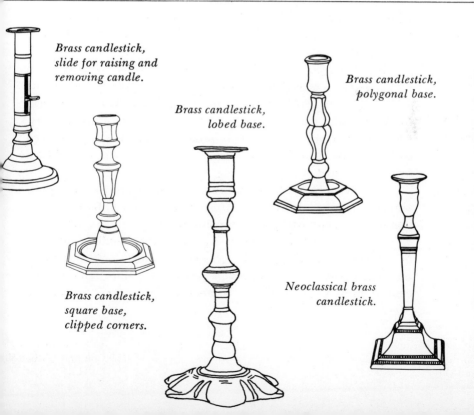

*Brass candlestick, slide for raising and removing candle.*

*Brass candlestick, lobed base.*

*Brass candlestick, polygonal base.*

*Brass candlestick, square base, clipped corners.*

*Neoclassical brass candlestick.*

1700s through the Chippendale period. Bases were round, square or octagonal until the Queen Anne period, when the lobed foot appeared. As the rococo style took hold, there was greater elaboration of bases especially, but also of sockets and stems. With the classical revival, bases became geometrical again (often round or square), and the baluster became less curvy and more geometrical or was transformed into a classical column. Ornament was symmetrical and balanced in such motifs as stylized leaves, reeding and beading.

In the last quarter of the century an alloy of zinc, copper and nickel called "paktong" came into fashion in England for chimney furniture and candlesticks.

Chandeliers and sconces were imported in larger numbers. Though chandeliers were occasionally made of pewter or silver, they were most often of brass. In the second quarter century, the globular stem was popular in America, and the fluted vase-shape shaft was coming into fashion in England. Later the urn motif was favored. Hall lanterns with glazed sides were another attractive brass lighting device of the period.

By the 1720s arched clock dials had come into style in England. Here again the engraver's skill is apparent, for many dials were very elaborately ornamented. Clock dials and works continued to be made of brass until the last quarter of the century, when wooden works were widely produced. The elegant engraved and enameled clock faces of former years were sometimes replaced by printed paper ones.

Another adjunct to furniture consisted of the handles, pulls and escutcheons known as "furniture brasses." Bail or ring handles on light backplates, sometimes engraved, are found on early eighteenth-century pieces. By 1730 drop handles had gone out of style altogether, and the heavier "batwing" form so familiar on Queen Anne and Chippendale pieces came into fashion. Mid-century brasses were made on a somewhat larger scale to conform

*Brass lantern, Engli*
Colonial Williamsb

to generous Chippendale proportions. Intricate rococo versions, elaborately pierced and with scrolling outlines, are typical of this period. Some, found especially on very high-style Chippendale highboys and similarly imposing pieces, were of ormolu, or gilded brass or bronze. (Ormolu was also used for some of the most elegant chandeliers and candlesticks in the rococo and neoclassical tastes; it was introduced into England by Matthew Boulton of Birmingham in 1762.) Brasses in the neoclassical style were nor-

*Queen Anne and Chippendale furniture brasses.*

*Brass chandelier, English.* Historic Deerfield, Inc

mally circular or oval in shape, sometimes rectangular with clipped corners. Such motifs as rosettes, eagles, baskets of flowers and classical temples decorated backplates and the flat, circular knobs used on smaller pieces. Some furniture hardware grew heavier in feeling in the last years of the century and the early years of the nineteenth as Sheraton-style furniture began the trend toward the greater massiveness of the Empire period. Lion heads supporting rings were handsome on such transitional pieces.

*Arched clock dial, engraved brass, possibly Baltimore.*
Baltimore Museum of Art.

*Neoclassical drawer pull.*

*Colonial kitchen equipped with utensils and vessels of iron,
brass and copper.* Colonial Williamsburg.

A number of pewterers, as well as an occasional silversmith,
worked in brass and copper. Eighteenth-century American makers
of brass and copper housewares include Daniel King, Benjamin
Harbeson (also of Lancaster), and Oat & Cooke of Philadelphia;
Philip Syng of Annapolis, Maryland; James Kip, Abram Montayne,
Richard Wittingham, and James and Aaron Rogers of New York;
Richard Lee, Sr. and Jr., of New England; Jeffrey Lang of Salem,
Massachusetts; and Bolton & Grew and Paul Revere of Boston.

# IRON

From brass and copper we move to iron—often less noticeable, but frequently just as thoughtfully designed. Chimney furniture, grates, firebacks, tools, andirons and so on were wholly or partly iron (in the case of andirons and fire tools, brass finials were common, and the horizontal bar for holding logs was always iron).

Firebacks were of cast iron with molded decoration. Early in the eighteenth century English examples showed Dutch influence in design and in thinner construction. Stoves, increasingly popular throughout the 1700s, were also of cast iron. Benjamin Franklin introduced an open stove with a hearth which extended into the room in the 1740s. The Franklin stove—actually not an invention but rather a synthesis of ideas about more efficient use of heat already current in England and France—has become a generic term for this type: many examples bear cast ornament in the neo-classical and Empire styles which became popular many years after Franklin launched his stove. In 1761 Thomas Maybury, also of Pennsylvania, cast the "ten-plate stove," important because it was the first designed for both cooking and heating.

Much of the most decorative wrought iron was made by Pennsylvania German craftsmen. Among their productions were kitchen implements of all kinds, latches and hinges, and weathervanes, most of which, when placed against a blank wall or similar background, may be enjoyed simply as graceful, well-balanced designs. Such articles were made elsewhere, too, of course, but

*Cast-iron fireback with the arms of the*
*Earl of Fairfax; Marlboro Furnace, Frederick County, Virginia.*
Museum of Early Southern Decorative Arts.

Pennsylvania is the home of many of the most interesting and imaginative.

Wrought-iron candlestands were more numerous, especially late in the century. Tripod or four-footed bases supported these attractive lighting devices, which had either a single or double arm. It is thought that the double-armed variety is American, for

*Cast-iron Franklin stove with neoclassical ornament; Frederick County, Maryland.* Museum of Early Southern Decorative Arts.

"most European examples have only single arms" (Fales, *Antiques,* December 1958). Candle sockets, knops and finials were sometimes of brass.

After 1750 iron was processed at Elizabeth Furnace (Jacob Huber and the famous Henry William Stiegel), Charming Forge (Stiegel again), and the Carlisle Iron Works, among others. After 1775 there were the Carlisle Furnace, Cumberland Furnace, Laurel Forge, Mount Holly and Pine Grove (Ege family) —all in Pennsylvania.

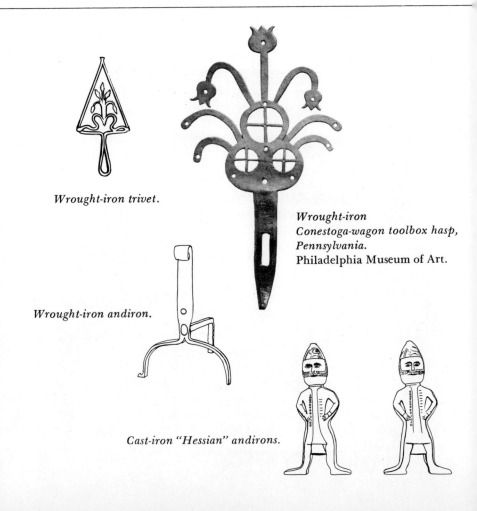

*Wrought-iron trivet.*

*Wrought-iron Conestoga-wagon toolbox hasp, Pennsylvania.* Philadelphia Museum of Art.

*Wrought-iron andiron.*

*Cast-iron "Hessian" andirons.*

# JAPANNED WARES

Attractive articles were made of painted and varnished metal in England from about 1720 and in America from the late 1700s. Tin (really sheet iron with a protective tin coating) was most often used, but metals such as pewter were also japanned. The object was to imitate Oriental lacquered wares, and although both the technique and the finished product were very different from Oriental models, English "japanned" goods have their own charm.

The industry got its start in Pontypool, Wales, where the necessary methods and processes were introduced by Major Hanbury and the Allgood family. Candlesticks, boxes, chestnut urns, teapots and tea caddies were among the earliest products. Trays were always one of the most popular japanned forms and came in several shapes: oval, rectangular, square and scalloped; round trays were called "waiters." A black, red or tortoise-shell ground painted in gold with chinoiserie and edges finished with pierced decoration are typical of early Pontypool work; for many years this factory turned out the finest japanned wares in England.

In 1761 two Allgood brothers set up a factory at Usk in rivalry with the family concern at Pontypool. Bilston, Wolverhampton and Birmingham were other centers of the industry, and though they flourished from the 1760s onward, they never managed to achieve the famous Pontypool quality. In the mid-1760s colors were added to the gold that had formerly been used alone, and landscapes, architectural designs and flowers (from the 1780s) broadened the decorator's scope. Exports of these wares furnished Americans with a practical yet pretty alternative to unpainted metal or pottery housewares.

Japanned tin, iron, brass, copper and pewter—objects of these metals appeal to today's collectors because they were so often transformed from humble necessities to handsome accessories.

*Tin tray, pierced edge; Pontypool, Wales.*
National Museum of Wales.

*1800-1825*
*The*
*Federal and Empire*
*Styles*

*A graphic depiction of
the engagement between the* CONSTITUTION
*and the British* GUERRIÈRE.
Ex coll. Irving S. Olds.

# Historical Background

GEORGE III; REGENCY OF PRINCE OF WALES, 1811–1820;

GEORGE IV, 1820–1830.

CONSULATE, 1799–1804;

NAPOLEON I, 1804–1814; LOUIS XVIII, 1814–1824;

CHARLES X, 1824–1830.

PRESIDENTS: THOMAS JEFFERSON, 1801–1809;

JAMES MADISON, 1809–1817; JAMES MONROE, 1817–1825.

Expansion is the keynote of this period—not only in terms of geography, but also in terms of knowledge, science and national attitudes.

When Jefferson took office in 1801, Washington, D.C., had just become the national capital. The city moved Gouverneur Morris to comment, "We want nothing here but houses, cellars, kitchens, well-informed men, amiable women, and other trifles of this kind to make our city perfect."

There were other frontiers, too. The tremendously important Louisiana Purchase of 1803 doubled the area of the United States and insured interior settlers dependent on the Mississippi an open route to the sea. It also brought into the Union a territory which President Jefferson predicted would "from its fertility . . . ere long yield more than half of our produce, and contain more than half of our inhabitants."

Deep in the wilderness Lewis and Clark were exploring the Northwest to the Pacific from 1803 to 1806, and Zebulon Pike the Southwest from 1805 to 1807. Both expeditions mapped further territory for expansion. States newly admitted to the Union were Louisiana, 1812; Indiana, 1816; Mississippi, 1817; Illinois, 1818; Alabama, 1819; Maine, 1820; and Missouri, 1821.

Access to the interior was imperative, so in 1811 the government began the Cumberland Road, a national highway from Cumberland, Maryland, to Wheeling, West Virginia. From the day it opened, the road was shared by dashing stagecoaches, lumbering Conestoga wagons and cattle and sheep being driven to market. The Erie Canal, begun by New York's Governor De Witt Clinton in 1817, the year the Cumberland Road was finished, was another kind of highway to the midlands. The importance of the canal, which went from Albany to Buffalo, was immense, for it transported people and goods relatively painlessly to the country west of the Appalachians. It also made New York a great commercial center, and Philadelphia was soon supplanted as the most populous and important American city.

The English actress Fanny Kemble wrote that she liked "traveling by canal boats very much. . . . The country through which we passed [was] delightful." But, she added, the low bridges obliged everyone to lie flat on the deck about once an hour "to avoid being scraped off it."

With the great westward movement and the need for communication between interior and coastal regions, the steamboat was enormously useful, because it could go *up*stream as well as down. Robert Fulton's *Clermont* made its first journey up the Hudson to Albany in 1807, in the face of almost universal disbelief: "The morning I left New York there were not perhaps thirty persons in the city who believed the boat would ever move one mile per hour," wrote Fulton. By 1811 the first steamboat was plying the Mississippi, and New Orleans became an even more important port than before. Other navigable rivers and lakes soon had steamboats, which revolutionized life on the frontier. Travel and shipping costs were reasonable, and civilization puffed into new territories within a short time of their opening up. By 1819 a steamboat had crossed the Atlantic.

American ships were arriving at even more distant ports. The Mediterranean offered much of interest to traders, but was dangerously full of pirates. After Americans had been worsted in several encounters, Jefferson sent warships to deal with the corsairs, and for two years the United States was at war with Tripoli.

In spite of vigorous shipping and trading in foreign parts, Americans were turning away from Europe and toward their own west, becoming more truly Americans. By the end of the War of 1812 this feeling of nationalism had solidified, for the new country had cause to feel pride in finally resisting the authority of the old.

Napoleon's ambition to control as much as possible of the world around him made for friction in all directions. France and England harassed each other, and both harassed the United States. In an effort to deal with them without going to war, Jefferson finally led Congress in declaring an embargo. The Long Embargo lasted from December of 1807 until the spring of 1809, and in forbidding American ships to leave American ports to trade in foreign countries, it infuriated the inhabitants of every seaport from Maine to Georgia.

The embargo failed in its object, however, and the United States entered the War of 1812. The first engagement, in which the British *Guerrière* surrendered to the *Constitution,* encouraged Americans. But things generally went very poorly, for in spite of the founding of the U.S. Military Academy at West Point several years earlier, the Army was untrained and of little use. The Navy was in much better shape and in 1813, after Oliver Hazard Perry had defeated British ships in the Battle of Lake Erie, he sent the famous message, "We have met the enemy and they are ours."

In August of the next year the British captured Washington, D.C., burning the Capitol and the White House. December found Andrew Jackson preparing for an attack on New Orleans, and although the battle took place after the war was officially over, Jackson's forces were victorious.

By the time Lafayette made his last visit to America in

1824–1825, he found a changed atmosphere. The small, isolated Colonies on whose side he had fought to gain freedom had become a nation. The great advances in transportation routes and methods and such landmarks as the early use of gaslight (in Philadelphia's Peale Museum) showed progress on scientific fronts; the constantly advancing frontier indicated the way of the future—westward.

# Development of the Style

About 1800 the purely decorative neoclassical style of the late eighteenth century began to take on ideological overtones. Americans, having gained their independence and established a republican system of government, saw themselves as spiritually akin to the ancient states of the Mediterranean. Greek and Roman decorative motifs began to appeal to them as symbolism, not merely as ornament. The French Revolution furthered this trend, and decorative arts of the Directoire period in France reflect Greek inspiration, as those of the Empire show marked Roman influence. Because of a feeling of brotherhood with the French public and because direct trade was now possible between France and the United States, a great interest in French arts and customs grew up in America in this period, and it has lasted to our own day.

The movement toward more exact reproductions of ancient classical styles was due in France to Napoleon's desire to identify himself with the Roman Empire under the Caesars. The Empire style was a conscious attempt to reflect imperial grandeur through massive and imposing forms and splendid gilded and crystal orna-

*Furniture and decorative objects of the Empire period.*
Winterthur Museum.

*A group of early nineteenth-century country furnishings.*
Henry Ford Museum.

ments. It was in this connection that Napoleon's military campaign in Egypt (1798–1799) had an impact on the decorative arts,
for Egyptian motifs stress the international, versus the national,
character of Napoleon's ambitions and achievements. Forms and
ornaments developed in France at this time were, at their best,
elegant and finely made, and they were quickly adapted by
English and American craftsmen.

With the arrival of the American Empire period about 1810
the decorative arts impart, as Alice Winchester has said, "a feeling
of roundness and solidity in contrast with the slender straight lines

and crisp curves" of the earlier neoclassicism. Furniture and decorative objects in ceramics and metals were often copied directly from ancient forms such as klismos and curule chairs, tripod stands and cylix and other ancient vase forms. Winged and caryatid supports, lion's paws, palmettes, lotus leaves, griffins and ram's heads were favorite motifs of the Empire period.

There was also much interest in national heroes and various patriotic symbols. Washington and Franklin were pressed into yet another kind of service as their portraits appeared on fabrics and ceramics, as well as in contemporary prints, paintings and statues. The eagle, too, was enormously popular and was inlaid, engraved, painted and carved by enthusiastic artisans.

As the second decade wore on, principles of design and workmanship began to change and decorative objects were made on an increasingly large scale. By 1825, craftsmen had in many ways ceased to adhere to the standards of the previous century, replacing them with new approaches that reflected the rise of the middle class and the accompanying development of labor- and cost-saving machinery.

# $\mathcal{F}$urniture

During the opening years of the nineteenth century New England, Philadelphia and Baltimore continued to make and enjoy furniture in the Hepplewhite and Sheraton styles. New directions in furniture design first appeared in New York with the work of Duncan Phyfe and Charles-Honoré Lannuier.

Duncan Phyfe went to New York City from Albany before the turn of the century and began producing furniture in a distinctive and personal style that was widely imitated. He was first to make the klismos, or Greek, chair, whose flowing curves unite the horizontal and vertical lines of seat and legs. A little later he began creating curule chairs, a Roman type with rounded, X-shape base. Also associated with Phyfe's work of this period are tables with vase pedestals and tripod supports, cloverleaf tabletops, paw feet, saber legs (like those of the klismos chair), carved waterleaves and thunderbolts, and lyre or cornucopia chair splats. Phyfe's cabinet-making career was unusually long, extending from the 1790s to the 1850s, and as styles and the public taste coarsened, so did his furniture. His admirable early pieces were supplanted in later years by what Phyfe himself called "butcher furniture."

While Phyfe derived inspiration largely from England, the other outstanding New York cabinetmaker of the period, Lannuier, drew on French design sources. He arrived in New York from his native Paris in 1803, and from then until his untimely death in 1819 he made furniture with a decidedly French accent. Characteristic of Lannuier's style were the use of ormolu (gilt-

*Card table with cloverleaf top, vase pedestal, waterleaf carving on legs and brass paw feet. All are considered characteristic of Duncan Phyfe's work, but the table bears the stamp of Michael Allison of New York.* Henry Ford Museum.

*Drum table with marble top and stenciled decoration, attributed to Lannuier.* Henry Ford Museum.

bronze) mounts and appliqués, brass inlay and marble columns and tops on pier tables.

After 1810 the Empire style spread throughout the country. Some widely recognized Empire motifs are the scroll, winged and caryatid supports, lion's-paw feet, Egyptian dog's-paw feet, and lyre splats and supports. A phase often called "late Sheraton" (1815–1820), characterized by twist turnings and spiral arms, stands between Empire and late Empire furniture. From 1820 to

*Pier table with mirror panel, ormolu appliqués, and gilded supports and feet; attributed to Charles-Honoré Lannuier of New York.* Brooklyn Museum.

1830 established shapes and motifs were simply enlarged and broadened. Lion's-paw feet, leafy bracket feet, bulbous turned feet, winged lion's paws, heavy spirals and heavy pedestals mark late Empire pieces. Stenciling, often used to simulate ormolu mounts, and wood graining were characteristic techniques, frequently executed with skill.

New forms of the 1800–1810 period include the semicircular commode, Sheraton dressing chest with attached mirror (a New England form) and the chest of drawers with projecting small columns at sides and a swell front. About 1810 klismos and curule

*Worktable of bird's-eye maple with painted decoration, probably Massachusetts.*
Mr. and Mrs. Reginald P. Rose.

*Convex mirror with girandoles.*
Henry Ford Museum.

chairs became popular and rolled backs or projecting top rails appeared on many chairs. Sofas with upcurved ends, often unequal in height, superseded the earlier type; these are sometimes called "Récamier couches." Sleigh beds, also with upswept ends, were the fashionable successors to high-post beds. As the period wore on, sideboards deepened, extending almost to the floor in the general trend toward massiveness. The convex mirror, with or without girandoles (candle branches), and mirror-back pier tables are two other very typical Empire forms.

Sheraton "fancy chairs" were an attractive lightweight

*Sofa with curule supports, attributed to Duncan Phyfe of New York.* Museum of Fine Arts, Boston; Karolik Collection.

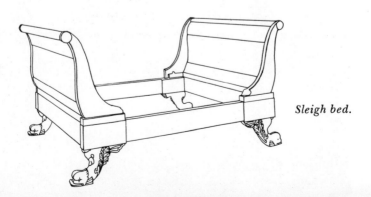

*Sleigh bed.*

painted or japanned type that preceded Hitchcock chairs. Windsor chairs were still very much on the scene, and spindles were sometimes bamboo-turned.

Clocks were more widely made in this period, for less expensive wooden works had made them available to the middle classes. Eli Terry's "pillar and scroll" clock was one of the first of the American mantel and shelf variety. Equally popular was Simon Willard's banjo clock, patented in 1802. This was an original

*Sideboard attributed to Phyfe.* Henry Ford Museum.

American form and was turned out, despite the patent, by many clockmakers besides Willard.

Late Empire forms include most of those introduced between 1800 and 1820, as well as two more massive ones: the cornucopia-arm sofa and the wardrobe.

These, then, were the trends in furniture of the Empire period, made for people who wanted the latest fashions. But much furniture of a simple, traditional nature continued to be produced

*Open armchair with lyre splat.*

*Side chair of modified klismos form with painted decoration, Baltimore.* Metropolitan Museum of Art.

*Open armchair, Philadelphia.*

as well. Among the groups that were relatively immune to changing fashions were the Shakers of New England and New York. Their furniture was in the classical country tradition—with some distinctive nuances. The style depends on good plain lines, good wood and superior craftsmanship; and its essential character is supposed to reflect the ideals of simplicity and purity that governed the life of the Shakers. The sect flourished from the early 1800s to the 1850s, spreading from the East to Ohio and Kentucky, so Shaker furniture made between those years is varied and representative. It was effective and attractive in its own setting, and it

*Windsor armchair with bamboo-turned legs and spindles.*

*Shaker side chair.*

*Banjo clock.*

*Pillar and scroll clock.*

appeals strongly to twentieth-century Americans who see in it many of the qualities that distinguish fine modern furniture.

In the years of westward migration after the Revolution, settlers in the Georgia Piedmont, Tennessee, Kentucky and the Northwest Territory were producing distinctive provincial versions of Hepplewhite, Sheraton and Empire designs. Locally available woods such as cherry, walnut and maple were used, and the early versions were often inlaid with fine lines of vines and swags, oval fans, geometrical bandings and similar designs. As communications improved and shipments from the big furniture-making

*Sofa with late Empire*
*cornucopia-arm motif, Southern.*
Ex coll. Mrs. Frederick S. Fish.

*Shaker sewing table.*
Privately owned.

centers increased, however, the furniture of this region lost its special character.

Besides those already mentioned, well-known cabinetmakers of the period include John and Hugh Finlay of Baltimore; John and Thomas Seymour (dominant until 1816) of Boston; Duncan Phyfe (dominant), Michael Allison and Charles-Honoré Lannuier of New York; François Seignouret of New Orleans; Henry Connelly and Ephraim Haines of Philadelphia; Samuel McIntire (dominant until 1811) and Nathaniel Appleton of Salem. Clock-

*Secretary of walnut with inlay of very fine lines, Georgia.*
Mr. and Mrs. Bolling S. Du Bose.

*Painted Pennsylvania German dresser, or china and kitchen cupboard, with incised and carved decoration that reflects restraining neoclassical influence.*
Philadelphia Museum of Art.

makers include Silas Hoadley, Joseph Ives, Eli Terry and Seth Thomas of Connecticut; Lemuel Curtis, Simon Willard, Aaron Willard and David Wood of Massachusetts.

The neoclassic style persisted in England, too, until about 1810, when the Regency style, the English counterpart of the Empire, took over. Mahogany and rosewood were widely used, as well as exotic veneers. The Roman and Egyptian forms described above were characteristic of Regency furniture, as were brass inlays, mounts and feet.

*Sugar chest (a characteristic*
*Kentucky form) of*
*cherry with delicate inlay.*
Ex coll. Walter M. Jeffords.

*Dressing chest with*
*attached mirror.*

Thomas Hope, whose book *Household Furniture* (1807) is now considered valuable in the study of Regency furniture, was a wealthy amateur designer. Among other contemporary designers who published their work were Thomas Sheraton, whose *Cabinet Dictionary* came out in 1803, and George Smith, whose *Household Furniture* appeared in 1808.

Percier and Fontaine, gifted French architects and interior designers who were responsible for the excellence of the architecture and furnishings of Napoleon's various establishments, published the second edition of their *Recueil de décorations intérieures* in 1812.

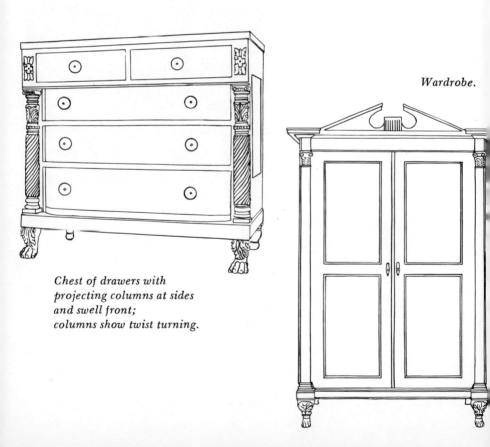

*Wardrobe.*

*Chest of drawers with projecting columns at sides and swell front; columns show twist turning.*

# Silver

From 1800 until about 1815 or 1820 silversmiths continued to work in the neoclassical style, though Empire elements began to appear very early in the century.

The first signs of the Empire were the enlarging and broadening of forms: ovals were lowered, widened and often decorated with chunky vertical lobes or melon reeding. The shoulders of such pieces began to dip, creating a boat shape. Round or polygonal forms were also typical and prestamped or -cast bands of ornament were added to stress the horizontal lines of rim, shoulder and base. Popular motifs for the applied bands included laurel, waterleaf and grapevine. Handles and spouts were often cast in curving shapes that ended in dolphin or animal heads. Other cast elements included large ball feet and supports in the form of winged paws or claws; and finials in the form of pineapples, bouquets of flowers, animals and balls. The art of Egypt provided suitable details here as in furniture: sphinxes were sometimes used as supports, snakes are seen coiling into handles or encircling bases and rims, and various stylized plant and flower forms make borders.

The coffin-end spoon joined the earlier Federal type about 1800; this lightweight spoon had a square, clipped end and was sparingly decorated with a monogram or delicate bright-cut ornament. Table, tea, salt, mustard and dessert sizes were made, as well as ladles and forks—though knives and forks were not generally made in American silver until the second half of the century. The fiddle-handle spoon succeeded the coffin-end in the second decade; this type had a down-curved handle with spatulate end often decorated with a stamped wheat sheaf, basket of flowers or shell pattern. Sugar tongs, forks and other types of flatware followed this pattern, too.

The tankard's long and illustrious history ended in this period, for while the form was still made, it had lost its early vitality. This was due in some measure to the widening temperance movement in nineteenth-century America, as a result of which spouts were added to many eighteenth-century tankards to make them suitable for use as pitchers and in church. The porringer, too, lost its earlier popularity.

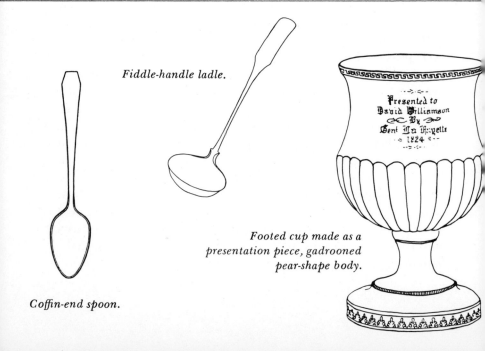

*Fiddle-handle ladle.*

Presented to
David Williamson
By
Gen¹ La Fayette
1824

*Footed cup made as a
presentation piece, gadrooned
pear-shape body.*

*Coffin-end spoon.*

Beakers, mugs, cups and similar vessels gradually took on swelling Empire curves and were often melon reeded or ornamented with some other bold pattern.

Presentation pieces were very much in vogue, especially after the War of 1812, when there were many heroes to honor. These pieces took various forms—tureens, punch bowls and tea sets were among them—but they were always of impressive size and decoration. Many were modeled after such classical forms as the Warwick vase, cylix and urn. The suggestion of kinship with earlier heroes was further stressed by decorative motifs inspired by ancient mythology. Symbols of the industry and plentiful harvest of agrarian America (wheat sheaves, beehives, baskets of flowers) or of the free republican spirit (acorns, eagles, stars) appeared frequently, too. Less awesome pieces of silver were also commissioned and inscribed with more personal sentiments expressing appreciation or admiration.

Early in the period the barrel-shape pitcher, modeled on a ceramic pitcher from Liverpool, was popular. Later, pitchers fol-

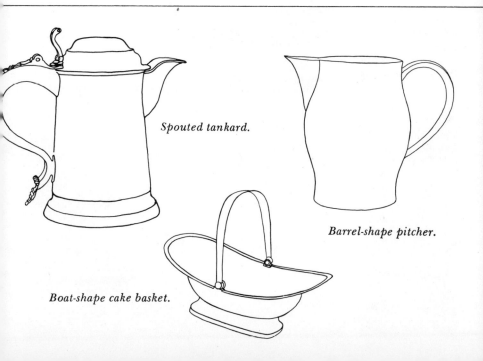

*Spouted tankard.*

*Barrel-shape pitcher.*

*Boat-shape cake basket.*

lowed the Empire trend toward roundness and a low center of gravity. The ewer, often of classically inspired Greek-vase shape, was another impressive contemporary piece.

The tea service and other imposing silver items had become especially popular as a result of the wide use of sideboards, which offered an ideal place for the display of special pieces. Tea sets and the newly important dinner services with matching serving pieces were to become increasingly important as the century went along, gaining in size and variety of forms.

Cake baskets, vegetable dishes, salt dishes and sauceboats are other typical forms of the period, frequently made in the boat

*Sugar tongs with fiddle-shape arms, basket-of-flowers and wheat-sheaf motifs.*
Privately owned.

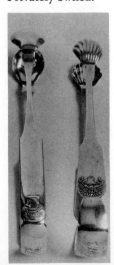

*Pitcher, or ewer, by Frederick Marquand, New York.*
James A. Williams.

*Waste bowl, early neoclassical motifs, by Joseph Richardson, Jr., Philadelphia.*
Museum of Fine Arts, Boston.

shape and sometimes ornamented with bands of gadrooning or stamped decoration.

Candlesticks were of classical-column form at first; and chambersticks, less imposing candleholders that were easily carried from room to room, were round in section with a round base. These were often accompanied by a conical snuffer.

In Albany silversmiths Isaac Hutton and Shepherd and Boyd were working; in Baltimore (where from 1814 to 1830 hallmarks based on the English system were required on all silver plate) Standish Barry, Samuel Kirk and John Lynch; in Boston Joseph Loring, Ebenezer Moulton and Paul Revere (until 1804) ; in New

*Tea set, applied floral bands, by William Thomson, New York.*
Museum of the City of New York.

York William G. Forbes (until 1809), Ephraim Brasher, John Forbes, John Vernon, Hugh Wishart, George Carleton and Frederick Marquand; in Philadelphia Joseph Anthony, Simon Chaudron, Thomas Fletcher and Sidney Gardiner (who were associated from 1814 to 1838 in the firm of Fletcher & Gardiner), Philip Garrett, Harvey Lewis, Edward Lownes, Joseph Lownes (until 1816), John McMullin and Christian Wiltberger.

English silversmiths abandoned the neoclassical for the Regency style about 1810, combining Greco-Roman, Gothic, Egyptian, Chinese and Indian motifs in a decorative idiom that also included a much wider use of cast ornament. Among Regency craftsmen were Paul Storr (dominant until 1834); Peter, Ann and William Bateman; Robert Garrard; Rundell, Bridge and Rundell (royal goldsmiths, for whom Storr worked for many years); and John Wakelin. A new development was the rise of designers, such as John Flaxman and Thomas Stothard, who did not actually work the metal. In 1806 Charles H. Tatham's *Designs for Ornamental Plate* appeared, giving impetus to the trend toward sculptural silver.

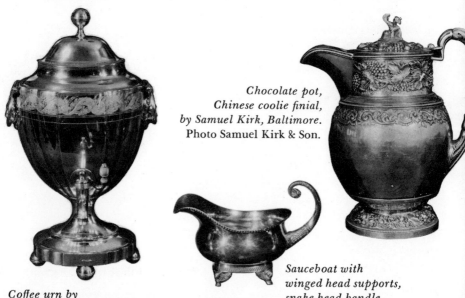

*Chocolate pot,*
*Chinese coolie finial,*
*by Samuel Kirk, Baltimore.*
Photo Samuel Kirk & Son.

*Coffee urn by*
*Christian Wiltberger, Philadelphia.*
Virginia Historical Society.

*Sauceboat with*
*winged head supports,*
*snake-head handle,*
*by Alexander Young, South Carolin*
Privately owned.

# Ceramics

With the end of the Revolutionary War and the consequent lifting of bans on trade and manufacture, the range of American-made products had greatly increased. But one important area in which English imports continued to dominate was that of ceramics, and the variety of appealing and colorful British earthenwares tempted American customers increasingly throughout the period. This meant, once again, that American potters were left to fill the need for crockery of a purely practical nature. Occasional attempts to compete in the dinner-, tea- and ornamental-ware market were met with the same lack of enthusiasm that had thwarted earlier efforts.

Noteworthy among makers of early nineteenth-century American ceramics was the Bell family, led at this time by Peter Bell of Hagerstown, Maryland, and Winchester, Virginia. The Bells and their fellow potters in the Shenandoah Valley made up a large and prosperous group who followed the old tradition of making slip-decorated redware. A little farther north, in New Jersey, Xerxes Price is known to have been producing stoneware at what is now Sayreville as early as 1802; his jars were stamped "XP." Paul Cushman of Albany, New York, operated a stoneware pottery from 1809 until about 1832. He is known for jugs and jars inscribed with his name, the date and the location of his factory. New England potters include Thomas Crafts of Massachusetts, noted for his grotesque jugs; Peter Cross of Hartford, at work by 1807 and the first New England potter to mark his stoneware with his name; and L. Norton & Company of Bennington, Vermont, which from 1823 continued the Norton family tradition of producing dairy and kitchen vessels in redware and stoneware.

Lura Woodside Watkins, authority on early New England pottery, has observed that in the nineteenth century "the whole art of potting deteriorated to the production of thick and utilitarian wares." Of stoneware jugs, pots and crocks in particular she says, "The appeal . . . for us today comes more from their decoration than from the objects." Simple arrangements of impressed

*Stoneware jug marked* XP (*for Xerxes Price*); *Sayreville, New Jersey.* Brooklyn Museum.

motifs such as hearts, crosses and tassels, sometimes enhanced by a touch of blue, were characteristic, while incised flowers, fish and birds are found on more imaginatively decorated stonewares. Nineteenth-century examples are often marked with the manufacturer's name and the date, so that from this time on tracing the history of American stoneware is considerably simplified.

Outstanding in the field of Pennsylvania-German *sgraffito* wares was David Spinner of Bucks County. Spinner is remembered especially for his plates decorated with pictures of horse racing, mounted huntsmen and so on, and for the red glaze that gave a smooth, finished effect to his work.

In 1816 Dr. Henry Mead of New York produced a glazed white soft-paste porcelain vase with molded handles, but no other example of the doctor's work in porcelain is known.

English potteries continued in the early nineteenth century to employ eighteenth-century techniques and, frequently, styles. By

*Slipware plate, Delaware Valley.*
Leah and John Gordon.

*Grotesque jug by*
*Thomas Crafts, Massachusetts.*
Privately owned.

far the most popular of the English ceramics exported to America were the transfer-printed wares that had begun as a specialty of Liverpool. The center for such pottery began to shift to Staffordshire about 1800, and a tremendous amount was produced there throughout the first half of the century. The favored jug shape of the Staffordshire manufacturers was globular with a straight, circular collar, and this gradually replaced the barrel shape of the Liverpool jug. The death of Washington in 1799 inspired many eulogistic designs and patterns, such as the one picturing America sorrowing before a monument to Washington inscribed "Washington in Glory—America in Tears." The War of 1812 and the visit of Lafayette in 1824 provided other very popular themes, usually printed in black, though other colors are found.

The "old blue" or "historical blue" transfer-printed wares of

*Liverpool jug with transfer-printed scene of America mourning the death of Washington.* Ex coll. Mrs. Frederick V. Geier.

*Coffeepot with transfer-printed view of Hartford State House, Staffordshire.* Wadsworth Atheneum.

Staffordshire were far and away the most widely produced. Continued ill feeling between Britons and Americans was damaging the lucrative Staffordshire-American pottery trade, so about 1820 Staffordshire manufacturers began decorating their tablewares with transfer prints of American scenery, public buildings and so on, which they hoped would appeal to American customers. Most were copies of contemporary prints and paintings but some were drawn especially for the potteries by artists sent for that purpose. Cities, obscure towns, historical events and patriotic emblems proved enormously popular when printed in medium to dark cobalt blue on a white ground. The borders which surround these central designs are often very elaborate and represent one of the most interesting aspects of the blue-and-white transfer-printed genre; they also help to identify the makers.

*Part of a Gaudy Dutch tea and coffee set, Staffordshire.*
Henry Ford Museum.

Another extremely successful group of wares was the Dr. Syntax series produced by J. & R. Clews of Staffordshire. The fictional Dr. Syntax had no specific association with America, but he was such an amusing adventurer that he had broad appeal. The series is based on illustrations by Thomas Rowlandson depicting the eccentric clergyman on his travels through the English lake country.

Well-known Staffordshire producers of American historical wares besides J. & R. Clews were E. Wood, J. & W. Ridgway, Ralph Stevenson, Andrew Stevenson, Thomas Mayer, William Adams and Joseph Stubbs.

Bright flower and foliage designs, in colors which were sometimes almost garish, decorated the Gaudy Dutch pottery produced in Staffordshire from about 1810 to 1830 primarily for the Ameri-

*Transfer-printed teapot in Empire shape; medallion shows Fulton's last boat, the* CHANCELLOR LIVINGSTON, *under full sail; by E. Wood of Staffordshire.*
Randall J. LeBoeuf, Jr.

*Spatterware group in peafowl pattern.*
Rochester Museum of Arts and Sciences.

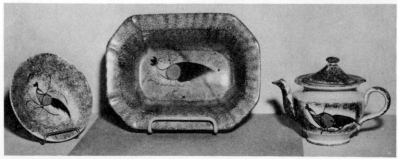

can market. The bold designs on these plates and tea wares had much the same feeling as traditional Pennsylvania German painted decoration in naturalistic and geometric patterns, and the underglaze blue and overglaze polychrome-enamel decoration of Gaudy Dutch pottery made it particularly attractive to color-loving Pennsylvania. The body of the ware was cream color and it was not, even in its own day, cheap; hand-painted decoration was time consuming and put Gaudy Dutch into a higher price range than some of the other earthenwares of the period.

One of them was spatterware, more quickly produced and therefore less expensive. It, too, was a brightly decorated earthenware and was intended by its Staffordshire makers to please all Americans with a taste for gay dishes. Sponged, or spattered, decoration was employed by English potters as early as the seven-

*Assorted shapes and types of English lusterware.* Privately owned.

*Teapot with silver-resist design, Staffordshire.* New-York Historical Society.

teenth century, but the nineteenth-century version was done in a wider range of colors and designs. Plates, tea and dinner wares, water jugs, platters and toilet sets with matching wash bowl and jug were turned out from 1820 to 1850 in nearly 40 patterns of spatterware. Those with the schoolhouse, peafowl and tulip motifs were among the most popular. Later spatterware was produced in ironstone.

Lusterware, more sophisticated than either Gaudy Dutch or spatterware, is another of the gay English ceramics that belong mainly to the nineteenth century. The technique had been practiced in the Near East from very early times; it was taken to Spain by the Arabs in the seventh century, and it spread from there to other European countries. It had been used in England in the latter part of the eighteenth century, but it was more fully ex-

*Spode dessert service.* Photo Parke–Bernet Galleries, Inc.

ploited now and by 1820 had become relatively cheap to produce. Luster decoration was often combined with transfer printing and enamel decoration, sometimes on earthenware, sometimes on porcelain. In the words of Geoffrey Bemrose (*Nineteenth-Century English Pottery and Porcelain*), "The facility of English luster to mince with Miss Austen or to roister with Rowlandson endears it to the collector." And the range of decorations, from prints of contemporary events and celebrities to "pious quatrains" and "licentious doggerel," proves his point. Among the centers for the production of lusterware were Staffordshire, Sunderland and Swansea.

A new ware which appeared in this period under a number of different names was essentially a heavy, almost indestructible white ware. One of the first to produce it was Josiah Spode II,

*Worcester dish with chinoiserie decoration.* Ex coll. Mrs. Andrew Varick Stout.

whose "Stone China" or "New Stone" was made into finely potted dinner and dessert services from 1805. In 1813 C. J. Mason of Lane Delph, Staffordshire, patented Mason's Ironstone, which found an immediate market and was copied extensively. It was cheap, very durable and as practical for large dinner services as for jugs, ornamental vases and bowls and so on. Shapes and decorations were copied during these years from Oriental porcelains.

Another development that belongs to this period and that affected American ceramics later in the century is the glaze used on pottery made on the estate of the Marquis of Rockingham in

*Two pieces from a dessert service by Chamberlain's Worcester factory.* Photo Los Angeles County Museum.

Vieux Paris *vas* *with portrait medallion* *Benjamin Frankli* Governor's Mansion, Georg

*Cadogan pot, English.*

Swinton. It originally covered the distinctive "Cadogan" coffee or hot-water pots produced by this factory and was of a manganese-brown color. A similar glaze was used by innumerable English potteries and was often referred to as the "Rockingham glaze," though "mottled glaze" is another name for it.

The rival firms of Spode and Minton, both of which had entered into the manufacture of porcelain in the 1790s, were two of the chief producers of fine tablewares in the first half of the nineteenth century. Only three of the most famous eighteenth-century porcelain factories had survived: Derby, Worcester and Caughley-Coalport. They continued to produce characteristic or popular eighteenth-century forms and patterns, and they imitated the neoclassic forms and ornaments of Sèvres, but they did very little in the way of innovative work. William Billingsley did contribute something new to the art of English soft paste: a body of lovely white color with great translucency, which he claimed was equal to that of Sèvres. He founded a porcelain factory at Nantgarw in Wales, but because the paste was so unreliable in the kiln he had great difficulties, and the factory was in existence only from 1813 to 1820. Nantgarw plates often had borders of raised flowers, and these and other tablewares, sometimes with painting and gilding in the Paris manner, were the main products.

On the Continent the manufacture of hard-paste porcelain continued at Buen Retiro in Spain (until 1808) and at Sèvres in France. The use of soft paste was given up completely at Sèvres in 1800, and the hard body was molded into classical forms and decorative motifs in imposing vases and other pieces made for diplomatic presentation.

Numerous Paris factories, usually referred to by the name of their street or quarter, also made hard-paste porcelain. Their wares were very similar—they all imitated Sèvres—and unmarked pieces are very difficult to place correctly. The whole group is often called by collectors "Vieux Paris" (Old Paris), and examples in the Empire style with floral decoration are frequently encountered today.

# Glass

Even though favorable conditions for establishing a prosperous native glass industry remained elusive, the glassblowing traditions which had persisted in the second half of the eighteenth century grew stronger in the early years of the nineteenth. Westward migration created new markets, and slowly improving methods of transportation gradually eased the problems of shipping.

There were many difficulties, however. Some were financial: an uneven economy made it hard for new businesses to become well established. And there was still the attitude of well-to-do Americans, who usually preferred imported glass even though American manufacturers copied European tablewares faithfully and sometimes remarkably successfully. Higher duties were imposed on imported glass, but European glassmakers were loath to lose such a profitable market and used every conceivable strategy, within and without the law, to keep their wares on the shelves of American emporiums.

There were two glass factories founded in this period that took firm root in spite of the vicissitudes: Bakewell & Company of

Pittsburgh, representing the new Midwestern glass industry; and the New England Glass Company of Cambridge, Massachusetts. Many smaller factories sprang up, most of them for the manufacture of bottles and window glass. Often they lasted only a short time, but some endured, and it is the wares produced in their workers' spare time or at the end of the day that we come to first.

These were practical and decorative items made for family and friends and probably for sale to nearby householders. Shapes were traditional and functional, so well proportioned that they have satisfied generation after generation. Forms, too, were traditional; everyday necessities such as bowls, pitchers and dishes have survived in the greatest numbers. Sometimes these craftsmen made purely decorative objects which had the doubly satisfying effect of allowing the glassblower to show off his skill and creating a unique ornament for the recipient. Some of the more commonly made ornaments, or whimsies, were hats, rolling pins, canes and witch balls. But many were unique—truly whimsies of their creators.

Most Midwestern glass was made by workmen trained in the tradition of Stiegel and Amelung. As new territories opened up, these craftsmen followed the settlers in the hope that they could fill the need for bottles, window glass and some tablewares. Those who settled in Zanesville, Mantua and Kent, Ohio, did have some success, for these are towns known to have been the sites of production of many Midwestern wares eagerly sought by collectors. Others settled in Wheeling, West Virginia, Pittsburgh, Pennsylvania, and other towns scattered throughout the territory. Their products for table use were made of high-quality window or bottle glass, relatively thinly blown and of considerable brilliance. The colors were usually those natural to glass—greens and ambers—but occasionally artificial colors such as blue and amethyst were used. Bowls and pans, pitchers of all sizes, small compotes, sauce dishes and sugar bowls are some of the most important items produced. Early Midwestern shapes were often similar to those of the eighteenth century, but as the period went on, forms took on the broader outlines of the Empire style. Some specifically Midwestern forms evolved, too, particularly in sugar bowls and in long-necked, swirled bottles.

In addition to free-blown articles, pattern-molded wares were widely made. Vertical and swirled ribbing, fluting, broken swirl (a pattern in which vertical ribbing is superimposed on twisted or swirled ribbing), allover diamonds and diamonds above flutes (a characteristic Zanesville pattern) were some of them.

The small glasshouses that were founded in New Jersey, New York and New England were staffed for the most part with workers trained in the South Jersey tradition, which had its be-

*Three Midwestern bottles
with swirled ribbing,
amber, cornflower blue and green.*
Toledo Museum of Art.

*Pitkin-type pattern-molded hat.*
Ex coll. George S. McKearin.

ginnings in the eighteenth-century glasshouse of Caspar Wistar. The Wistars' long and successful career as glassmakers allowed plenty of time for many workers to be trained in their factory. As men left to take jobs elsewhere the tradition spread, until, by the early nineteenth century, "South Jersey" glass was being made throughout the Northeast.

This was the era when increasing numbers of settlers headed for upper New York State, and many glasshouses were founded to cater to them. As always, bottles and window glass were the staples, but the tablewares that were so often a sideline fall into the South Jersey category. One of the best-known New York factories was the Mount Vernon Glass Company of Oneida County,

*Small compote and dish in characteristic Zanesville ten-diamond pattern, amber and light green.* Henry Ford Museum.

New York, founded in 1810; it produced a variety of forms and styles over a long period.

Articles in the South Jersey tradition were free-blown from bottle and window glass and finished with applied-glass ornament. Some of the most often encountered are threading, rigaree (pinched trailing), bird finials and prunts. These are employed alone or in combination on many forms. Vases, pitchers of all sizes, compotes, drinking vessels and candlesticks are some of them. Here, as in the Midwest, shapes remained the same for long periods because of the lack of commercial pressure, so South Jersey glass is often difficult to date.

Another more or less indigenous American type of glass was

*Blown-three-mold group showing*
*Baroque, Geometric, and Arch patterns.* Toledo Museum.

blown three mold, made from about 1820 into the 1830s. The technique was known in England and Ireland but was apparently not used nearly so extensively there as in America. Full-size molds were used to form both the shape and the pattern in objects of flint glass in blues, greens, amethyst, amber and clear metal. The molds were usually made in three parts—hence the name—and a blown-three-mold piece was impressed with the mold's design both inside and out. This is different from the later pressed glass, in which designs can be felt on one side only. Blown-three-mold glass was made as a substitute for the cut crystal of Ireland and England, but of the 150 patterns recorded by G. S. and H. McKearin (*American Glass*), many are apparently distinctly American.

*ree-blown sugar bowl of*
*lear lead glass,*
*hape and engraving*
*ypical of Pittsburgh area.*
*Ienry Ford Museum.*

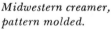

*Midwestern creamer,*
*pattern molded.*

*Midwestern sugar bowl.*

Because of the large number of different patterns, the Mc-Kearins divided them into three basic categories, Geometric, Arch and Baroque. The first is by far the largest category and is made up of objects in many different combinations of ribs, flutes, circles, ovals, diamonds and sunbursts. The Arch group included patterns in which Roman and Gothic arches are prominent. Baroque patterns are composed of hearts, palmettes, guilloches and trefoils.

The objects made in blown-three-mold glass were many, including a variety of bottles and decanters, pitchers, dishes and barrel-shape and straight-sided tumblers.

Pictorial and historical flasks, also made in full-size (two-piece) molds, form another characteristic group of American glasswares. Just as these flasks have attracted a large number of modern-day collectors, so they appealed enormously to nineteenth-century buyers, for by 1820 they were almost universally used as containers for all kinds of liquids—mostly spirituous. Their attractive colors and topical or decorative designs have been described by Alice Winchester (*How to Know American Antiques*) as being

*Blown-three-mold bottle in sunburst pattern.*

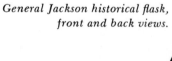

*General Jackson historical flask, front and back views.*

to glass "what Currier and Ives prints are to pictures: they are virtually a record of historical, social, and economic events through the period of their production."

The earliest are thought to be those bearing Masonic emblems and decorative designs of geometric motifs such as scrolls and sunbursts. The historical flasks bore portraits of prominent citizens; national emblems such as stars and eagles; scenes of purely local interest, and so on. Some collectors focus on old flasks of specific subjects, but many are pleased to acquire any that take their fancy. This latter group has great scope, for pictorial flasks are still being made today.

The kind of popular art with a very definite national flavor that is represented by historical and pictorial flasks was far removed from the cut and engraved lead glass being made here to compete with European imports. Patterns were copied from English and Irish examples and every year there were more glass-cutters coming from those countries to do the actual cutting. Thomas Caines, working at the South Boston Crown Glass Company, is given credit for establishing the manufacture of lead glass in the East. During the War of 1812 he introduced it in the hope that he could fill the vacuum in the luxury glass market created by the cessation of trade with England. The two glassmaking giants of these years, Bakewell & Company and the New England Glass Company, were major producers of high-quality cut glass. Other noteworthy Eastern glasshouses were the Flint Glass Works on Marlboro Street in Keene, New Hampshire (1815–1822, when they stopped making lead-glass tablewares), the Bloomingdale Flint Glass Works (in Brooklyn), the Brooklyn Glass Works and the Jersey Glass Company (in Jersey City).

Benjamin Bakewell established his firm in 1808; he made cut and engraved decanters, a variety of drinking vessels, large bowls designed to hold punch or fruit centerpieces, and the like. Bakewell's cut glass was so highly regarded that President Monroe ordered a large service engraved with the arms of the United States for the White House. Another contemporary tribute was paid by Mrs. Anne Royall, writing in 1828: "The glass of Pittsburgh and the parts adjacent, is known and sold from Maine to New Orleans. Even in Mexico they quaff their beverage from the beautiful white flint of Messrs. Bakewell, Page & Bakewell of our city." The glasses from which they were quaffing in Mexico need not have been cut or engraved, however, for Bakewell also made blown, blown molded, blown three mold and other types of the period, including window glass and ordinary bottles.

The New England Glass Company was formed under the direction of Deming Jarves in 1818. There, too, all sorts of domestic glasswares were made in lead glass, clear and colored, cut and engraved, free-blown, molded and later pressed. Cutters were imported from abroad, and indeed, from the beginning the company produced glass which was "in quality and purity . . . not excelled by any other manufacturer in America or for that matter in any country" (McKearin, *American Glass*).

Most of the engraved and cut glass turned out by these factories and after 1820 by many smaller factories as well was of

Goblet with cut flutes
at base of bowl.

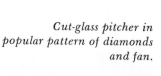

Cut-glass pitcher in
popular pattern of diamonds
and fan.

clear glass. Some European glassmakers, on the other hand, were working out elaborate decorative effects to enhance fine glass further.

Cameo encrustations, or sulphides, as they were also called, gave glasswares something of the neoclassical look made so popular by Wedgwood's jasperware. The technique involved enclosing a white-paste medallion—often a portrait bust of a famous personage—in the glass substance. Some noteworthy work of this kind had been done in Bohemia and France, and in 1819 the Englishman Apsley Pellatt (Jr.) patented his own version. Paperweights, decanters, wineglasses and scent bottles are some of the forms decorated in this way.

The glass excise tax was still drastically affecting glass production in England and was probably the cause of glassmakers' turning to bottle glass for the manufacture of everyday tablewares. The tax on bottle glass was only one-fifth that on lead glass, so it was obviously a much more economical material. The glasshouse at Nailsea is credited with the production of a whole class of tablewares of leadless glass. The earliest so-called Nailsea type was of dark green metal splashed with colored enamel chips. Another type was of a lighter smoky green metal with threads of white trailed around the rim or lip. The third—and perhaps most famous—type was boldly looped or striped. Bottles, jugs and flasks most often bore the distinctive looped decoration, but more sophisticated novelty items with refined looping which can really be classed as latticinio were also made. Pipes, shoes, bells and hats were some of the novelty forms blown in pale green glass with decoration in white, pale pink and occasionally other colors.

According to tradition, round glass "witch balls" were hung in cottages to ward off evil spirits. Whether the spirits in the neighborhood of Nailsea were predominantly evil is not known, but witch balls, decorated with bright daubs of color, are today attributed to that factory. There is no documentary evidence, in fact, of the Nailsea establishment's having produced any of this glass—and these same types are known to have been made at other factories—but it has become customary to call it "Nailsea" all the same.

Ireland, meanwhile, continued to do an excellent business in cut glass. Prominent in this period was the Waterloo Glasshouse Company of Cork, established in 1815. Large cut-glass table services were its specialty. Characteristic motifs of Irish glass in general in these years were pillared fluting, or half-round flutes used in broad bands, and scalloped borders, which consisted of continuous arches of scallop-shell shape. Both were admired and adopted by American glassmakers, who were on the verge of achieving their great dream: a firmly rooted *American* glass industry.

*Nailsea pitcher with
broad looped decoration.*
Victoria and Albert Museum.

*Nailsea vase, dark body
splashed with white.*
Victoria and Albert Museum.

*1825-1850*

*The*

*Late Empire and Early*
*Victorian Styles*

*Wallpaper with view
of Battle of Chapultepec
(from the war with Mexico), 1847.*

# Historical Background

PRESIDENTS: JOHN QUINCY ADAMS, 1825–1829;
ANDREW JACKSON, 1829–1837; MARTIN VAN BUREN, 1837–1841;
WILLIAM HENRY HARRISON, 1841; JOHN TYLER, 1841–1845;
JAMES K. POLK, 1845–1849

Reason, cultivated and exercised with pride by eighteenth-century men, was swept away by the Romantic wave of the nineteenth century. Inspired by ancient civilizations with whose greatness they identified themselves, yet fascinated by the possibilities of their own political independence and the industrial revolution, Americans in all walks of life felt capable of rising to great heights. They were looking away from Europe toward their own culture and, especially, toward the West. This shift in focus was encouraged by Andrew Jackson, champion of the common man and enemy of privilege and monopoly. He looked after the interests of factory workers in the cities and farmers migrating westward, and he fought to break the hold of Eastern power over the country's economy. Jackson's election in 1828 was in fact one of the turning points of the century, for it represented the coming of age of government by all the people.

America was coming of age in other areas too, and one of the most important was transportation. The first American steam locomotive began a regular run in South Carolina in 1830, and in

1838 the first steamship from England to America arrived in New York. From about 1833 to 1858 the clipper ships, those beautiful vessels that seemed to fly across the water, were an important factor in the booming shipping trade. They transported many things—opium and gold among them—but were especially active in the China tea trade, for they could deliver the tea while it was still relatively fresh. Not only were the possibilities of travel and communication considerably enlarged by these new conveyances, but the means for expanding the nation into the wilderness were all at once present. Explorers pushed farther and farther west, displacing Indians and Mexicans in their zeal to add feathers to the cap of the new republic. Arkansas joined the Union in 1836, Michigan in 1837, Florida and Texas in 1845, Iowa in 1846, Wisconsin in 1848 and California in 1850; in 1847 Salt Lake City was founded by the Mormons. Western expansion was so rapid, in fact, that in 1837 it caused a great commercial panic.

The Mexican capture of the Alamo in 1836 was one of a series of incidents that led to the declaration of war with Mexico in 1846. With the end of that war in 1848 the United States acquired land in the Southwest as far as the Pacific Ocean. In Florida the Seminole Indians had risen up to protest against being pushed out; in a bloody war from 1835 to 1842, they were finally defeated. Treaties with Britain fixed northern United States boundaries, the northeast in 1842 and the northwest in 1846. Enthusiasm for charting new territory spilled over national frontiers, and in 1840 Commander Charles Wilkes discovered the Antarctic Continent.

The democratic impulse was effective in small things as well as large, and some contemporary observers were shocked by the careless manners and rowdy behavior that confronted them everywhere. Frontier habits were understandably rough, but there was a lack of regard for the niceties even in the cities. Charles Dickens, describing in his *American Notes* a visit to the two houses of Congress in 1842, said, "Both houses are handsomely carpeted; but the state to which these carpets are reduced by the universal disregard of the spittoon with which every honourable member is accommodated, and the extraordinary improvements on the pattern which are squirted and dabbled upon it . . . do not admit of being described."

Trains and boats were carrying people rapidly from one place to another, and in 1844 another invention allowed them to stay put while their *words* traveled. On May 24 Samuel Morse's telegraph was put into operation between Washington and Baltimore. The inventor's first message was "What hath God wrought!" and indeed the sense of amazement and wonder expressed in that telegram seemed to pervade the age. With each new development the feeling of special American endowment grew; this feeling was not limited to those already here, for 1846 saw the beginning of large-scale German and Irish immigration. The discovery of oil near Pittsburgh in 1845 and of gold in California in 1848 (resulting in the famous Gold Rush of 1849) opened new areas and new horizons. Labor-saving devices appeared: the reaping machine was patented in 1833, and Elias Howe invented the sewing machine in 1845.

Events of a cultural nature also convey the spirit of the age: the National Academy of Design, founded in New York in 1826, was dedicated to "warm[ing] into life the seeds of native talent"; and the establishment of the Smithsonian Institution in 1846 provided a showcase for our native arts. Among literary landmarks James Fenimore Cooper's *Leatherstocking Tales* of 1823–1841 explores the effects of the frontier clash between civilization and nature; and Ralph Waldo Emerson's *Essays,* published in 1841, express the widely felt sense of being part of an all-powerful universal force for good. Godey's *Lady's Book,* a repository of "improving" stories and information about domestic and minor arts, originally appeared in 1830, one of the first products of the popular press. In 1834 William Dunlap published *The History of the Arts of Design in the U.S.,* a lively—if somewhat biased— account of American artists of the author's own generation as well as preceding ones.

As the nation grew, so did national feelings and institutions.

The number of voters increased dramatically during this period. In 1831 the first nominating convention of a national political party was held for the purpose of naming a Presidential candidate. (Candidates had formerly been chosen by Congressional caucus.) From 1833 to 1855 tariff laws were enacted to protect American manufacturers from foreign competition. And in 1845 the United States Naval Academy was established at Annapolis. Among other events of importance were the Great Fire of 1835 in New York (which destroyed 674 buildings), and, in England, the coronation of Queen Victoria in 1837.

# *Development of the* *Style*

Defining stylistic trends becomes increasingly difficult as the nine-teenth century moves on, for the turmoil, bustle and energy that characterize this fiercely democratic and aggressively experimental age are reflected in its decorative arts. The effort to express them-selves led craftsmen to turn once again—as their predecessors had done—to the arts of earlier times. By reviving designs of the Gothic, Elizabethan, Renaissance, Louis XV and Louis XVI styles they hoped to associate their own period with the high ideals and grandeur they felt were characteristic of other centuries. Though there was a certain amount of strict adherence to specific revival styles, in general the democracy of the streets also reigned in the uninhibited mixing of decorative elements. The consistency in-herent in eighteenth- and early nineteenth-century styles seemed to matter much less than the search for self-expression.

The cornucopia, a classical motif which gained increasing importance as the Empire style developed, served as a kind of advance symbol of the course the decorative arts were to take. Its ornateness is a quality that decorative objects of the Victorian era were to display in very definite fashion; it signifies abundance, and home furnishings were produced in quantity as never before; it contains a wide variety of fruits and grains, and variety can be said to be the hallmark of Victorian design; and it represents an optimism and faith in continuing prosperity typical of the nineteenth-century Romantic. It symbolizes, in short, the opulence that was so dear to the Victorian heart. Deep, rich colors, dark woods, bold patterns and lavish use of marble, gilding and mirrors reinforced the middle-class Victorian's image of himself as a deserving participant in the good life that America offered all men.

This unprecedented affluence was due in part to the arrival of the machine age, enabling textiles, wallpapers, glasswares and metalwares to be produced in quantity and at relatively low cost. Developments in furniture-making machines occurred regularly in this period, but that craft was not revolutionized so completely as many others until the succeeding quarter century.

Classical Empire forms and motifs continued throughout the period, although there were hints of the neorococo as early as the 1820s, and the 1830s saw the first of the many lesser revivals. Luxuriant and unrestrained naturalism in ornament was the first sign of the rococo, and curving lines and fruit-and-flower motifs became more and more dominant until they triumphed in the 1850s.

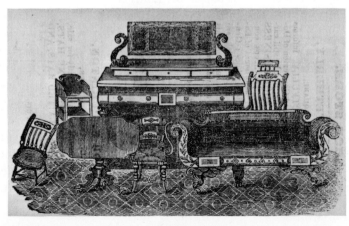

*Advertisement for Stephen Toppan's cabinet furniture manufactory, Dover, New Hampshire, 1830.* New Hampshire Historical Society.

# *Furniture*

After 1825 furniture made in the late Empire style no longer embodied the spirit of ancient classical art. Inspiration, when it derived directly from classical sources, seems to have come from an admiration of the splendid monumentality of architectural and decorative elements of the public buildings of ancient Greece and Rome.

As time went on, a new phase developed in which heavy lion's-paw and leafy bracket feet and the large spirals of late Empire forms gave way to large, plain surfaces, heavy, flat scrolls and projecting columns. Adapted from French *Restauration* furniture of the 1820s, this is often called "scroll furniture," and it was popular during the 1830s and 1840s. Examples are set forth in the 1833 broadside of the New York firm of Joseph Meeks & Sons—a document which has achieved fame because it is one of the first concrete indications we have of exactly what was being made and used in a given year. John Hall, an English architect working in Baltimore, published *The Cabinet Makers' Assistant* a few years later, showing a variety of simple designs for furniture ornamented with flat scrolls. The advent in 1840 of the power-driven band saw increased the appeal of such designs enormously, for they could be turned out cheaply and quickly with the new machine.

Another trend was the Gothic revival. It was popular here in architecture, given impetus by architect A. J. Davis' houses in the Gothic style and, at the end of the period, by A. J. Downing's

*Stenciled sideboard in the high Empire style, flanked by slightly earlier klismos chairs.* Bayou Bend Collection, Museum of Fine Arts of Houston.

*Architecture of Country Houses* (1850). Both Downing and Davis made suggestions for furniture in the Gothic taste, and Davis designed furniture specifically for his Gothic interiors, but the style never attained more than moderate acceptance. It was limited largely to pointed arches on doors of secretaries and wardrobes, and to decorative details such as carved cusps, rosettes and fretwork designs.

*Worktable with stenciled decoration and distinctively Empire carved feet, rosewood.*
Metropolitan Museum of Art.

*Circular pedestal table with Italian-marble top, by Quervelle, Philadelphia.*
The White House.

*Anthony Quervelle's engraved label incorporates several Empire motifs in a fanciful pier table.*
Privately owned.

The Elizabethan revival also began in the 1840s. There seems to have been some confusion in the Victorian mind about which details went with which revival styles, but the ones called "Elizabethan" included spiral twist turnings, spool turnings and split turnings in the shapes of bobbins and knobs. Cottage furniture, painted in the Sheraton fancy tradition and intended for use in country houses, often incorporated Elizabethan-revival details; it remained popular for several decades.

*Painted and stenciled
side chair labeled
by Lambert Hitchcock.*
Privately owned.

*Side chair in the
Elizabethan-revival style.*
Museum of the City of New York.

*Design for a footstool
from John Hall's*
THE CABINET MAKERS' ASSISTANT.

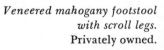

*Veneered mahogany footstool
with scroll legs.*
Privately owned.

One of the first to use the assembly-line method for furniture was Lambert Hitchcock, whose stenciled chairs, also descendants of Sheraton fancy furniture, are among the most famous of all nineteenth-century products. Hitchcock stenciled his name on the seat back of his own work, but there were numerous other crafts-men who produced similar chairs in his day. Now the name has become a generic term and many such chairs have been repro-duced in recent years. The Boston rocker is another well-known

*Horsehair-upholstered sofa in the early rococo-revival style.* Henry Ford Museum.

*Design for a* méridienne *from John Hall's* THE CABINET MAKERS' ASSISTANT.

painted and stenciled type that belongs to this period and to the Hitchcock tradition. It was a comfortable chair with a shaped seat and high back made of spindles.

Mahogany continued to be widely used in this period, sometimes in the form of veneer over an inexpensive wood; and rosewood was also very popular. Marble tops were much admired on sideboards, tables, washstands and many other forms. Carving, painting and stenciling remained in favor as decorative techniques, occasionally supplemented by japanning.

Many forms from the preceding period continued to be made,

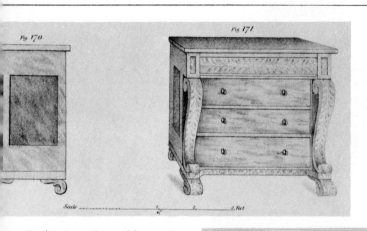

*Design for a "consol bureau"*
*from John Hall's*
THE CABINET MAKERS' ASSISTANT.

*Marble-topped*
*rosewood washstand.*
Mrs. Richard C. Aldrich.

and bedroom, parlor and other kinds of sets, or suites, became fashionable. The *méridienne,* a short sofa with one end higher than the other, was used in bedrooms; one reclined with the back against the higher end. The whatnot, a series of open shelves for the display of knicknacks, is another typical Victorian parlor piece. A new type of desk, called a "davenport," appeared; it was a small, solid rectangular form that resembled a lectern and had a variety of pigeonholes within.

The late Empire chair with wide fiddleback was joined about 1840 by the balloon-back chair with uprights and top rail united

*Cabinet in the Gothic taste,*
*black walnut.*
Ex coll. Frances Parkinson Keyes.

*Dresser, part of a set, decorated*
*with motifs from a number of*
*revival styles, walnut.* Privately owned.

in a curving balloon outline. Chairs with over-the-seat upholstery were also becoming popular; they were sometimes tufted with buttons, foreshadowing the great interest in upholstered furniture that arose in the 1850s.

Clocks for wall and mantel found favor in this period and appeared in a wide variety of shapes and materials. Among the best liked was the steeple clock of the 1840s; this was a plain rectangular form with a painted panel below the dial and a pointed steeple-shape top. The typical mirror of the 1840s was

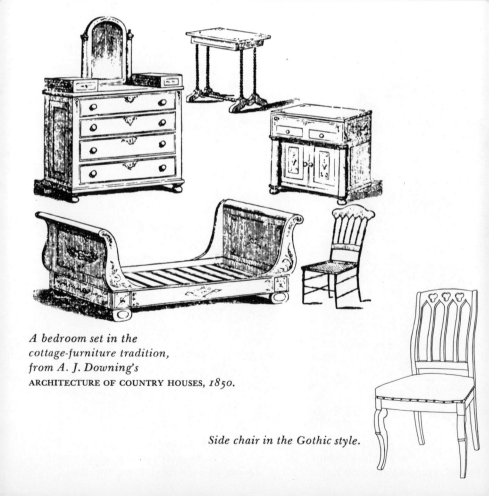

*A bedroom set in the cottage-furniture tradition, from A. J. Downing's* ARCHITECTURE OF COUNTRY HOUSES, *1850.*

*Side chair in the Gothic style.*

rectangular, too, in a painted, stenciled or gilded frame. Some examples have a decorated panel above the mirror, and some have two mirror sections.

Makers of the period include John Needles of Baltimore; Prudent Mallard and François Seignouret of New Orleans; John Jelliff of Newark; Charles A. Baudouine, Joseph Meeks & Sons of New York; Elijah Galusha of Troy, New York; and Anthony Quervelle of Philadelphia.

The English were much busier reviving past styles than the

*Steeple clock.*
Privately owned.

*Carved and lacquered desk,
or davenport, made in China for
the American export trade.*
Photo Childs Gallery.

Americans. Gothic and Elizabethan forms appeared in design books of the 1830s and the rococo gained the ascendancy in the 1840s, accompanied by a spate of less important revivals of such diverse styles as Renaissance and Arabesque. The balloon-back chair took the lead in the 1830s, and papier-mâché furniture and allover-upholstered furniture also came into style. Among important English publications of the time were J. C. Loudon's *Encyclopaedia of Cottage, Farm and Villa Architecture,* 1833; A. W. N. Pugin's *Gothic Furniture in the Style of the Fifteenth Century,* 1835; and Henry Wood's *A Series of Designs of Furniture Decoration, c.* 1845.

In France the rococo was revived in the 1830s, and there was much experimentation with allover-upholstered furniture. As a result of this interest, several new forms were introduced, most of which turned up in England and America in the 1850s.

*Empire looking glass.*

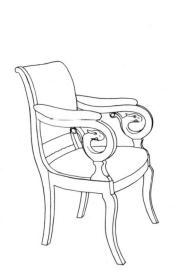

*Armchair with scroll arms.*

*Balloon-back side chair.*

# *Silver*

The catalogue of the Crystal Palace Exhibition held in New York in 1853 stated:

> Works in the precious metals occupy no inconsiderable space in the exhibition, and attract attention by their beauty and the great intrinsic value which they represent. In the American department, and to some extent in the English, they are more remarkable for their value as bullion than as works of art. In works of this kind, as we have before remarked, we are not satisfied with ordinary artistic merit. The ornament must be so rare and rich in design and execution as to give additional value to materials already rich.

The period 1825–1850, which eventually produced both the foregoing point of view and the silverwork in question, was one of considerable experimentation with form and ornament and with joining them in objects both useful and pleasing to contemporary society. Many critics of our own age have felt that they did not always succeed, and it is apparent that they were not accepted unreservedly by connoisseurs of the Victorian era; but designers and workmen were dealing with the wholly new problems of a vastly expanded market and recently invented machines that relieved them of work they were used to doing themselves and, at the same time, opened many new decorative horizons.

Round and polygonal Empire shapes and occasionally the simpler early neoclassical forms were produced in this period. The urn shape was a favorite, especially when it was set upon a high, molded base, or pedestal. It was often accompanied in pitchers and ewers by a high, looping handle that rose above the body. With the increasing popularity of the rococo, fat pear-shape pieces were much in favor, usually elaborately embossed or decorated with cast ornament. The bases of such pieces were often simply a continuation of the body itself, with a low, scrolling apron and foliated feet. Parts made in the forms of flowers, vegetables and other products of nature were another aspect of the rococo revival. This ebullient use of naturalistic elements extended to cast

*Ladle with fiddle-shape handle, by George Doty, Detroit.* Henry Ford Museum.

*Teapot with* repoussé *ornament, by Samuel Kirk, Baltimore.* Photo Samuel Kirk & Son.

handles in the forms of tree branches and grapevines; of finials in the forms of oak leaves and clusters, bunches of grapes, roses, vegetables and, in a somewhat different line of naturalism, Chinese coolies.

The rococo was given an early start by the *repoussé* work of Samuel Kirk, who began to experiment with the revival of this old technique in 1822. He evolved an over-all floral-and-foliage pattern that is widely associated with the Kirk firm, but that was actually employed by many of his contemporaries. He was also one of the first to revive chinoiserie motifs, which proved so congenial to rococo-revival designers.

Other techniques of the period include casting, engraving and chasing (used, as well, in conjunction with *repoussé* work: the design was chased on the outside to highlight it after it had been hammered into relief from the inside).

Ornament of the period had many sources besides the rococo

*Presentation piece with ornament drawn from natural and ancient sources, by Thomas Fletcher, Philadelphia.* Joseph Sorger.

*Sugar urn with acorn and oak-leaf mid-band, by John Ewan, Charleston.* Privately owned.

and the classical: nature in all its aspects was glorified, and diverse luxuriant growths can be observed thriving on late Empire silver. The Greek revival, which was the notable architectural style of the 1830s, provided another source, and Greek-key, waterleaf and anthemion borders, and engraved and cast laurel wreaths were used as ornaments for silver that was otherwise left quite plain. As everybody knows, the Victorians were sentimental—about the past, about nature, about the simple life (an understandable reaction, perhaps, to their red plush and rosewood interiors)—so the popularity of rustic scenes emphasizing milkmaids, cows and windmills is not surprising.

Spoons were again foremost among forms of the period. The fiddle shape was dominant, and after 1830 the handle began to turn up instead of down and was sometimes outlined by a molded thread. Toward the end of the period Gorham began stamping out a variety of flatware patterns by machine.

Presentation pieces remained in favor, frequently based on

*Tea set, once the property of President James K. Polk, by Charters, Cann and Dunn; also marked by retailer, Ball, Tompkins & Black, New York.* Henry Ford Museum.

classical forms with classical and allegorical ornament. Tea and dinner services grew in popularity, too; the tea set often had two teapots, a coffeepot or urn, sugar bowl, creamer and waste bowl.

Pitchers and the more elaborate ewers were still in demand, frequently made in the urn shape mounted on a high pedestal and fitted with a high loop handle. The cake or fruit basket was another typical form, sometimes pierced in an elaborate pattern. Centerpieces in general were an important luxury item, incorporating such elements as allegorical figures, cupids or swans supporting extravagant chariots, baskets and other containers for fruit or flowers. Candelabra offered a splendid opportunity to the designer beguiled by nature, for the arms obviously lent themselves to gnarled-branch and twisted-grapevine forms. Candlesticks were at first more restrained, usually round in section with a round base, but as the rococo revival drew nearer, they began to curve and flow in naturalistic shapes.

Salt cellars and mustard pots offered the designer considerable

*Coffee service, gold washed, by Edwin Stebbins & Company, New York.*
Henry Ford Museum.

scope. Liners of blue or ruby glass, to protect the silver from corrosion, were supported by frames pierced or molded into exuberantly rococo shells, waves and leaves.

Some well-known silversmiths and firms of the period include, in New York, William Adams (who moved to Troy, New York, in 1844), Ball, Tompkins & Black, John W. Forbes, William Forbes, William Gale & Son, Baldwin Gardiner and George S. Gelston; in Philadelphia Bard and Lamont, Thomas Fletcher and Sidney Gardiner (associated as Fletcher & Gardiner until 1838); in Boston Jones, Ball, and Poor (now Shreve, Crump, and Low) and Obadiah Rich; in Baltimore Samuel Kirk (who was joined by one of his sons in 1846 to form Samuel Kirk & Son) and Andrew E. Warner.

American silver was undergoing the same kind of development that occurred in England in this period. The acanthus and

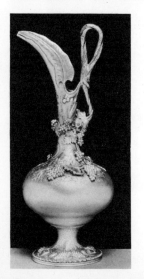

*Wine ewer decorated with sculptured leaves and grapes, by Samuel Kirk, Baltimore.* Photo Samuel Kirk & Son.

*Ewer, one of a pair, retailed by Ball, Tompkins & Black, New York.* Henry Ford Museum.

*Sugar bowl by William Forbes, New Y* Henry Ford Museum.

vine, prominent features of Regency silver, grew more and more unrestrained, sometimes threatening to engulf the objects they decorated. Rococo scrolls, waves and flowers appeared increasingly and the use of ornament based on natural forms in general was very important from the 1830s onward. Tropical-plant forms sprang up in the 1840s, along with the delicate tracery, engraved and pierced, of Moorish art. Elizabethan strapwork and cartouches and Gothic motifs appeared in this period, too, foreshadowing the Renaissance revival. There was great variety in surface effects, achieved through the use of parcel gilding, burnishing and mat and frosted-white surfaces.

Other very characteristic motifs were military and symbolic figures, and exotic ones representing subject peoples, for this was, of course, England's great period of colonial expansion in far-off lands such as India and Africa.

*Compote with openwork basket, molded base, by Gregg, Hayden & Company, South Carolina.* Henry Ford Museum.

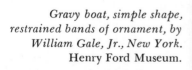

*Gravy boat, simple shape, restrained bands of ornament, by William Gale, Jr., New York.* Henry Ford Museum.

# *Ceramics*

In the second quarter of the nineteenth century American potters finally began to compete with some success against the English wares that had dominated the market since the earliest Colonial days. The ceramics of England, and to a lesser extent of France and Germany, continued to find eager acceptance among Americans, but a handful of skilled men were for the first time turning out native pottery that rivaled European work.

D. and J. Henderson's American Pottery Manufacturing Company, founded in Jersey City in 1828, was the earliest of these successful enterprises. David Henderson was the guiding spirit, and until his death in 1845 the company produced wares of the most popular Staffordshire types. His example was followed by numerous small potteries throughout New Jersey, which became known as the "Staffordshire of America."

Henderson's first product was molded stoneware, followed by molded yellow and Rockingham. Yellow ware was a practical ceramic body of light clay covered by a glaze ranging from straw color to deep yellow, and "Rockingham" had by this time become a generic term for brown-glazed earthenwares whose quality ranged from coarse to fine and whose color varied from rich dark brown to tortoiseshell with amber highlights. American Rockingham is often called "Bennington ware"—incorrectly, for although it was certainly produced at Bennington, it was also made by countless other potteries. Henderson copied from England the technique of fashioning pottery with molds instead of throwing it on a potter's wheel. The method was soon taken up by other factories, for it provided a simple and inexpensive means of producing objects with elaborate relief decoration, and its widespread use marked the beginning of the age of industrialization in ceramic shapes.

Among the designs molded on pitchers, tea sets, flowerpots, spittoons, mugs, jars and so on were naturalistic plant and floral motifs—grapes and grapevines were especially popular—and hunting, genre and sentimental scenes. Two forms particularly characteristic of this period were apostle and hound-handled pitchers, both produced by many different potteries. The quality of modeling of the hound varied tremendously, depending on where it was made; Bennington models are generally considered superior. The apostle motif, in which the apostles stand side by side in pointed Gothic arches, is also occasionally found on other forms, such as the water cooler or—incongruously—the spittoon.

Shortly after opening his pottery, Henderson developed a Rockingham ware known as "flintware." Henderson's flint stoneware was awarded a silver medal by Philadelphia's Franklin Institute at its exhibition of 1830 on the basis of its being "superior to any made in this country."

The range of Staffordshire-type ceramics made by the American Pottery Manufacturing Company also included transfer-printed tablewares and spatterware, both of which were copied quite successfully, though they were never produced in great quantities. One important factor in the firm's success with such wares was probably the succession of English-trained potters employed there. The best-known is Daniel Greatbach, who arrived in this country in the late 1830s and worked for Henderson as a modeler until sometime between 1845 and 1848. He is thought to be responsible for some of the pottery's most successful molded items, and also for several of those produced at Bennington, where he was working for Christopher Webber Fenton by 1852.

Norton & Fenton, in which Julius Norton of the established Bennington potting family was associated with Fenton, operated as a firm from the early 1840s until 1847 (though pottery was made at Bennington over a much longer period). "Christopher Webber Fenton," according to Richard Carter Barret, curator of the Bennington Museum, "is credited with being one of the greatest potters of his time. Wares produced under his direction include a greater number of types and varieties than was produced by any other potter in America during the period from 1844 to 1858." Among those types were common white and yellow wares, granite ware (harder and whiter than white ware but less fine than ironstone), flint-enamel and Rockingham wares, slip-covered redware, scroddled ware (related to the agateware of eighteenth-

*Stoneware pitcher, hunting scene molded in relief, marked by David Henderson's compar Henry Ford Museum.*

*Blue spatterware pitcher, attributed to the American Pottery Manufacturing Company, Jersey City, New Jersey. Newark Museum.*

*Paneled pitcher in rich-toned flint-enamel ware, made at C. W. Fenton's works, Bennington, Vermont. Ex coll. Mark La Fontaine.*

century England in being made of mixed clays of different colors), white porcelain dinnerware and Parian ware.

From the early years of the factory we have Rockingham in such forms as the paneled or rounded jug or pitcher, which was one of the period's typical shapes, tea and tablewares, Toby jugs, spittoons and water coolers, often with molded decoration of floral or Gothic ornament or hunt scenes. Fenton developed a flint enamel which had flecks or streaks of green, blue and yellow in the brown. Fenton's method of applying the color was different from former ones, and Lyman, Fenton & Company (a new partnership established after Norton & Fenton was dissolved) patented it under the name of "Fenton's Enamel" in 1849. FENTON'S FLINT ENAMEL was often impressed with an oval mark in which the date 1849 was the central inscription, and the mark continued to be used for some years thereafter—not always on flint-enamel wares, for the workmen apparently regarded it as an all-purpose mark for the firm's products.

Other utilitarian wares were produced in this period, but they

*Flint-enamel lion from Fenton's pottery, Bennington.* Yale University Art Gallery, Mabel Brady Garvan Collection.

*Hound-handled Rockingham hunt pitcher, made at the Salamander Works, Woodbridge, New Jersey.* Brooklyn Museum.

do not compare in importance with Parian, developed by Fenton with the aid of John Harrison, a modeler from the Copeland works in England, where the Parian body is said to have been invented. It is named for Parian marble, which it resembles in whiteness, texture and translucency, and Fenton used it for many different items, including statuettes and other figures, vases and pitchers.

A similar interest in decorative unglazed porcelain can be seen in the "biscuit busts of celebrated Americans" produced by the firm of Charles Cartlidge & Company of Greenpoint (Brooklyn), New York. Cartlidge opened his factory in 1848, and he made porcelain of excellent quality with a brilliant white glaze and bright gilding. Dinner wares, pitcher sets and such novelties as buttons and cane handles were among the items he made. A glazed porcelain pitcher with molded decoration in an acorn and oak-leaf pattern is characteristic.

The 1840s saw the westward migration of potters—several of them English immigrants—who hoped to capitalize on the needs

Stoneware jug, incised clipper ship, by Daniel Goodale, Jr., Hartford, Connecticut. Henry Ford Museum.

*Glazed white porcelain pitcher, molded oak-leaf pattern outlined in gold, by Charles Cartlidge & Company, Greenpoint, New York.* Brooklyn Museum.

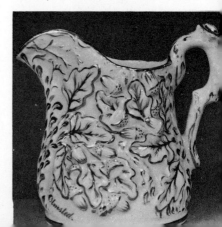

of settlers in developing territories. One of the most important pottery centers grew up in East Liverpool, Ohio, where clay of high quality was to be found. East Liverpool eventually surpassed the potteries of northern New Jersey in the production of various practical and decorative wares. The useful yellow and Rockingham objects made there in this period are typical of those of similar potteries that sprang up from east to west—in Baltimore, New York, Pittsburgh and Indiana.

The first really successful porcelain factory in America was that begun in Philadelphia by William Ellis Tucker and operated under a variety of partnerships from 1826 to 1838. Tucker's wares were patterned after contemporary French porcelains, with classical forms and decoration of gilding, flowers in enamels, or landscapes and local scenes in sepia (a rich reddish brown). In 1827 Tucker received a silver medal from the Franklin Institute for "the best porcelain made in Pennsylvania, either plain white or gilt." The judges commented, in what seems a somewhat disparaging vein, "Some of the cups and other articles bear a fair compari-

*Porcelain teapot, painted landscape, by Tucker & Hemphill, Philadelphia.*
Philadelphia Museum of Art.

*"Cottage" vase, porcelain with painting, gilding and flower encrustation; French.*
Cooper-Hewitt Museum of Decorative Arts and Design.

son with those imported." But it does indicate the attitude that made it so difficult for American potters to compete successfully against their European counterparts. Tucker forms included teapots with spirit lamps, tureens, gravy boats, shell dishes, custard stands, mantel ornaments and pitchers, besides more ordinary dinner wares.

The factory was in existence for only about a dozen years, however, and could not have begun to supply the increasing demand for the rich porcelains so admired by Victorians. European factories continued to meet this demand—those of England primarily, but Meissen, Sèvres and other Continental factories contributed too. The Haviland china made at Limoges, France, for the American market was enormously popular here from the 1840s onward.

The taste of the times seems to have run, after about 1830, to elaborately decorated and highly colored porcelains. Such firms as Minton, Spode, Rockingham, Coalport, Davenport, Ridgway and Worcester were only too happy to supply dessert, dinner and breakfast sets; centerpieces; vases; ewers; and garden pots decorated with floral, scenic or fruit centers and rich gilt borders, and

*Transfer-printed "New Orleans" plate, pink lace border, by Ralph Stevenson, Staffordshire.* Philadelphia Museum of Art.

sometimes with flower encrustation (applied, molded flowers). The heavy classical forms typical of Empire styles of the 1820s and 1830s were joined by rococo shapes, and porcelains of the early Victorian period are frequently curved and recurved almost to the point of confusion.

"The enormous gallery of parian statuary which garnished the vestibules and drawing rooms of the early Victorians was a triumph of the Staffordshire potters," observes G. Bernard Hughes (*Victorian Pottery and Porcelain*). Copeland and Garrett, successors to Spode, are thought to have developed Parian, which remained popular for statues and various other forms for a quarter of a century after its introduction in 1842. It was soon being produced by numerous other factories, and by 1850 Minton was the leading manufacturer of Parian statuary. All kinds of subjects were modeled in this body, from royal to mythological personages, nudes, and romantic and sentimental figures with such titles as "Prisoner of Love" and "Erin Awakening from her Slumbers."

The formula that was used for statues was somewhat different from that developed for hollow and tableware, called "standard Parian." This was harder than statuary Parian and lent itself to the casting of hollow ware with high-relief ornament. Copeland, Minton and Coalport were among the firms that produced vases, molded jugs and similar forms in Parian. One interesting use of the ware was in conjunction with glazed porcelain for ornate figure-supported centerpieces.

English earthenwares continued to arrive on American shores in quantity and in great variety. After about 1830 the transfer-printed Staffordshire pottery was made in many colors besides cobalt blue, including light blue, sepia and green, as well as the very popular pink; two colors were sometimes used together, one for the central motif and one for the border. Ridgway's *Beauties of America,* Clews' *Picturesque Views on the Hudson River* and other such series depicting actual sites and views were gradually replaced by romantic and imaginary scenes. Toward the end of the period ironstone bodies were used for transfer prints, some of which show Gold Rush or romanticized California scenes. The distance between Staffordshire and California is especially evident in one portraying gold miners floating about a lagoon in gondolas in what appears to be more a fantastic Venice than a bawdy frontier territory.

Luster continued popular, the most common item from the 1820s to 1840s being globular, straight-necked pitchers with gold- or copper-luster decoration. Tea and dinner wares and numerous decorative forms were also made. In the late 1820s a number of ground colors were added to the earlier white: buff, pink, apricot, blue and yellow. A splashed or mottled pink luster is often associated with Sunderland although it came from other places as well.

The Rockingham wares which had become so popular in American versions continued to be made in large numbers by English potters. Molded hound-handled and apostle pitchers in the round or paneled shapes that reflect the Gothic-revival style of the 1830s and 1840s were favorites, and all types of Rockingham-

*Covered tureen, or sauceboat, with stand, part of a set of Gaudy ironstone in the strawberry pattern, Staffordshire.* Henry Ford Museum.

*Castleford teapot and creamer, English.* Mrs. William Guthman.

glazed household forms such as bowls, pans, pudding molds and even picture frames were made by numerous potteries.

Also usual for utilitarian objects was the "banded creamware" that had been in production since the late eighteenth century. This was a creamware or pearlware body to which slips of different colors were mechanically applied in bands. Marbled and mocha decorations were often used in combination with the banding, producing very decorative as well as useful wares in the old English slipware tradition. The marbled type had two or more shades of slip blended into a variegated pattern, while the mocha bore a pattern suggestive of trees, bushes or moss. To achieve this effect, a pigment, usually brown but occasionally also blue, green or black, was mixed with tobacco juice and other ingredients and applied to the ceramic surface. It spread into a feathery pattern resembling one of the plants mentioned above; its "delicate brown traceries" also resembled the "markings of the Mocha stone, a variety of quartz from Mocha on the Red Sea in Arabia."

*Banded creamware jug with marbled and mocha decoration, English.* Henry Ford Museum.

*a service, porcelain, by Ridgway & Company, Staffordshire.* From the catalogue :o The World of Art and Industry, New York Crystal Palace, 1853.

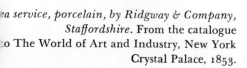

David Dunderdale's factory at Castleford originated a style now known generically as "Castleford," though it came to be made by many other factories. It is a kind of white jasper molded into neoclassical shapes with relief decoration. Most common are teapots, though other forms were occasionally made, and a bright blue was frequently used to accentuate outlines.

Ironstone continued in favor in this period; much of it was undecorated, though transfer-printed ornament in lacy patterns is not uncommon. Shapes were characteristic heavy classical ones in the Empire style, admirably suited to this heavy white ware. All kinds of items besides dinner ware were made, and it was found particularly practical for washstand sets of matching jug and basin. Sprigged ware, made in similar simple Empire shapes with rounded or paneled sides and decoration of scattered raised sprigs of flowers against a white ground, was also characteristic; it is often miscalled "Chelsea."

The making of decorative figures was undertaken by innu-

*Fruit dish, Parian and glazed porcelain, by Minton & Company, Staffordshire.* New York Crystal Palace catalogue.

*Terra-cotta group representing French peasants, by Pierre Adrien Graillon, Dieppe, France.* New York Crystal Palace catalogue.

*Banded creamware mug.*

*Toby jug of type called "Ben Franklin."*

*Water cooler in the "mediaeval style," by Henry Doulton & Company, Lambeth, England.*
New York Crystal Palace catalogue.

merable Staffordshire earthenware potters of the period, and a large and often appealing group of "cottage figures" has survived. John Walton of Burslem was a prolific maker of these figures of important people of the day or of typical English characters. Ralph Salt was a member of the "Walton school," and Obadiah Sherratt produced groups "direct and vigorous almost to the point of brutality" (G. Haggar, *Staffordshire Chimney Ornaments*). There were many more, some of whose names are known but most of whom have remained anonymous. Another important group of figures is that of Staffordshire dogs, turned out by the thousands in the period 1810 to 1870. They were most often made in pairs for use on the mantel, and the most popular of the many breeds portrayed were spaniels, greyhounds and whippets.

This period of great diversity in ceramics—in which simply shaped and decorated wares coexisted with elaborately molded, colored and gilded porcelains—closed with the Great Exhibition of 1851 in London, at which all types of ceramics characteristic of the second quarter of the century were shown.

# Glass

There is probably nothing so uniquely American among the decorative arts as pressed glass. American character is molded into a lacy cup plate just as surely as are its outline and pattern. A kind of pioneer spirit fostered the technical and mechanical know-how that produced machinery for pressing tablewares. Fresh, new patterns suitable for pressed glass were created by moldmakers using traditional motifs in combination with patriotic symbols, local and national landmarks, and profiles of well-known Americans. And when it turned out that lead glass lost much of its brilliance in the pressing process, an ingenious use of stippling restored the lost sparkle.

Pressing machines naturally took over much of the work hitherto done by individual blowers, who recognized the trend away from handwork and toward assembly-line procedures and, not surprisingly, resented it. Lura Woodside Watkins (*American Glass and Glassmaking*) writes that when Deming Jarves of the Boston and Sandwich Glass Company perfected a machine for pressing hollow wares, the glassworkers went so far as to threaten

Jarves' life, "forcing him to remain inside his house for six weeks." Jarves was eventually able to go out again and the glassblowers found work, but they were correct in foreseeing that from this time on the old hand methods would be largely superseded in the field of moderate-priced commercial tablewares. Skilled blowers were forced to make way for mold designers and makers, men who were entirely independent of the glassmaking and -working process, but who designed both the forms and the decorative details of pressed wares.

Beginning in the late 1820s, pressed glass was made in all centers of commercial glass production, with regional variations in pattern and form. The process was simple: lead glass, clear or colored (but usually clear in the early period), was pressed into the mold by a plunger to produce an object that was smooth on one side and patterned on the other. The cost of the early lacy molds was high, but the time saved and the great increase in daily output enabled manufacturers to sell pressed glass very reasonably. The earliest patterns were inspired by such cut-glass motifs as strawberry diamonds, fine-cut diamonds and scallop-shell or fan rims. Lacy glass, made from 1828 until about 1840, was made in patterns whose elements were drawn from many unrelated sources. Generous Empire shapes, often round or rectangular, were covered with leaf and floral designs, cornucopias, architectural elements such as arches and scrolls, and American symbols, to create allover patterns against a lacy, or stippled, background. The "lace" in these early patterns was a clever cover-up for technical faults and loss of luster in the glass.

Forms commonly made in lacy glass include cup plates, tea plates, sauce dishes, salts and sugar bowls. Cup plates are eminently collectible little items that were placed under teacups while tea cooled in the saucer. Monuments, landmarks, national heroes and other subjects of historical interest often served as their central decorative motifs. Salt dishes are another appealing form for the collector. Those made in the second quarter of the century were usually rectangular, with boat, basket and round variations.

Some are marked, making them doubly desirable from the point of view of the student and collector, and Mrs. Watkins suggests that they served as advertisements for their makers.

Lamps were sometimes made with pressed cup-plate bases and free-blown fonts, later with a pressed stepped base or a variant of the traditional baluster stem. Candlesticks came in a variety of new shapes made possible by the pressing process—the most sought after is undoubtedly the dolphin.

About 1840 lacy glass was superseded by a type known as pressed-pattern glass. Lacy stippling required expensive molds, but it had become possible to restore brilliance to pressed glass by fire polishing, so that glass could be pressed in plain geometric patterns which were perhaps a welcome change from the busyness of lacy designs. Panels, flutes, thumbprints and diamonds were used in various combinations on an increasingly varied range of tablewares. The new pressed-pattern wares came in whole sets of dishes,

*Very early pressed bowl,
pattern imspired by cut glass.*
William J. Elsholz.

*Lacy salt dish,
boat shape, Sandwich.*
Ex coll. Dr. Charles W. Green.

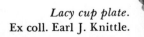

*Lacy cup plate.*
Ex coll. Earl J. Knittle.

and it is theoretically possible to assemble a complete dinner service in one pattern. Color, too, became more important, extending further the ability of pressed wares to appeal to a public fascinated by novelty.

Color was also an important aspect of the appeal of historical flasks, being made in ever greater numbers in this period. Eastern flasks were often in the greens and ambers natural to glass, but Midwestern examples were made in the same dazzling artificial blues, greens and amethysts that distinguished the free-blown and expanded blown-molded tablewares of the Midwest. Pictorial and historical flasks were made in molds and here again it was the moldmaker rather than the glassworker who was the artist. Shapes varied from the traditional rounded, bulging flask to canteen and flattened straight-sided forms. An especially handsome variant was the violin-shape flask whose curving contour was reinforced by molded scrollwork.

*Salt dish, Greek sarcophagus shape, marked by the New England Glass Company.* Toledo Museum of Art.

*Lacy compote.* Henry Ford Museum.

Historical flasks, like cup plates, provide a charming review of political and social events of the period. Flasks whose central design is a bust of Andrew Jackson, William Henry Harrison or Zachary Taylor perhaps served something of the same purpose as present-day campaign buttons: they were attractive, eye-catching propaganda. The Jenny Lind, Masonic and railroad flasks commemorate other public figures, organizations and inventions. Some of the most pleasing historical flasks were made by Thomas W. Dyott. "In the glass world from 1816 to the early 1830s, Dr. Dyott passed from the status of glass factor to proprietor of the largest, most prolific glass manufacturing complex in the East. But except for a few Historical Figured Flask designs, his products—vials, patent medicines, bottles of all kinds, druggists' and confectioners' glassware—are anonymous, as is the vast majority of similar hollow ware from contemporary glassworks" (Helen McKearin, *Bottles, Flasks, and Dr. Dyott*). Dr. Dyott's productive glassmak-

*Lamp with lacy foot, blown stem and font.*
William J. Elsholz.

*Pressed candlestick, dolphin support and petal socket.*
Ex coll. Dr. Charles W. Green.

ing career ended in the 1830s, when he was forced into bankruptcy.

A different expression was that of the workers in Eastern bottle and window-glass houses. The South Jersey tradition was not only preserved but expanded there by workers who continued to practice age-old techniques of blowing and ornamenting glass. Their work represents the continuity of the glassblowing tradition in America, while that of the pressers and molders represents the new spirit of an industrial age.

The history of the country glasshouses in which South Jersey-type pieces were made is unclear in many instances, for not only did glassworkers and factory owners move about with disconcerting frequency, but because their business was primarily in utilitarian bottles and window glass, we are left without the advertisements and factory records that sometimes assist the student of factories whose main line was commercial tablewares.

*Pair of pitchers with looped decoration, South Jersey.* Photo Richard T. Dooner.

*baque-white pressed*
*np with architectural*
*se, marked by the*
*w England Glass Company.*
*s. Samuel Schwartz.*

*Scroll, or violin, flask.*
Corning Museum of Glass.

The offhand wares made in bottle- and window-glass houses of this period were similar to earlier pieces, except that Empire influence can often be detected. Similarly, decorative techniques were traditional with occasional nineteenth-century modifications: lily-pad decoration, prunts, swirled ribbing (sometimes in imitation of the broad gadrooning of late neoclassical silver), swagging, threading and rigaree.

In New Jersey numerous glasshouses were operating in this period, some of the most important in Millville. One very effective innovation especially characteristic of New Jersey wares (though not exclusive there) from about 1830 was that of looped decoration in the glass itself. To obtain this effect, glass threads of one color were added to a gather of glass of another color, and the secondary, or decorative, color was dragged into loops or swags. Usually the body was of clear metal with white or aquamarine loops, though aquamarine with white loops and other, rarer

*Pitcher, dark amber
with opaque-white looping,
South Jersey.*
Henry Ford Museum.

*Sugar bowl
with lily-pad decoration.*
Henry Ford Museum.

*Vase engraved with
flower-and-leaf and chain
patterns, probably
from Washington, D.C.*
Brooklyn Museum

combinations are also found. Some examples have very broad loops, others are finely looped into a pattern that approaches latticinio. Another variation in New Jersey work involved using two different colors for two different parts of one piece. Most frequently encountered is aquamarine with amber or blue. Adding a rim of one color to a body of another was one more way of creating an interesting contrast. Bowls, pitchers and vases were common New Jersey forms; decanters, candlesticks and salts were less usual.

South Jersey-type glass from some of the New York State factories is very handsome. The northern factories at Redford, Redwood and Harrisburg produced "more fine examples of individual lily-pad pieces, and in a wider range of forms or types . . . than . . . any other glassmaking area in America" (McKearin, *American Glass*). The lily pad was a South Jersey applied-glass ornament perhaps more suggestive of waves than of flat lily pads.

*Decanter, flat-cut panels and rings.* Photo Toledo Museum of Art.

*Decanter, clear glass with blue pillar-molded ribs, probably Pittsburgh.* Dean and Mrs. Earl C. Seigfred.

It occurs in variations which the McKearins have classified in three types. New Jersey workmen had taken the technique to New York and, once there, they were inspired to use it very imaginatively. New York forms, often in a brilliant aquamarine or turquoise, included the ubiquitous pitcher, bowls of all sizes, compotes and sugar bowls—all occasionally mounted on a baluster foot, which added an Empire touch and gave the object very nice balance. Witch balls are found as well—usually serving as covers for pitchers and vases.

Other characteristic ornaments on New York pieces are threaded necks and crimped feet; the looping typical of New Jersey work is seldom found in New York.

Many glasshouses besides those mentioned produced offhand tablewares in New York, but because we lack space to list them all (and because the McKearins presented the known material about them in *American Glass*), we mention only the Mount Vernon

*Pitcher with cut pattern
very similar to English and American
ones, Bohemian.*
Photo Robert M. Vetter.

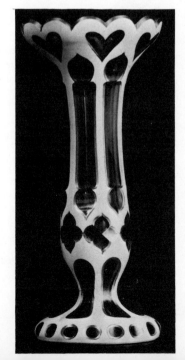

*Vase with opaque-white
overlay, probably Sandwich.*
Ex coll. Ruth Webb Lee.

Glass Works (of Oneida County), interesting and important because excavations on the site have yielded knowledge about the wares produced there: besides free-blown bottles and decanters, blown-three-mold wares, lead-glass tablewares and pressed salts were made. Glasshouses in Connecticut, New Hampshire and Massachusetts turned out South Jersey-type pieces, and there were probably many more whose existence is still unsuspected.

The market for finer wares—free-blown and molded with cut and engraved decoration—was considerable in this quarter century. Protective tariffs had finally been instituted, making it profitable for factories from Massachusetts to West Virginia to produce beautifully made glass for table and parlor. A problem in discussing these wares is that comparatively little study has been devoted to them, and identification of specifically American patterns can seldom be attempted. Another stumbling block is that American manufacturers were imitating first English and Irish

*Goblet with engraved allegorical scene and deep sculptural cutting, Bohemian.*
Photo Robert M. Vetter.

*Beaker, opaque violet Lithyalin with gilt chinoiserie, Bohemian.*
Ruth Bryan Strauss Memorial Foundation.

and then German and French wares, and they achieved such a high degree of success that telling import from American is never easy.

Engraved patterns of the first part of the period are restrained but usually charming: floral and leaf designs, buildings, ships and patriotic emblems. Among cut designs the strawberry diamond in combination with a fan motif, and bands of very fine diamonds, continued to be used early in the period, but flatter cutting and bold paneling dominated in the late 1830s and 1840s. Typical Empire shapes include round or boat-shape compotes and serving dishes, squat pear-shape decanters and pitchers, and large, round sugar bowls.

A technique known as "pillar molding" was used in Wheeling and Pittsburgh for the decoration of "heavy decanters, cruets, vases and candlesticks—all with wide bases" (Tracy and Gerdts, *Classical America, 1815–1845*). These heavy forms were originally made for use in public houses and riverboats.

The Bakewell firm in Pittsburgh produced very high-quality

*Decanter and wineglass with overlay, English.* Ex coll. Mrs. Applewhaite Abbott.

cut and engraved wares and every other popular type including pressed tablewares. The New England Glass Company of Cambridge also made all kinds of vessels for table and ornamental use. Their cut and engraved wares, like Bakewell's, were the equal of any imported. The Boston and Sandwich Glass Company, founded by Deming Jarves in 1825, was another producer of a wide range of household wares from their famous pressed to their now less well-known cut and engraved. Other important manufactories of fine wares were the Fisher Brothers of New York, John L. Gilliland of the Brooklyn Flint Glass Works, the Jersey Glass Works of Jersey City, the Union Flint Glass Company of Philadelphia, and the Wheeling, West Virginia, firms of M. & R. H. Sweeney & Company and Ritchie & Wheat. These factories employed their own cutters and engravers, but there were also free-lance artists who ran shops devoted solely to glass cutting and engraving. They worked on undecorated items of high-quality lead glass, called "blanks" in the trade, and, of course, they add another dimension to the problem of identifying specific makers of specific pieces.

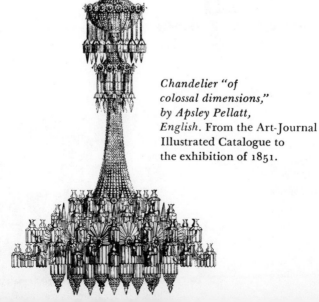

*Chandelier "of colossal dimensions," by Apsley Pellatt, English.* From the Art-Journal Illustrated Catalogue to the exhibition of 1851.

As the period wore on, interest shifted from the sparklingly clear cut and engraved wares of England and Ireland to the colored, cased and overlay, painted, stained and gilded glass of Europe, known as "Bohemian glass." By 1852, a visitor to Boston was impressed enough to write of the New England Glass Company, "We were repeatedly struck with the fact, new to us, that most of the exquisite, richly colored and decorated glass ware, which is so much admired under the name of 'Bohemian Glass,' is manufactured at these works."

Cased glass was one of the most admired Bohemian types; it was made by coating the basic color with one or more layers of different colors. "Overlay" is the name given when cut designs expose the lower layers. Solid-color glass was also typically Bohemian—ruby was a favorite, though many other hues appeared as well. Staining was another variation in which clear glass was given a transparent coating of color.

Bohemia, where all these techniques first gained popularity, was busily producing and exporting glass throughout the century. In addition to rich colors, there were also clear-glass vases, bottles,

*Wineglasses, all but the left-hand example showing Venetian influence, by Apsley Pellatt, English.* Art-Journal Catalogue.

*Dessert set, elaborate cut design, by Richardson, English.* Art-Journal Catalogue.

tumblers and the like, elaborately cut and engraved. Engraved designs tended to be of sentimental or romantic scenes, but the cutting, even when small motifs were used, was often deep enough to be called carving and produced a bold result. All these techniques, in fact, created striking effects—if not in deeply carved or cut patterns, then in color or unusual shapes. Black glass, called "Hyalith," and marble-like glass, called "Lithyalin," were other eye-catching types.

English and French glass manufacturers were as taken with Bohemian styles as the Americans, so they, too, copied and exported it, adding another note of confusion to the international glass scene: obviously it would be tremendously difficult to pin down the origin of an unidentified piece of Bohemian glass.

Foremost among makers of sophisticated glasswares in England were Apsley Pellatt of London and Benjamin Richardson of Stourbridge, the latter "known in mid-nineteenth-century England as the father of the glass trade" (Hugh Wakefield, "Richardson Glass," *Antiques,* May 1967).

"It is, however, in pure white crystal glass that this fabric

*Opal vase with decoration in gold and enamel colors, by Benjamin Richardson, English.*
Art-Journal Catalogue.

*Sugar bowl in an Empire shape with broad swirled ribbing, South Jersey tradition; New York.*

*Plain bottle with witch-ball top, South Jersey tradition.*

*Ornamental base with looped witch ball, South Jersey tradition.*

[glass], now as of old, displays its highest sphere of beauty and usefulness," stated the author of a prizewinning essay entitled "The Exhibition as a Lesson in Taste," published in the Art-Journal catalogue of the Great Exhibition of 1851. The repeal of the burdensome glass tax in 1845 paved the way for heavy pieces with deep cutting. And here the offerings of the Richardson and Pellatt firms stood out. The work of both showed Greek influence in pitcher, decanter and similar shapes. Richardson's clear crystal was deeply cut in bold geometric patterns that covered the entire object. Forms embody the Victorian passion for specific articles for every conceivable use—and some that seem inconceivable today. Decanters were numerous here as in all exhibits; wineglasses, vases and pitchers were other relatively common forms. More elaborate were covered compotes, a fruit stand and a dessert set with three sizes of goblet, a decanter, ewer, footed bowl and large centerpiece. Opal glass (having a "milky iridescence," according to Webster) with gilt and enamel painted decoration was another well-known Richardson type.

Apsley Pellatt showed many of the same forms, but his specialty was glass in the Venetian manner. In fact, the catalogue claimed that he excelled "in most particulars, the works of the old Venetians." Pellatt's wineglasses show very definite Venetian influence in their air of fragility and delicate decoration. Chandeliers were another of this firm's specialties and they were grand enough to gladden the heart of any lover of opulence. They were enormous, with thousands of glittering prisms, and they embody excellence of design and craftsmanship. Pellatt was noted as well for his pillar-molded decoration, a style in which bold molded ribs, widely spaced, created a striking design. Overlay and painted clear or opaline glass were other products of the Pellatt firm.

Clearly European glasshouses were still producing much of interest to American consumers, but the combination of effective protective tariff laws and a solid financial base made possible by the success of pressed wares had finally given American glassmakers the firm footing for which they had been groping for over 200 years.

*1850-1875*

*The*

*Victorian Style*

*Detail of* VIEW OF LIBERTY-STREET NEW-YORK,
*published by W. Stephenson & Company (1854–73).*
Museum of the City of New York.

# $\mathcal{H}istorical\ \mathcal{B}ackground$

PRESIDENTS: ZACHARY TAYLOR, 1849–1850;

MILLARD FILLMORE, 1850–1853; FRANKLIN PIERCE, 1853–1857;

JAMES BUCHANAN, 1857–1861; ABRAHAM LINCOLN, 1861–1865;

ANDREW JOHNSON, 1865–1869; ULYSSES S. GRANT, 1869–1877.

America was truly the land of opportunity in the third quarter of the nineteenth century, and if the streets were not quite paved with gold, they could lead, for those with initiative and a feeling for the times, to the success every poor boy dreamed of. It was a time of tremendous activity in almost every field imaginable, and it was during this period that the cornerstones of modern America were laid. The Civil War brought an end to slavery. The industrial revolution went inexorably forward until it had transformed American industry and agriculture. Our cities became the country's power centers, attracting rural Americans as well as great numbers of immigrants. Our present two-party political system emerged. Society changed as a new class of resourceful, self-made men challenged the social leadership of old aristocrats.

One activity that reached a point of equilibrium during this period was that of land acquisition. After the Gadsden Purchase of 1853, by which the United States gained land in the southern part of Arizona, and the acquisition of Alaska from Russia in 1867, we had reached our continental territorial limits. Commercial expansion was another matter, however. Even though business was booming within our borders, Commodore Matthew Perry negotiated a commercial treaty with Japan, ratified in 1854, which opened that country to Americans. Another very profitable venture outside our national boundaries was the whaling industry, which was still strong in the 1850s and 1860s.

Back on the American continent, the first railroad train between Philadelphia and Pittsburgh was put into service in 1852; a suspension bridge was erected at Niagara Falls in 1855; and the Pony Express between Missouri and California began running in 1860. (Mechanization was outrunning even the Pony Express, however, and the next year the telegraph supplanted that remarkable service.) Larger enterprises included the laying of a successful Atlantic cable in 1866 and the completion of the first transcontinental United States railroad in 1869.

Interspersed among all these successes were the inevitable failures. There were financial panics in 1857, 1869 and 1873. Chicago was devastated by the Great Fire of 1871 (begun, according to legend, when Mrs. O'Leary's cow kicked over a lantern and set her barn on fire). In 1874 the notorious Boss Tweed was convicted of fraud, an event regarded by some New Yorkers with distress and by others with satisfaction.

The greatest upheaval of the period was, of course, the Civil War, which racked the country from 1861 to 1865. In 1852 Harriet Beecher Stowe's book *Uncle Tom's Cabin* strengthened already hardy abolitionist sentiment; and in 1857 the Dred Scott decision, in which the Supreme Court declared that Negro slaves did not become free when taken into free states and therefore could not exercise the rights of citizens, became another cloud in the darkening sky. One of the severest critics of the decision was Abraham Lincoln, and shortly after his election in 1860 six Southern states seceded from the Union to form the Confederacy (South Carolina, Mississippi, Florida, Alabama, Georgia and Louisiana). They elected Jefferson Davis provisional president and were soon joined by Texas, North Carolina, Arkansas and Virginia. The Civil War began, and two years later, in 1863, Lincoln issued the Emancipation Proclamation, freeing 3,000,000 slaves. Just as the war was ending in the spring of 1865, Lincoln was assassinated.

This period of expansion, division and tragedy saw the publication of some of our greatest native works of literature, each expressing a different aspect of the American character: Hawthorne's *House of the Seven Gables* and Melville's *Moby Dick,* both in 1851; Thoreau's *Walden* in 1854; and Whitman's *Leaves of Grass* in 1855. There were no such highlights in our decorative arts, but nevertheless the first American international exhibition, held in 1853 at the specially erected Crystal Palace in New York, was a landmark. Titled "The World of Science, Art, and Industry," it was launched in the hope of promoting "a correct appreciation of what is really beautiful in the arts of design" among its viewers and of encouraging American manufacturers "by placing before them the productions of European taste and skill." Other events of cultural importance include the founding of the first agricultural college in the United States in Cleveland in 1855; the formation of the partnership of Currier and Ives in 1857; the establishment of Mount Vernon (George Washington's home) as a national shrine in 1858; and the founding of both the Metropolitan and the Boston museums of art in 1870.

# *Development of the Style*

Makers of our decorative arts during the Victorian period tried new styles and designs with enthusiasm, and they were fascinated by new materials and techniques. The only common denominator among Victorian furnishings is therefore their diversity. Revivals continued to occur with startling frequency and designers had not lost their willingness to combine the shape of one period with the ornament of another—or indeed of two or three others.

The rococo-revival style reigned throughout the 1850s, affecting every one of the decorative arts. Serpentine curves, florid fruits, flowers and vines transformed the objects that had for almost a century conformed to a classical mold of some sort. In the 1860s the rococo was joined by a new classical style inspired by the art of the Renaissance. There were other revivals, too, though they were not so prevalent: various eighteenth-century French styles besides the rococo, and Near and Far Eastern. Renaissance-revival forms were more architectural than rococo ones, and motifs included lion and ram heads, grotesques, strapwork, caryatids and acorns and oak leaves. A sampling of other popular motifs would

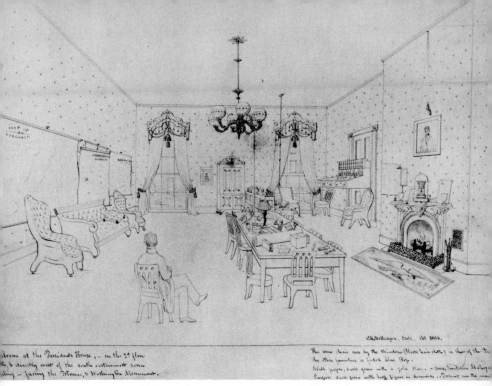

*Sketch of Lincoln's Cabinet Room, 1864, by C. K. Stellwagen.*
Western Reserve Historical Society.

include acanthus leaves, rural and historical scenes, flowers, floral scrolls, Chinese figures and scenes, and the Greek key.

Eighteenth-century craftsmen had catered to a relatively small group of well-to-do citizens along the eastern seaboard, but by the third quarter of the nineteenth century there was a much larger market, and it was scattered across the continent. Mechanization in all the crafts made it possible to meet the demands of the new market—to supply large quantities of goods in the latest styles and at medium prices. The advantage was, of course, that comfortable, modern furnishings were available to increasing numbers of people and that upholstered furniture, carpets, draperies and other such niceties, which had formerly been luxuries, were now easily attainable. The disadvantage was that the stamp of the individual craftsman, except in costly high-style furnishings, was almost totally erased.

The summing up of this period of diversity came a year after its close, at the Centennial International Exhibition held in Philadelphia in 1876 to celebrate the hundredth anniversary of American independence. The wares displayed there were apparently so well received that a critical handbook of the exhibition declared: "We may safely pronounce that the Centennial Exhibition will exist in the annals of history long after the vaunted pyramids of Egypt, of which the builders and the object are already alike unknown, shall have crumbled into dust."

# *Furniture*

The rococo-revival style was well established by 1850. Its inspiration was, of course, the eighteenth-century French rococo style, but as it was interpreted and adapted by nineteenth-century furniture makers, it was transformed into a valid expression of nineteenth-century character and spirit. New technical processes were used in the laminated, molded furniture of John Henry Belter and his contemporaries, and each piece was hand-finished with deep, rich carving of flowers, vines and fruits that expressed the romantic nature of the nineteenth century. The forms themselves, curving as they do to conform to the body and often luxuriously upholstered, express the Victorian love of comfort.

Characteristic nineteenth-century rococo forms differ from their eighteenth-century prototypes: chairs have high backs surmounted by high crests of lacy carving; their cabriole front legs sometimes end in a plain cone instead of a scroll; and their rear legs are a reverse, or upside-down, cabriole curve. The balloon-back side chair remained a popular rococo chair form throughout this period as well. Sofas are often made in a three-sectioned

BROOKS'

CABINET WAREHOUSE.

2 T. BROOKS 2

127 T. BROOKS 12

T. BONAR 121 NASSAU ST. N.Y.

127 FULTON ST. COR. SANDS BROOKLYN.

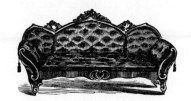

*Two rococo-revival sofas and a chair from the bill head of
the Boston firm F. M. Holmes & Company, dated 1863.*

medallion shape with a raised, carved crest on the center section.
Alternatives to this type are the tête-à-tête, or love seat, made in an
S curve with one seat facing forward and one backward; and the
single-end sofa, a descendant of the *méridienne.* Center tables
were an important element of the Victorian parlor, and examples
in the rococo-revival taste were usually made with cabriole legs,
undulating skirts of lacy carving and marble tops.

John Henry Belter, who came to this country from Germany
and set up shop in New York, is widely associated with rococo-
revival furniture, although it was made by several other very
capable cabinetmakers, among them Elijah Galusha of Troy, New
York; Charles Baudouine and Joseph Meeks & Sons of New York
City; Daniel Pabst of Philadelphia; François Seignouret and
Prudent Mallard of New Orleans. Belter's original contribution
was the steaming of laminated layers of rosewood veneer in molds
to give them the curving shapes that characterize the style. He
patented his process, but it was pirated by others. Belter's own
furniture is also distinguished by the imaginative, tastefully designed and executed carving that ornaments it.

The Renaissance was another revival style of the period and
was extremely popular for two decades. It was not, in many cases,
historically accurate, and motifs from a number of sixteenth- and
seventeenth-century styles were often amalgamated in Renaissance-
revival pieces. In general, the forms were rectangular with such

architectural features as heavy moldings, broken pediments surmounted by crests, sculptured busts and columns, and applied
medallions. Other characteristics of the style include incised linear
decoration (especially when the furniture was machine-made) and
acorn turnings. Legs on chairs and tables were often stiffly turned
and vaguely reminiscent of trumpet-turned legs of William and
Mary furniture; they also recall the round, turned legs of ancient
Roman furniture. Center tables are frequently supported by angular pedestals, which are in turn usually surrounded by additional
scrolls. Forms were basically the same as those of the rococo and
other Victorian styles, though the Renaissance style did lend itself
to large, impressive wardrobes and sideboards, dressing bureaus,
cabinets and other such storage pieces. Inlay was lavishly applied

*Rococo-revival whatnot, stool, center table, chair and single-end sofa,*
*the last three by John Henry Belter; rosewood.* Photo Brooklyn Museum.

to the most sophisticated of these and various eighteenth-century French revival forms, many of which were made by European craftsmen working here. Makers of Renaissance-revival furniture would include Thomas Brooks of Brooklyn, New York; L. Marcotte & Company of New York City; and the Berkey & Gay Furniture Company of Grand Rapids, Michigan.

So-called Louis XVI elements were often merged with Renaissance-revival ones, but the style also appeared in what its creators considered strict reproductions of eighteenth-century neoclassical furnishings. The Victorian origins of such pieces are nearly always discernible, however.

Rococo, Renaissance and eclectic forms, besides those mentioned as belonging to specific revivals, were varied, though there

*Side chair with balloon back, rosewood.* Museum of the City of New York.

*Laminated and carved tête-à-tête, rosewood.* Metropolitan Museum.

*Side chair by Belter, rosewood.* Photo Metropolitan Museum of Art.

weren't a great many new ones. *Étagères,* essential for the display of Victorian bric-a-brac, were glorified whatnots which were curved, carved, scrolled and further enhanced with marble and mirrors. Bedrooms might now include, in addition to the usual bed and dressing table or mirrored bureau, a washstand, shaving stand, cheval glass and towel rack, besides assorted chairs.

Upholstery, important even before midcentury, came into its own in overstuffed chairs and sofas. By the 1870s, it had spread over the entire frame of some types of furniture and was tufted, buttoned and fringed besides. This was originally a French fashion, and many allover-upholstered pieces were borrowed from France; among them were easy chairs, taborets (stools) and otto-

*Side chair with Renaissance-
and Louis XVI-revival
elements, by Thomas Brooks.*
Ex coll. Arthur W. Clement.

*Rococo-revival* étagère
*by Elijah Galusha, rosewood.*
Munson-Williams-Proctor Institute.

mans. The ottoman, in fact, replaced the center table in some fashionable parlors of the 1870s.

From 1850 another trend was toward unusual pieces with moving parts, such as reclining chairs, swivel chairs and tilting chairs. Such forms are often classed as patent or innovative furniture. George Hunzinger of New York is known to have made furniture of this type.

Other novelties include iron and papier-mâché furniture. Garden furniture and such incidentals as hat and umbrella stands were made of cast iron; in the 1870s iron-and-wire furniture for the garden was new. Papier-mâché, sometimes inlaid with mother-of-pearl, was a lightweight, colorful alternative to wood for small

*Victorian grouping showing rococo- and Renaissance-revival motifs and a small papier-mâché fire screen.* Henry Ford Museum.

chairs, tables and stands. It is thought that very little papier-mâché furniture was actually made here, but it was imported from England, where large quantities were made.

Among the woods most used for more conventional furniture were figured tropical rosewood, mahogany and black walnut (new in this period). Stained hardwoods were used when a cheaper product was desired. Veneering was still fashionable, and marble tops for tables, stands and similar pieces remained *de rigueur* throughout much of the period.

Makers of furniture active from 1850 to 1875 include, as well as those already listed, Roux & Company, Pottier & Stymus, Cottier & Company, Robert Ellin & Company and Christian Herter of New York City; John Jelliff of Newark, New Jersey.

While much Victorian furniture was still to some extent

*Renaissance-revival wardrobe, part of a set.*
Henry Shaw House,
St. Louis.

*Renaissance-revival cabinet,*
*rosewood with light wood inlays and*
*black and gilt decoration.*
Metropolitan Museum.

handmade, machines were increasingly employed in shaping, turning and producing scrolls and incised carving designs. Large furniture-making establishments in the East, especially in New York, had been shipping furniture to other parts of the country for years (the Meeks firm and Duncan Phyfe, for example, shipped quantities south and west). In this period the business of turning out standard furniture by machine came into its own, most particularly in Grand Rapids, Michigan, from which it was shipped to customers throughout the Midwest and eventually even to other countries. The pieces made there were simplified versions of high-style forms being made in the East.

It was in reaction to cheap furniture of this kind, made from inexpensive materials with shortcut methods, that the "arts and crafts" movement sprang up in England. The protest against

*Advertisement for a bedroom set in the Renaissance-revival style.*
Museum of the City of New York.

inferior workmanship and design standards was begun by John Ruskin and William Morris in the 1850s, and it was taken up and pursued with vigor by Bruce J. Talbert and Charles L. Eastlake. Eastlake's *Hints on Household Taste,* first published in America in 1872, was a tremendous success. His "hints" include such delicate suggestions as those implicit in his comment on the furnishing of a modern house: "The dining-room may have succumbed to the influence of fashion in its upholstery; the drawing-room may be crowded with silly knickknacks, crazy chairs, and tables, and all those shapeless extravagances which pass for elegance in the nineteenth century." He urges instead simple forms based on what he took to be medieval prototypes, carefully constructed and thought-

*Victorian library.* University of Rochester.

fully ornamented with flat carving or inlay. His first choice for wood was oak, but he found unpolished mahogany and natural-grain rosewood and walnut acceptable substitutes. The forms illustrated by Eastlake are not numerous but they include standard items such as tables, chairs and bookcases in rectangular shapes modeled on medieval and Jacobean forms. The flat-carved decoration derived from a wide range of sources. One of the motifs is a sort of zigzag or sawtooth pattern for borders or bands of ornament; others are simplified flower and plant motifs, as well as more elaborate medieval designs. Eastlake did not confine himself to furniture, but suggested appropriate treatments for curtains, walls, floors, picture frames, metal lamps and hardware, and so on.

*Victorian room setting with upholstered ottoman.* Brooklyn Museum.

It is ironic that while some designers (notably Christian Herter and Leon Marcotte) did grasp and implement the heart of his message—sound design, suitable ornament and honest joinery—many manufacturers of cheap furniture found that his suggested patterns lent themselves admirably to production-line techniques. Much "Eastlake" furniture, therefore, travesties the principles of its namesake.

Since improved communications was one of the great achievements of the nineteenth century, America was able to keep pace with developments in English decorative arts during most of the Victorian period. The stylistic trends outlined for American furniture therefore correspond to those in England during the same time. The Great Exhibition of 1851, held in the Crystal Palace in London, was responsible for the reaction among sensitive English-

*Papier-mâché table, English.*

*Design for a chest of drawers from Charles L. Eastlake's* HINTS ON HOUSEHOLD TASTE, *1872.*

men to what William Morris later called the "long neglect of art—and neglect of reason, too, in this matter" which had allowed poor design and construction to dominate the decorative arts. The crusade spread, as we have seen, to America; in England it was the beginning of the arts and crafts movement, in which William Morris was a leading figure. Sometimes also called the "Queen Anne" style in furniture because it complemented the new "Queen Anne" houses, it was based on "truth in construction" principles of simple forms and surface decoration. But this style did not become prevalent until late in the century, and in the interim highly ornate furniture with naturalistic carving of fruit, flowers and game, and with inlay, boulle work and marquetry was as much admired in the land of Morris and Eastlake as it was in our own.

*Cast-iron garden settee.*
Photo Parke–Bernet Galleries, Inc.

*Upholstered,
tufted, fringed armchair.
Joseph T. Butler.*

# Silver

Fantasy in silver probably reached its greatest heights in this period, when the combinations of shapes with motifs derived from an almost endless number of exotic, historical and contemporary sources seem more unexpected than those of any other era.

The real flowering of the rococo revival in silver occurred in the 1850s, with emphasis on the recurving line and luxuriant naturalism. Along with this trend there was, however, an oncoming Renaissance-revival style and a continuing use of neoclassic shapes from the eighteenth and early nineteenth century.

This period thus saw great variety in shapes. Besides the rococo pear form, a characteristic one adapted from Greek jar and jug forms was basically urn or egg shape, with a narrow neck rising from a gracefully swelling body, sometimes with two handles high on the shoulder, sometimes with one high-rising handle. The cylix form remained in style, too, with its shallow bowl mounted on a pedestal foot. Also typical was a low, squat form, circular or oval, set on either a low molded foot or a high pedestal.

Renaissance-revival motifs became dominant in the 1860s.

They were usually applied with more restraint than those of the rococo revival, stressing bands of ornament made up of Greek key, anthemion, guilloche, classical-frieze patterns and strapwork. Beading was employed once again, and decoration was often confined to the surface, without embossing or high relief. Legs and feet might consist of scrolled acanthus leaves or animal heads and hoofs; handles and finials were frequently cast masks, putti, lion heads or swans. Mythological and allegorical figures were popular as well.

The 1870s saw an increase in angularity in body shapes and especially in handles. The Greek-jar shape was given a more angular and abrupt shoulder, slanting sharply toward the top of each piece. Japanese and neoclassical Adam influences can be

*Beaker, a modest presentation item, by Eugene Jaccard & Company, St. Louis, Missouri.* Henry Ford Museum.

*Goblet made as presentation piece by Edward and David Kinsey, Cincinnati, Ohio.* Henry Ford Museum.

discerned in the wares of this period. Surface decoration was likely to be either engraved or chased in Japanese plant, bird or animal motifs; and handles might simulate bamboo.

The wide use of electroplated metals instead of solid silver and the almost complete mechanization of silversmithing which had occurred by this time had a democratizing effect. People of moderate means could now possess tea and coffee services, a luxury that had, two or three generations before, been available only to the wealthy. Because of this wide use of electroplated metals, the word "plate," which up to this time had meant solid silver, took on its modern meaning of a base metal covered with a thin coat of silver. Solid silver pieces were then referred to as "sterling," as

*Commemorative trowel,*
*used to lay cornerstone*
*of Tammany Hall,*
*by Francis W. Cooper, New York.*
Henry Ford Museum.

*Centerpiece used at*
*wedding of Samuel Clemens;*
*sphinxes support base.*
Mark Twain Memorial.

*Silver-plated cruet set,*
*simple, geometrical lines and*
*restrained decoration, by*
*Reed and Barton, Massachusetts.*
Museum of the City of New York.

they are today. Rolled Sheffield plate, either imported from England or made in the United States, also continued to be used.

Mechanization meant that all kinds of effects which had never before been possible could be produced: high-relief ornament and free-standing figures, animals and many other forms were turned out by machine. Surface variation by means of frosting, oxidizing, matting, burnishing and gilding was also achieved as a result of new technical developments. Engraving, flat chasing, piercing, casting, embossing and enameling were other techniques used to ornament silver.

Flatware as we know it—in matching sets—developed during this period: sets of silverware contained not only spoons, but also

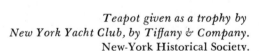

*Christening bowl marked by Tiffany & Company.* Mark Twain Memorial.

*Teapot given as a trophy by New York Yacht Club, by Tiffany & Company.* New-York Historical Society.

*Fruit stand; relief ornament shows up well against matted ground.* Museum of the City of New York.

knives and forks and all kinds of serving pieces. In fact, implements were available for serving almost every conceivable kind of food. There were fish knives and forks, crumb knives, nut picks, orange knives, and cheese knives and scoops—to mention only a few. A great variety of flatware patterns was created and patented by the major producers of silver, plated and solid.

Presentation pieces of all kinds grew still more numerous. And tea and dinner services were turned out in great quantity. A tea set of the period might include three pots, two for tea and a larger one for coffee; creamer and sugar bowl; pitchers; spoonholder; and a butter dish. Dinner services were made with pieces such as tureens, entrée and vegetable dishes, and centerpieces.

Individual centerpieces and ornate candelabra were very typical forms which gave the designer an opportunity to indulge

*Coffeepot, creamer and sugar bowl from a six-piece service by Tiffany & Company.* Museum of the City of New York

*Inkstand with military insignia, simple lines, classical ornament.* Museum of the City of New York.

almost any flight of fancy: figures, flowers, chariots, cupids, wild animals and exotic plants modeled in high relief or in the round were some of the elements that were combined with "visionary mania."

Pitchers, vases and ewers, made in the classical Greek-vase shapes mentioned earlier, are also typical. And all manner of small objects, such as thimbles, inkstands and other desk accessories, small boxes, tea balls, bells, strainers, salts with matching spoons and mustard pots. Extra items for the table included napkin rings and domed butter dishes. A new and popular form was the card receiver, a bizarre construction of decorative glass and silver, in which the caller could leave his card.

Church silver of the period was made in Gothic and other medieval forms, richly ornamented. Gothic chalices with hexa-

*Soup tureen, hand-chased floral decoration, by Kirk.* Photo Samuel Kirk & Son.

*Butter dish, Reed & Barton.* Privately owned.

gonal knop and base and baluster stem, flagons, alms basins and so on appealed very much indeed to American designers. Architectural elements, sculptured figures and engraved religious scenes were also employed.

After about 1850, because of the great quantities of ready-made wares, many men who had formerly made and sold silver stopped production entirely and turned to selling manufactured pieces; silversmithing shops declined and silver factories and jewelry stores proliferated. The designer, whose job was confined simply to making designs for silver, rose to prominence in place of the silversmith. A partial list of important firms of the period follows: S. Kirk & Son in Baltimore; Shreve, Crump & Low Company and its forerunners in Boston; Meriden Britannia Company in Meriden, Connecticut; Bailey & Company, J. E. Caldwell & Company and R. & W. Wilson in Philadelphia; Gorham Manufacturing Company and Whiting Manufacturing Company in Providence; Ball, Black & Company, Tiffany & Company, Wood & Hughes in New York; Reed & Barton in Taunton, Massachusetts; and Rogers Brothers in Waterbury, Connecticut.

England and America were closer than ever before in design developments. Classicism and a subdued naturalism existed side by side in English silver throughout much of the period, but the edge was given to classicism in 1857 with the publication of Owen Jones' *Grammar of Ornament.* Jones stressed the importance of restrained ornament of a flat, stylized nature that reinforced rather than competed with the structural lines of the piece itself.

The 1860s brought an increasing regularity in form, often highlighted by molding, but this disappeared with straighter-sided forms of the Adam revival of the 1870s. A taste for Japanese ornament was also developed in this decade.

Domestic plate throughout the period showed more restraint than had formerly prevailed, in contrast to the very showy presentation pieces and racing trophies that continued to appeal widely to the Victorian public.

*Water jug and tray, dolphin-head*
*spout, made as a presentation piece by Kirk.*
Photo Samuel Kirk & Son.

# Ceramics

By midcentury the traditional small potshop where wares were thrown on the wheel and decorated by hand had given way in many areas to factories where pottery was shaped in molds. Professional designers created the molds, which were then used to mass-produce objects with elaborate relief decoration. The simple shapes and earthy colors of early American pottery were replaced by classical and rococo shapes decorated with motifs that were not necessarily related to the piece and its function.

Stoneware had by this period replaced red earthenware for all but the humblest pots and crocks. English and American manufacturers of high-fired earthenwares, such as white, yellow and Rockingham, had taken over the market for unpretentious tablewares, teapots, molds and similar forms, and as these newer wares were reasonably priced and relatively durable, they, too, cut into the redware potter's market. Small country potters could not compete with the established American and English factories, so they were left to fill what need there was for simple dairy and kitchen pottery in handmade redware and stoneware.

Typical nineteenth-century redware forms include jugs with narrow necks and globular bodies (made very early and throughout the nineteenth century), pie plates with glazed interiors, flatbottomed platters and straight-sided pots. The earliest colored redware glazes were browns and greens, but as time passed black glazes began to appear, giving a less countrified though not so natural and warm effect.

In the period 1850 to 1875, stoneware was much more elaborately decorated than formerly. In fact, according to Lura Woodside Watkins, "a wholly new traditional art developed." The new designs were trailed or brushed onto stoneware pots, jugs and jars in cobalt blue or brown. Instead of abstract floral or plant motifs or geometrical shapes, the designs were now much freer personal interpretations of the birds, deer, chickens, people, houses and trees in the potter's own neighborhood. Among stoneware forms, made in bodies that ranged from buff to dark gray depending on the clay, were the crocks, jugs and pots already mentioned, as well as small flasks, water coolers and the curved and lidded pots known as "bean pots."

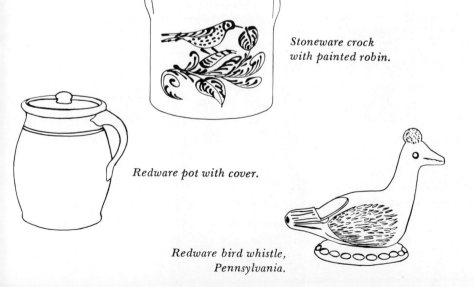

*Stoneware crock with painted robin.*

*Redware pot with cover.*

*Redware bird whistle, Pennsylvania.*

Bennington's Norton Pottery was one of the major manufacturers of mass-produced stonewares in this period. Some objects have decoration painted in cobalt blue, and one frequently encountered design, of a recumbent deer in a quiet pasture, is particularly fresh and charming.

Of the two major American potteries of the first half of the century, that of Christopher Webber Fenton in Bennington was the only survivor. David Henderson had died in 1848, and with him went the concern for quality as well as the business acumen which made the American Pottery Manufacturing Company so successful.

Fenton's factory, called by 1853 the United States Pottery Company, continued to produce useful dishes in yellow and white wares as well as in Rockingham and flint-enamel glazes. He con-

Stoneware water cooler,
unusually elaborate,
by Norton Pottery,
Bennington.
Smithsonian Institution.

*Parian Indian Queen.*
Ex coll. Dr. Karl C. Smith.

Parian pitcher
in corn-husk pattern,
United States
Pottery Company,
Bennington.
Brooklyn Museum.

tinued the production of Parian as well, and as time went on shapes became increasingly encrusted with high-relief ornament in the form of bunches of grapes, sinuous vines and florid naturalistic motifs. Smaller molded pitchers were produced in Parian in fairly large numbers, and they reflect the typical Victorian interest in naturalism applied to form as well as ornament. The Niagara Falls Pitcher, molded to resemble the rushing waterfall itself, is an example of naturalism carried to greater lengths than ever before. The pond-lily pattern which appears in relief on other pitchers is equally characteristic, though it does not encompass the form itself.

Another development was the use of a blue (or, rarely, tan, pink or green) and white body with applied Parian ornament, sometimes incorrectly referred to as "blue-and-white Parian." As

*Molded porcelain pitcher, blue and gold decoration, Union Porcelain Works, Greenpoint, New York.* Henry Ford Museum.

*Blue-and-white molded bisque porcelain pitcher, United States Pottery Company.* Brooklyn Museum.

Parian is by definition *white* biscuit, named for its resemblance to white Parian marble, the correct name for the colored ware is "blue-and-white porcelain." This combination was much favored for decorative items such as vases, ewers and pitchers with natural-istic ornament or sentimental scenes in relief.

A number of objects, such as the famous Bennington poodle holding a basket of flowers in its mouth; the recumbent doe and stag, a pair thought to have been modeled by the talented Daniel Greatbach; and numerous others, were made in more than one body. That is, the poodle or a relief-decorated pitcher might appear in Parian ware and the same model also in both flint-enamel and Rockingham ware.

Among other types produced in the short period between 1850 and the closing of Fenton's pottery in 1858 was white porce-lain dinnerware in sturdy classical shapes with narrow gold-band decoration. This was made widely in America and Europe, so it is very difficult to identify the Bennington ware (which was un-marked) positively. Granite-ware toilet sets, presentation pitchers and ornamental objects were also characteristic and were often decorated with gilding and colors. Granite ware was not marked either and is difficult to identify as the work of one specific factory (it was made by several) without historical evidence.

Utilitarian wares of yellow and red earthenware and stone-ware as well as Rockingham wares for the table continued to be the staple products of Midwestern potters. After 1870, however, the East Liverpool factories gave up Rockingham for granite ware or ironstone. American potters in general had begun in the 1860s to produce the ironstone and granite ware that had heretofore been imported from English factories, and plain white granite was for many years, according to Arthur W. Clement, "the customary cheaper tableware used in this country." In the later years of the period, some porcelain was also produced by East Liverpool potters.

Among other important manufacturers at work during this time were two new Brooklyn firms: William Boch and Brother, established in Greenpoint in the early 1850s, and Morrison and Carr, also of Greenpoint, founded in 1853. Both produced highly glazed white porcelain, a common form being that of a molded pear-shape pitcher, and both exhibited their porcelains at the Crystal Palace Exhibition of 1853. A pitcher typical of the Boch firm has molded decoration depicting the young Bacchus in a grape arbor, but other productions included a variety of small knobs and ornaments for doors, shutters, drawers and so on. Morrison manufactured Parian busts and ornamental pieces, which were sometimes lavishly decorated.

The Civil War disrupted all areas of life in America, and when it was over, new trends developed in ceramics. Eclecticism was apparent in the more pretentious wares, which show Near and Far Eastern influences as well as classical and Renaissance ones. The firm of William Boch and Brother had been taken over in 1862 by Thomas C. Smith, trading under the name of Union Porcelain Works. In anticipation of the coming 1876 exhibition, the firm secured the services of the talented German sculptor Karl Müller, who modeled the well-known Poets' Pitcher, Liberty

*Tea set designed by Karl Müller for Union Porcelain Works, eclectic mixture of motifs.* Brooklyn Museum.

Cup and Century Vase. These were elaborate display pieces with skillful portraits and other ornaments in high relief. The use on the Century Vase of nationalistic motifs (the American eagle, a portrait of George Washington, allusions to technical progress in America) with classical ones and a vaguely Oriental leaf-and-vine motif illustrate the eclecticism that typifies the period. The varied techniques used—biscuit and glazed porcelains, painting and gilding—make the same point.

Another well-known firm of the period was Bloor, Ott and Booth, founded in Trenton, New Jersey, in 1863 as a manufacturer of high-fired earthenware. In 1871 the firm became Ott & Brewer and began producing porcelain. They, too, hired a professional sculptor to design exhibition pieces, but these were apparently outshone by the Union Porcelain Works display.

In order to achieve the cluttered, crowded look that seems to

*Meissen watch holder.*
Staatliche Porzellan-Manufaktur, Meissen.

*Century vase designed by Müller for Union Porcelain Works.*
Brooklyn Museum.

have been the ambition of every Victorian housewife, it was necessary to have objects of all sorts. English and Continental potters had been catering to this need for years, but American potters became especially active in this area during the second half of the century. Aside from the sophisticated Parian statues and figures, there is a whole class of considerably less highly finished figures. Most are of animals, and most probably date after 1850. The Rockingham-glazed lions, poodles and cow creamers of Bennington come first to mind, and indeed they were among the most appealing of the group, but various similar figures were made at many other potteries throughout the East and Midwest. Pennsylvania potters made an even wider variety of animals, including horses, birds, monkeys, bears and bird whistles. Banks in the form of Empire chests of drawers or of buildings are also found.

While American potters confined themselves largely to rela-

*Vases by Daniell & Sons, London.*
From The Masterpieces of
the Centennial International
Exhibition, 1876.

*Sèvres vase, "Etruscan
in form."* From the Descriptive Catalogue of the Dublin
International Exhibition, of 1865.

tively simple animals, Staffordshire potters continued to make much more elaborate pottery figures of well-known personages of the day: kings and queens, singers and actors, historical characters and, for those with a taste for such subjects, notorious murderers and their victims. These figures were made of high-fired earthenwares and decorated with bright colors and shiny glazes, making them attractive to the "humble folk of town and country alike."

Other figures which might have been found on an American Victorian *étagère* were sentimental portrayals of children in pastel *bisque* (biscuit) from France, and colored and glazed figures of shepherds, shepherdesses and the like from France and Germany, many of them copies of eighteenth-century figures from Sèvres and Meissen (or Dresden, as it was called at the time).

More practical English earthenwares of the third quarter of the century include ironstone and other utilitarian wares, which continued to be produced in quantity and to appeal to Americans. A new ware called "majolica," earthenware covered with colored glazes and intended to imitate porcelain, was introduced by Minton in the 1850s. It was at first used for decorative wares, but was later employed in the manufacture of domestic utensils and as tile for the decoration of buildings. The technique was known in the United States in the 1850s, but it was not adopted to any significant degree until the 1880s.

Minton was the leader among English manufacturers of dinner and decorative wares from the 1840s onward. Like Wedgwood in the previous century, the firm of Minton overshadowed its contemporaries in the production of a great variety of skillfully made pottery and porcelain. "All the important factories vied in producing elaborate wares and each had its own speciality," according to Geoffrey Bemrose. Minton specialized in porcelains of the Sèvres type, and French artists were imported to produce authentic designs. Classical Greek forms were employed by some factories. Gothic designs were favored by Meigh & Company of Old Hall, and Worcester turned out a series of wares imitating Japanese ivory carving. To quote Bemrose again, "It is a little surprising that no enterprising firm thought of giving the world designs in Japanese Gothic."

An Irish porcelain that achieved great popularity was that made by the Belleek Pottery. Established for the purpose of making Parian statuary that would undersell that of Staffordshire on the American market, this firm became most famous for the hard Parian body covered with a mother-of-pearl luster. The combination of this lustrous, eggshell-thin ware with elaborately molded forms associated with marine life—seashells, mermaids, corals and underwater plants—was a happy one and had enormous appeal. Tea wares, small bowls and vases, and fantastically delicate flower-encrusted twig baskets are typical Belleek forms. Haviland china remained an important American import, as did some other Continental porcelains, most of which shared the same virtues and faults of design and decoration as English porcelains of the day. Many of them were shown, along with American wares, at the 1876 exhibition in Philadelphia, where more than one display moved the author of the catalogue to a tribute such as this: "We shall endeavor to give the reader an idea of the appearance of these remarkable works of art, as far as words can do it; but we urge all who would have a realizing sense of their beauty to take an opportunity of viewing for themselves."

*Majolica flowerpot and stand,*
*Minton & Company.* From The World of Art and Industry, New York Crystal Palace, 1853.

# *Glass*

As everyone knows by now, one of the chief characteristics of Victorian art is abundance of detail. In many instances, the quantity of different decorative elements seems to have taken precedence over the beauty of the material itself and over the appropriate combination of form and ornament, but on the other hand, mid-nineteenth-century design is fascinating as a reflection of the Victorian character. The common man had come of age as a conspicuous consumer: his delight in owning glass tablewares and parlor ornaments, for example, increased in direct proportion to the amount of color, gilding, engraving and cutting to be found on them, because to him lavish ornament represented a tremendous step up, putting him on a level with the aristocrat, who, in the past, had had a monopoly on richly decorated accessories.

Respect for the glass itself and for form appropriate to use was maintained most consistently in country bottle- and window-glass houses. South Jersey types and free- and mold-blown Midwestern types discussed in earlier sections are the two main components of this tradition.

In the case of pressed glass, mold designers and cutters were the artists, and although there are many quite simple geometrical patterns, these craftsmen were often influenced, especially after the Civil War, by the need to elaborate on basic designs.

High-style luxury glasswares, the category into which the various Bohemian types and cut and engraved clear wares fall, display the most frequent disregard of the potential beauty of pure lead glass simply shaped and decorated. Technical and chemical experiments had made many showy new effects possible—and therefore irresistible—and glassblowers, cutters and engravers themselves were eager to exhibit their often considerable virtuosity.

Commercial glasswares of this period display tremendous technical competence. A wide range of color was at the glass-blower's disposal, and effects such as staining, silvering and frosting (very popular for glass lamp shades or globes) increased his versatility. Most astonishing of all, the building in which London's Great Exhibition of 1851 was held was called the Crystal Palace because it was actually made of glass. This remarkable feat of construction was repeated in the New York Crystal Palace of 1853.

Glass from all over Europe and America was on display at both these exhibitions. The Bohemian style had become international, and the German exhibits were rivaled, if not surpassed, by those of other countries. Chief among these were the English, and it was pointed out in the catalogue:

> Though the English manufacturers may yet find some difficulty in competing in cheapness with Bohemia, the Islington glass-works of Rice, Harris, & Son, of Birmingham, seem to have surpassed this famed manufacture in every other respect; they exhibit an equal beauty of color with the Bohemian, a general superiority of taste, and uniformly superior workmanship; and this notwithstanding Bohemia displays some very beautiful examples, for they often owe more of their beauty to their decoration than to their shape or colour.

Many other English firms showed Bohemian wares, Benjamin Richardson's among them, and though Rice, Harris did have an impressive array of overlay and colored glass, they also displayed cut and engraved lead glass, pressed and molded drinking vessels and other tableware, and threaded "Venetian" glass—a good cross section of commercial glasswares popular at the time in England and to a large degree in America also. This is not to say that Americans didn't find much to emulate among the Continental and English glass exhibits. They were influenced particularly by styles and motifs in the exotic and "antique" modes.

In spite of protective tariffs and fine American-made wares, there was still plenty of European glass to be found in American homes. This was the era, too, in which high-style design became

From The Masterpieces of the Centennial International Exhibition, 1876.

international, so native and imported glasswares were often similar or indistinguishable.

An elongated silhouette derived from the ancient amphora and other vessels was popular for jugs, vases, cruets and similar containers. Handles were placed well up on the shoulder and sometimes looped high above it. The pear shape was common. There were ambitious pieces of indescribable shape, often appearing to be a series of unusual forms rising one above the other. Decanters, stoppered bottles for dining or dressing table, pitchers and vases came in such shapes.

Goblets and wineglasses were very frequently shown. Bowl shapes varied—round, tulip and bell were popular—and stems, feet and rims were lavishly faceted and boldly carved.

*Bohemian vase, ruby and amber with cut and engraved ornament, German. Ex coll. Ruth Webb Lee.*

*Bohemian vase decorated with view of Crystal Palace, made as a souvenir of the 1851 exhibition; German. Ex coll. Koopman.*

*Ruby vase and footed goblet, Bohemian style of Louis Vaupel, flashed, cut and engraved decoration. Toledo Museum of Art.*

Glass of various colors and overlay were decorated with gilt and enamel, cutting and engraving. Motifs were eclectic: naturalistic grapevines and oak leaves appeared alone or in combination with Moorish, Baroque and Greek-revival elements. Renaissance-revival shapes (simpler, more accurate copies) paralleled the silver and furniture of the 1860s. And the 1870s saw even more eclecticism and the addition of Near and Far Eastern motifs. Ornamental objects were very popular, along with such forms as tazzas, compotiers, liqueur services, toilet bottles and claret jugs, and all the more traditional forms.

The English had commented in the 1851 catalogue, "There is enough novelty of form in these works [from the Brooklyn Flint Glass Works] to assure us that our transatlantic brethren are fully aware of the mercantile value of Art." The objects illustrated in connection with this observation were of clear crystal cut in

*Pressed and cut crystal-and-ruby goblet, New England Glass Company, Massachusetts.* **Toledo Museum of Art.**

*Clear glass decanter made by the N. E. Glass Company for the Centennial exhibition.* **Toledo Museum of Art.**

unusual prismatic designs; the whole effect was much sparer and more streamlined than that of European exhibits and as a matter of fact, American wares were frequently simpler than European. Nevertheless, elaborate overlay, colored, cased, engraved and gilded glass continued to be made in America, and among its most renowned producers in this quarter century were the New England Glass Company; the Boston and Sandwich Glass Company; Christian Dorflinger, first in Brooklyn and later (by 1865) in White Mills, Pennsylvania; and Gillinder and Sons of Philadelphia and Greensburg, Pennsylvania.

Among the best-known individual craftsmen of this period are Louis Vaupel, who went to work at the New England Glass Company in 1853, and Nicholas Lutz, who came to America from the famous French glassmaking town of St. Louis. Vaupel worked in the Bohemian style: hunting scenes, animals, trees and foliage

*Clear cut-glass compote, N. E. Glass Company.* Toledo Museum of Art.

*Kerosene lamp, blue-and-white overlay font on gilded opaque-white base, engraved blown-glass shade; attributed to the Boston and Sandwich Glass Company, Massachusetts.* Henry Ford Museum.

*Decanter with delicate lines and ornament of Adam revival; "Venetian" influence also apparent.* From The Masterpieces of the Centennial International Exhibition.

are engraved in a "fine, delicate, light feathery cut, and whenever needed, an intaglio cut" (from a statement by Louis Vaupel's grandson John Vaupel, quoted in *Antiques,* May 1971). Lutz worked first for Dorflinger and then, from about 1870, for the Boston and Sandwich Glass Company. Though most famous today for its pressed wares, Sandwich, "from its very inception . . . ranked with the New England Glass Co. and the Bakewells of Pittsburgh in the variety and quality of its wares of all types" (McKearin, *American Glass*). Lutz was one of the most talented blowers at Sandwich and is particularly noted for his work in the so-called Venetian style, which became popular in America after the Civil War. Very thin glass with delicate allover engraving, and straw-stemmed wineglasses and goblets were hallmarks of this style, as well as Lutz's specialty, "striped," or latticinio, glass.

Besides the popular Bohemian and clear glass there was

*Decanter and stemmed glasses with decoration of Oriental inspiration.*
From The Masterpieces of the Centennial International Exhibition.

silvered, or mercury, glass, patented in 1855 by the New England Glass Company and sometimes made in forms meant to simulate silver. Accessories such as furniture, door and window knobs, and lamp bases were made in mercury glass, too. Etching, painting, enameling and transfer printing were widely used as decorative techniques. As the period drew to a close, ornament grew more and more obtrusive, and shapes became more and more eccentric, possibly in an attempt to avoid disappearing altogether.

Paperweights, made with great skill and artistry in the Baccarat, Clichy and St. Louis factories in France, as well as in many other European countries, were another branch of glassmaking that grew in this period. The New England Glass Company was outstanding in this area as in so many others, turning out weights in the very popular millefiori (thousand flowers) pattern, with fruit and flower centers, with miniature apples and pears against a

*St. Louis paperweight, overlay decoration, French.* Photo Sotheby & Co.

*Paperweights: N. E. Glass Company pear, and Sandwich poinsettia on latticinio ground.* Henry Ford Museum.

latticinio background, and with medallion centers. A weight very often associated with this company was composed of a large apple or pear on a clear base. But paperweight production was by no means limited to this one factory: Sandwich, Millville (New Jersey) and some Midwestern houses were other sources.

Pressed wares of the 1850s, made by many Eastern and Midwestern firms, belong in the pattern-glass category. Early pattern glass had been relatively simple, combining ovals, printies (or thumbprints) and flutes. Ribbed designs were popular in the 1850s, and as the 1860s dawned, patterns again became more elaborate: motifs of all kinds, some in high relief, were grafted onto the basic geometric arrangement. Each pattern had a name, many simply descriptive and some fanciful. With the change from lacy to pattern had come a concurrent increase in forms; large sets

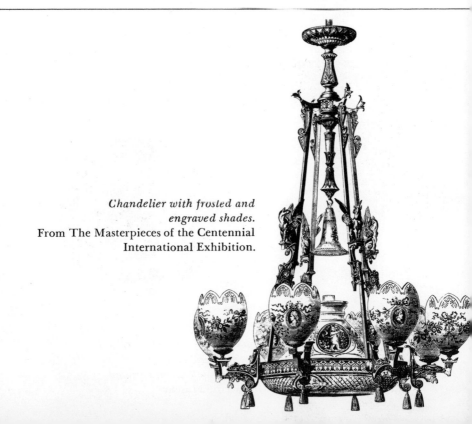

*Chandelier with frosted and engraved shades.*
From The Masterpieces of the Centennial International Exhibition.

of pressed pattern glass became enormously popular. The color range also increased greatly—early pressed wares had usually been clear but particularly after the Civil War color was the keynote. Spoon holders, butter dishes, celery vases, nappies (small dishes), goblets, wineglasses, lamps and vases, in addition to the traditional plates, cup plates, dishes and so on, came in blue, white, yellow, green, amethyst and other bright hues, transparent, translucent, opaque and frosted.

Patterns such as Pioneer (now Westward Ho!), first made in the 1870s, express the spirit of the age. The name itself is revealing, and the combination of motifs—an Indian finial, restrained neoclassical border designs and Western scene complete with log cabin, buffalo (a very meek-looking specimen) and mountain sunrise, exemplified the interest in ornate patterns that suggest a

*Pressed pitcher in ribbed bellflower design.*
Ex coll. George S. McKearin.

*Pressed pitcher, shell motif.*
Privately owned.

*Pressed goblet, "champagne,"
and egg cup in morning-glory pattern.*
Ex coll. Ruth Webb Lee.

story. The westward trend was of particular importance in American glass history, for "one of the vital factors in the gradual shift of the industry to the Midwest—Western Pennsylvania, Ohio, West Virginia, and later Indiana" was the depletion of the wood fuel supply in the East, and the finding of coal in the Midwest. "Discovery of natural gas in western Pennsylvania in 1859 and later in other Midwestern areas proved to be of tremendous importance to the glass industry" (McKearin, *American Glass*).

One westward migrant was William Leighton, longtime employee of the New England Glass Company, who had gone to work for the Wheeling, West Virginia, firm of J. H. Hobbs, Brockunier & Company. In 1864 he perfected a formula for lime glass as a substitute for lead glass. This proved to be of enormous importance in the manufacture of tablewares, for it lowered the price substantially. Most producers of commercial glass for the table switched to lime glass, but one important holdout was the New England Glass Company, which decided to continue with lead glass only. Its decision had much to do with its eventual decline and its move, in 1888, to Toledo, Ohio, to begin a new life as the Libbey Glass Company. The downfall of one of our greatest glass factories as a result of competition from cheap, sometimes ill-made wares provides an interesting and instructive twist in the history of the American glass industry—and industry in general—in the nineteenth century.

*Pressed milk glass, covered dish in sawtooth pattern, bowl in thumbprint pattern.* Photo Toledo Museum of Art.

# 1800-1875
# Britannia and Other Metals

Most early nineteenth-century metalworkers continued the trends and techniques of the eighteenth century. Fashionable fireplace equipment and lighting devices reflected the styles and decorative motifs of the classical revival, while everyday items of pewter, copper, tin and iron embodied careful workmanship in well-established shapes and forms. As the second quarter of the century approached, however, the venerable traditions of craftsmanship began to give way to mechanized methods of production, and the old forms gradually disappeared as a whole new way of living and working created different needs. "Just as in the making of large machinery itself the original wooden structure was soon replaced by metal, so, too, was almost everything that was touched by the process of industrialization, from clocks, farm tools, and household gadgets to wheels, rails, and vehicles," writes Herwin Schaefer in *Nineteenth Century Modern.*

Pewter and britannia metal, brass, bronze, iron and japanned tin were all used for lighting devices. Some were wholly metal, others had metal bases, shafts or frames in combination with glass shades and prisms and marble bases. The process by which eighteenth-century silversmiths had produced fine cast spouts, handles and so on was used increasingly in the nineteenth century for lamps, candelabra and chandeliers in complex revival styles.

Candlesticks more or less held their own until midcentury. Early forms were precise and restrained, with the emphasis on uncluttered lines. As the Empire period approached, candlesticks, like everything else, became heavier. A common Empire brass stick had a round base and shaft; pewter examples had shafts composed of knops and balusters mounted on rounded, often domed bases.

Real elaboration was generally reserved for candelabra and other multiple-light apparatus. Ornate bases, branches and sockets were made up of popular Empire forms such as classical and heroic figures and groups, architectural elements and national emblems. Many were further enriched by dangling glass prisms. These were also referred to as "girandoles," an overworked term which has come to mean single candlesticks with prisms, branched candlesticks, round convex mirrors with or without candleholders, as well as wall brackets with lights and sometimes mirrors. Later candelabra were occasionally unrestrained tangles of rococo leaves, vines, grapes and other swirling forms.

Another very attractive candleholder that achieved some popularity in early nineteenth-century America was the *bouillotte,*

*Lithograph of an 1840s parlor showing astral lamp.* Privately owned.

a French type which consisted of a flat dishlike base supporting a shaft from which extended arms with candle sockets. The addition of a painted-metal shade resulted in a form so attractive that it is still being used today (with electric lights, of course).

Lamps were the great new development in lighting. In 1783 the Swiss Aimé Argand had brought out what C. Malcolm Watkins (*Encyclopedia of American Antiques*) has described as "the most revolutionary innovation in artificial lighting prior to the electric light." His invention, which involved a new wick arrangement that produced a much brighter light, was quickly seized upon by other Europeans, and in 1786 a visitor to London reported that one shop devoted to Argand and other lamps created "a really dazzling spectacle; every variety . . . crystal, lacquer and metal ones, silver and brass in every possible shade." Argand burners were known in eighteenth-century America, too; Washington and Franklin were among the first owners of these "New-constructed Lamps . . . that will consume their own Smoke, and at the option of the Buyer, can be made to give a light equal to three, six, or one hundred Candles" (from a Boston newspaper of 1787). During the nineteenth century the use of Argand and Argand-type burners became much more widespread.

One variation on the original Argand lamp was the Carcel, which had a clockwork pump that kept the burner saturated with fuel. More popular, because they were less expensive, were astral and sinumbra lamps, both of which had ring-shape fuel reservoirs to reduce shadow. These two French inventions were the most widely used Argand types in America in the 1830s and 1840s, and they were made in a broad selection of materials: Sheffield plate, brass, cast iron, bronze and so on, topped by an etched- and cut-glass shade. They often came in sets of two or three so that they

*Pair of Argand lamps owned by George Washington, French. Mount Vernon.*

*Gilt-bronze candelabrum by Messenger & Phipson.* Governor's Mansion, Georgia.

could be used as mantel ornaments. Here, too, rococo curves were combined with Greek-revival urns, columns and classical figures, and with Gothic- and Renaissance-revival motifs. Some had hanging prisms. Solar lamps were a clever variant which created an intense white flame; these were at the height of their popularity during the 1840s and 1850s.

All these devices were made by, among others, the firms of Baldwin Gardiner and Mitchell, Vance & Company of New York; Cornelius & Company and Baker, Arnold & Company of Philadelphia; and Henry N. Hooper & Company of Boston.

Whale-oil lamps, also known as "common," "patent" and "agitable" lamps, were extremely popular during the first half of the century. They were well liked for their tidy shape, cleanliness and resistance to spilling fuel when tipped, even though they

*Lamp with frosted shades, glittering prisms.*
Privately owned.

*Design for solar lamps.*
Old Sturbridge Village.

didn't give so much light as Argand-type lamps. "Burning fluids" were used from 1830 as a cheaper substitute for whale oil. A number of lamps were devised in the next two decades to use these fuels, but they were highly explosive and no completely safe burner was ever invented.

Kerosene lamps superseded all earlier devices after the discovery of oil in Pennsylvania in 1859. They, too, were made in a number of forms: chandeliers, table lamps and wall fixtures. By 1869 Catherine Beecher and Harriet Beecher Stowe, in their *The American Woman's Home or, Principles of Domestic Science,* reported that "good kerosene gives a light which leaves little to be desired. Candles are used only on rare occasions, though many families prefer to manufacture into candles the waste grease that accumulates in the household." And as everyone who has ever spent any time in the country knows, kerosene lamps are still a necessary precaution against those stormy nights that bring down wires and plunge the household into disconcerting blackness.

Gas light wasn't really available to private houses until after the Civil War, and then only in cities, where it was possible to arrange a system of pipelines. Gas fixtures had to be stationary, so they were usually wall lights, hall lights and chandeliers. As they came at a time when elaborate ornament was dominant, they are ornate, displaying elements drawn from most of the later nineteenth-century revival styles.

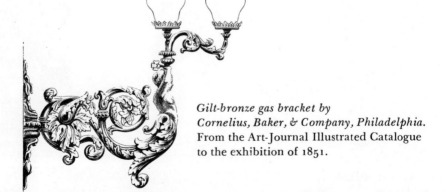

*Gilt-bronze gas bracket by Cornelius, Baker, & Company, Philadelphia.* From the Art-Journal Illustrated Catalogue to the exhibition of 1851.

# BRITANNIA

"Britannia metal is the best pewter ever made," Percy E. Raymond has written (*Antiques*, September 1949). His point is made in reference to the composition of the metal, and it is generally conceded that the alloy was in many ways more practical than pewter. Pewter collectors have felt, however, that production-line processes and forms render most britannia less interesting than pewter, which was the work of individual craftsmen practicing a carefully learned art. There is the additional feeling that while britannia metal is a superior alloy in being hard, bright and durable, it lacks the charm of the softer, mellower pewter.

"Plates, dishes, spoons, mugs, tankards, and porringers were the backbone of the pewterer's business in the days of the Pilgrim Fathers, and the same forms (tankards excepted) made up the bulk of the pewter-maker's stock when James Monroe became President in 1817" (Ledlie Laughlin, *Pewter in America*). Pewterers of the first quarter century include Thomas Danforth Boardman and partners, Samuel and William Danforth (these representatives of the respected pewter-making families of Danforth and Boardman continued to fashion pewter in the old way throughout the first half of the century, although they met the demands of the market by supplying machine-made wares as well), Ashbil Griswold and Jehiel Johnson of Connecticut; R. Austin, Samuel Green and Samuel Pierce of Massachusetts; Samuel Kilbourn of Maryland; Timothy Brigden of New York; Parks Boyd, Robert Palethorp, Jr., of Pennsylvania; and William Calder and Samuel E. Hamlin of Rhode Island.

Britannia lent itself to Empire shapes. The pear and inverted pear were favorites, sometimes with melon reeding and broad fluting like that of late Empire silver. Pedestals lifted some of these forms to an impressive height. Characteristic tall, tapering, cylindrical pots, thought for many years to be coffeepots, are now

*Britannia teapot.*

*Pewter pitcher with cover,
by D. Curtiss of Albany, New York.*
Yale University Art Gallery,
Mabel Brady Garvan Collection.

*Tall, cylindrical
britannia teapot.*

believed to be ample teapots. Handles were often of the scroll or double-scroll type, and the mid-bands of earlier pewter tankards and mugs were sometimes transformed on britannia pieces into conspicuous ridges.

An idea of typical britannia forms may be gained from an advertisement placed by Roswell Gleason in the *Norfolk Democrat* for February 11, 1848: "Splendid Communion Setts, Tea and Coffee Pots, Urns, Sugar Bowls, Creamers, Pitchers, Tumblers, Cups, Porringers, Tea and Table Spoons, Spittoons, Wash Bowls, Lamps, Candlesticks, Ladles, Castors and Castor Frames."

The lamps mentioned were very probably whale-oil or burning-fluid lamps, made in britannia in quantity. The peg lamp, fitting into the socket of a candlestick, the saucer-base chamber

*Whale-oil lamp.*

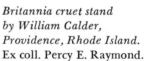

*Britannia cruet stand by William Calder, Providence, Rhode Island. Ex coll. Percy E. Raymond.*

*Burning-fluid lamp.*

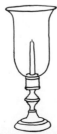

*Candlestick with glass shade.*

lamp, and the petticoat lamp, with a flaring base resembling that garment, are all whale-oil variants. The lamp portion might be of bell, inverted-bell, cylindrical, lemon or other shape, sometimes rising directly from a base and sometimes mounted on a stem resembling a candlestick. Bases for the short type were often round saucers, while a domed base frequently supported stemmed examples. J. B. Kerfoot (*American Pewter*) says that most of these lamps were not marked, probably because they were made to be sold to retailers, "a breed . . . that had not existed up to the time of the excitement over the revolution in lighting notions that swept the country between the 1830s and the sixties."

The process of spinning on a lathe, by which many of these things were formed, was augmented by casting and stamping. In this last method the various parts were machine-stamped out of rolled sheets and soldered together to create such forms as the octagonal teapot; alternatively, the sheet was "stamped," or pressed, into the required form. Both spinning and stamping produced pieces which have sharp, crisp outlines, in contrast to the rounded contours of earlier pewter.

Although there were manufacturers scattered throughout the republic, britannia was at first produced mainly in New England. It was displaced in the 1860s by pressed glass, decorative ceramics and inexpensive electroplated wares. Some prominent britannia manufacturers, in fact, switched to electroplating their products when they saw how quickly that process was catching on.

Foremost producers of britannia, working during the middle years of the century, would include Connecticut's Babbitt, Crossman & Company, Thomas and Sherman Boardman, Griswold, Thomas R. Holt, R. Wallace and Company (producers of plated britannia from 1855 to the present), and H. Yale & Company; Massachusetts' Roswell Gleason, J. H. Putnam, Smith & Morey, Taunton Britannia Manufacturing Company, Israel and Oliver Trask; Maine's Rufus Dunham and Freeman Porter; Rhode Island's George Richardson (much of whose ware was marked "Glennore Co."); New York's Endicott & Sumner, Henry Hopper and J. Weekes; Philadelphia's William McQuilkin and J. H. Palethorp and partners; and Cincinnati's Homan & Company and Sellew & Company.

During this period mergers of some of these firms created big companies whose names are familiar today. Examples are Reed and Barton, founded in 1840 by the successors of the original partnership of Babbitt & Crossman, and the International Silver Company, successor to the Meriden Britannia Company, which was itself the result of a merger in 1852 of several of the principal britannia manufactories in and around Meriden.

English makers who exported a great deal of pewter and britannia to America were James Dixon & Company and Townsend and Compton.

*Nineteenth-century kitchen with stove, utensils, lamp.* Stowe-Day Foundation.

# BRASS AND COPPER

The handsome eighteenth-century copper teakettle survived into the nineteenth century with little change, but finally it responded to innovations in living. In later versions the old gooseneck spout which had complemented the softly rounded eighteenth-century form was replaced by a straight spout, which went well with the more streamlined shape of the new kettles. Craftsmen no longer took the trouble to mark their products after about 1850, so it is difficult to date late examples or identify their makers.

Other types of simple kettles continued to be made, but now brass kettles—spun on a lathe from sheet brass after the middle of the century—outnumbered copper ones. Hiram Hayden patented a process for spinning brass kettles in 1851, and examples with his name and the date of manufacture may still be found.

Kitchen utensils, funnels, braziers, coal hods and oil-lamp fillers are some of the other ordinary products of the nineteenth-century metalworker. Dry and liquid measures, usually cylindrical in form, were another characteristic product. Dry measures are now very rare.

According to Kauffman (*American Copper and Brass*), and-irons were made in America in the second half of the eighteenth and first half of the nineteenth century because English braziers made fewer and fewer andirons as coal replaced wood. Since the fuel situation was not considered so desperate in the New World, Americans continued to use wood and, therefore, andirons, well into the nineteenth century. When American cities did begin to find wood in short supply and switched to coal, they placed their coal grates on their andirons, preserving the life of these attractive fireplace accessories until about midcentury. Brass-and-iron or steel fire tools followed roughly the same pattern as andirons, being used for coal after wood fires were no longer universal.

Short andirons remained popular in the early years of the nineteenth century; they were topped by large urn, lemon, ball or acorn finials, but, as was to be expected, Empire examples were heavier and sometimes lacked the grace of earlier andirons.

John Molineux and Paul Revere's apprentice William C. Hunneman, both of Boston, signed quite a number of andirons during the first half of the century. The type most frequently associated with them had a low column with ball finial; this front

*Brass andirons by William C. Hunneman, Boston.* Privately owned.

*Fireplace converted to use of coal.* Ex coll. A. G. Bailey.

column was connected to an identical but shorter column by a flat, curved piece.

Besides Molineux and Hunneman, Paul Revere was a well-known producer in Boston; in New York Isaac, Richard and Richard Wittingham, Jr. (known especially for their andirons) were at work; and William Heyser and W. O. Hickok are noted Pennsylvania craftsmen.

# IRONWORK

Elegant fireplace implements became less important with the rise of the cast-iron stove, which is found in a variety of forms. Empire examples came in controlled geometrical shapes which echoed the classical architecture of the day. Ornament was also drawn from classical sources: columns, arches, flat scrolls, friezes and linear bands of leaf, urn or geometrical motifs. Later, parlor stoves were cast in rococo, Gothic and Renaissance designs and shapes. Stoves were also made for the kitchen, laundry and other rooms, with special built-in work savers. One type had brackets for several flatirons so that when the one in use got too cold to do the job, another was always ready.

Furniture (discussed under *Furniture*), lamp bases and mirror frames were cast in up-to-the-minute revival styles, while in the kitchen pots and kettles were joined by cherry pitters, apple corers and peelers, and coffee grinders. Iron implements were made in large numbers for use out of doors, the domain also of perhaps the most famous iron (or other metal) form of all—the weathervane.

*Painted cast-iron
looking-glass frame.*
Sleepy Hollow Restorations.

*Cast-iron wood-burning stove,
classical motifs.*
Privately owned.

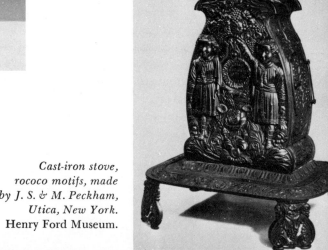

*Cast-iron stove,
rococo motifs, made
by J. S. & M. Peckham,
Utica, New York.*
Henry Ford Museum.

## JAPANNED TINWARE

We usually concentrate on the japanned, pierced and punched wares that lent such a bright, cheery note to nineteenth-century country kitchens and dining rooms, but according to contemporary advertisements, most tinware was plain. A great deal of it has disappeared for the same reason that lowly crocks and pots have disappeared: they were too commonplace to merit special care. But so many different things were made of tin that one nineteenth-century tinsmith considered it an appropriate material from which to fashion a grandfather-clock case.

Most objects were less bizarre. On the farm, tinware was used in the dairy, in the kitchen and throughout the house for lighting. Milk cans; dishes; bread, bun and apple trays; cake and pie pans; cookie cutters; mugs; dippers; measures; strainers; colanders; boxes; tea caddies; and coffee- and teapots are some of the items that the fabled Yankee peddler might have brought forth from the "maze of secret compartments, drawers and hooks" of his wagon. Tin mirrors and picture frames, popular especially in the Southwest, sometimes had scalloped edges and pierced and punched patterns, or were made in imitation of beveled wooden frames. Foot warmers with wooden frames and pierced-tin sides were another useful item.

Lighting equipment of tin was especially important: quantities of candlesticks of a very simple kind with round saucer base and shaft were made. And in the late eighteenth and early nineteenth centuries chandeliers with graceful, curved arms and simple candle sockets hung in many taverns and churches.

By 1850 japanned tinwares had reached the zenith of their popularity, having been carried from New England to the South, Midwest and even Canada by the zealous peddler. The industry's home was Berlin, Connecticut, where the Pattisons are said to have established it and where the founders of other Northeastern centers almost always got their start. A characteristic Berlin type includes apple dishes, coffin trays (octagonal with clipped corners), boxes of all sizes, and banks, with transparent red, blue, green or asphaltum (a reddish-yellow brown) backgrounds on which were stenciled designs in bright blues, reds, greens and

*Tin-peddler's wagon.*
Henry Ford Museum.

*Punched-tin coffeepot by P. Shade of Bucks County, Pennsylvania.*
Philadelphia Museum of Art.

yellows. In addition to the stenciled ornament, hand-painted flowers, fruit and other naturalistic forms, sometimes very uninhibited and imaginative, are found.

Owing to the exertions of Zachariah Stevens, Stevens Plains, Maine, was the center of a flourishing tin industry from 1825 to 1850. Well-known workers there were Elisha and Elijah North and Oliver and Mary Ann Buckley. Other successful manufacturers of japanned wares include Oliver Filley, who had branches in New York State and Pennsylvania; the Butler family of East Greenville, New York; and the American Tea Tray Works of Albany, manufacturers of oval trays from 1860. The Litchfield Manufacturing Company specialized in japanning on papier-mâché; pearl shell, metal leaf and paint were applied by imported English decorators. This work was, in general, much more detailed than the American type, which was characterized by bold designs quickly executed. This makes for an entirely different product and has a charm unlike that of finer work.

The importation of English decorators, however, stressed the

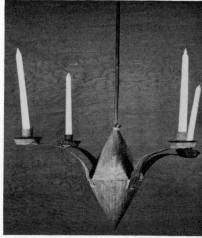

*Tin chandelier probably designed for a tavern ballroom.* Old Sturbridge Village.

*Group of hand-painted tinwares.* Old Sturbridge Village.

fact that japanned tin was originally an English craft, and one very good reason for this was that England had the tin mines. She supplied the raw material and probably blank trays, besides exporting enormous quantities of finished japanned tinware to the United States. Decorated English trays were, in Shirley Spaulding DeVoe's words, "as familiar in American homes as Staffordshire pottery" (*Encyclopedia of American Antiques*), and they came in oval, octagonal, rectangular and Chippendale (scalloped) shapes, painted or stenciled in ornate designs.

But fancy English trays were probably most numerous in urban areas. Country folk had to rely for their decorated trays on the peddler, and his wares were the work of native artists. If it were possible to transport ourselves back to a mid-nineteenth-century country lane, we might arrive in time to see a peddler rounding the bend. His call conveys the audacity of his fraternity and, perhaps, something of the spirit of the age:

"I'll take old copper, old brass, old iron and pewter, old rags, anything except cash and old maids!"

*Pennsylvania German painted-tin tray.*
Dr. Earl F. Robacker.

*Stenciled tray, probably English.*
Henry Ford Museum.

# $\mathcal{B}$ibliography

In a survey such as this we could not hope to offer original research, but drew instead on the work of others who have made specialized studies. To indicate some of the sources for this book and to guide the reader who wishes to inform himself more fully, we include a limited bibliography of basic and comprehensive books in each of the categories discussed in the text.

Much indispensable information was taken from the pages of *Antiques* itself. A list of specific articles would be far too long for this space, so we refer the reader to *Antiques'* cumulative indexes, 1922 to the present.

## FURNITURE

### AMERICAN:

COMSTOCK, HELEN. *American Furniture: Seventeenth, Eighteenth, and Nineteenth Century Styles.* New York: The Viking Press, 1962.
DOWNS, JOSEPH. *American Furniture: Queen Anne and Chippendale Periods in the Henry Francis du Pont Winterthur Museum.* New York: The Macmillan Co., 1952.

MILLER, EDGAR G., JR. *American Antique Furniture: A Book for Amateurs.* 2 vols. Baltimore: The Lord Baltimore Press, 1937.

MONTGOMERY, CHARLES F. *American Furniture: The Federal Period in the Henry Francis du Pont Winterthur Museum.* New York: The Viking Press, 1966.

NUTTING, WALLACE. *Furniture Treasury (Mostly of American Origin).* 3 vols. Framingham, Mass.: Old America Company, 1928 and 1933.

OTTO, CELIA JACKSON. *American Furniture of the Nineteenth Century.* New York: The Viking Press, 1965.

ENGLISH:

FASTNEDGE, RALPH. *English Furniture Styles from 1500 to 1830.* London: Penguin Books, 1955.

MACQUOID, PERCY, and EDWARDS, RALPH. *The Dictionary of English Furniture from the Middle Ages to the Late Georgian Period.* Revised and enlarged by Ralph Edwards. London: Country Life, Ltd., first published 1924–27; rev. ed. 1954.

## SILVER

### AMERICAN:

AVERY, C. LOUISE. *Early American Silver.* Reissue. New York: Russell and Russell, 1968.

ENSKO, STEPHEN G. C. *American Silversmiths and Their Marks III.* New York: Privately printed, Robert Ensko, Inc., 1948.

FALES, MARTHA GANDY. *Early American Silver for the Cautious Collector.* New York: Funk and Wagnalls, 1970.

PHILLIPS, JOHN MARSHALL. *American Silver.* ("American Crafts Series," edited by Charles Nagel.) New York: Chanticleer Press, 1949.

THORN, C. JORDAN. *Handbook of American Silver and Pewter Marks.* New York: Tudor Publishing Co., 1949.

### ENGLISH:

JACKSON, SIR CHARLES JAMES. *English Goldsmiths and Their Marks.* 2d ed., rev. New York: Dover Publications, 1964.

———. *An Illustrated History of English Plate.* 2 vols. London: Holland Press, 1967.

HEAL, SIR AMBROSE. *The London Goldsmiths 1200–1800.* Cambridge: University Press, 1935.

## CERAMICS

### AMERICAN:

CLEMENT, ARTHUR W. *Our Pioneer Potters.* York, Pa.: Privately printed, The Maple Press Co., 1947.

GAINES, EDITH. "Dictionary of Pottery and Porcelain," *Woman's Day,* August 1962, pp. 19–34.

WATKINS, LURA WOODSIDE. *Early New England Potters and Their Wares.* Cambridge, Mass.: Harvard University Press, 1950.

### EUROPEAN:

BEMROSE, GEOFFREY. *Nineteenth Century English Pottery and Porcelain.* ("The Faber Monographs on Pottery and Porcelain," edited by W. B. Honey.) New York: Pitman Publishing Corp., n.d.

HAGGAR, REGINALD G. *The Concise Encyclopedia of Continental Pottery and Porcelain.* New York: Hawthorn Books, Inc., 1960.

HONEY, WILLIAM BOWYER. *European Ceramic Art from the End of the Middle Ages to about 1815.* London: Faber and Faber, Ltd., 1952.

MANKOWITZ, WOLF, and HAGGAR, REGINALD G. *The Concise Encyclopedia of English Pottery and Porcelain.* New York: Hawthorn Books, Inc., n.d.

SAVAGE, GEORGE. *Porcelain Through the Ages.* London: Penguin Books, 1954.

———. *Pottery Through the Ages.* London: Penguin Books, 1959.

## GLASS

### AMERICAN:

GAINES, EDITH. "Dictionary of American Glass," *Woman's Day,* August 1961, pp. 19–34.

———. "Dictionary of Sandwich Glass," *Woman's Day,* August 1963, pp. 21–32.

———. "Dictionary of Victorian Art Glass." *Woman's Day,* August 1964, pp. 23–34.

MCKEARIN, GEORGE S. and HELEN. *American Glass.* New York: Crown Publishers, 1941.

———. *Two Hundred Years of American Blown Glass.* Garden City, N.Y.: Doubleday and Co., Inc., 1950.

REVI, ALBERT CHRISTIAN. *American Pressed Glass and Figure Bottles.* New York: Thomas Nelson and Sons, 1964.

EUROPEAN:

ELVILLE, E. M. *The Collector's Dictionary of Glass.* London: Country Life, Ltd., 1961.

HAYNES, E. BARRINGTON. *Glass Through the Ages.* London: Penguin Books, 1948.

HONEY, W. B. *Glass: A Handbook.* London: Ministry of Education, 1946.

## PEWTER AND OTHER METALS

AMERICAN:

COFFIN, MARGARET. *The History and Folklore of American Country Tinware 1700–1900.* Camden, N.J.: Thomas Nelson and Sons, 1968.

KAUFFMAN, HENRY J. *American Copper and Brass.* Camden, N.J.: Thomas Nelson and Sons, 1968.

KERFOOT, J. B. *American Pewter.* Boston and New York: Houghton Mifflin Co., 1924.

LAUGHLIN, LEDLIE IRWIN. *Pewter in America: Its Makers and Their Marks.* Reprint (2 vols. in 1), 1969; Vol. III, 1971. Barre, Mass.: Barre Publishers, 1969.

ENGLISH:

COTTERELL, HOWARD HERSCHEL. *Old Pewter: Its Makers and Marks in England, Scotland and Ireland.* Reprint. Rutland, Vt.: Charles E. Tuttle Co., 1963.

## GENERAL

THE ART JOURNAL. *Illustrated Catalogue of the Industry of All Nations.* London: George Virtue, 1851. A Catalogue of the Great Exhibition.

DAVIDSON, MARSHALL B. *The American Heritage History of Colonial Antiques.* New York: American Heritage Publishing Co., 1967.

———. *The American Heritage History of American Antiques from the Revolution to the Civil War.* New York: American Heritage Publishing Co., 1968.

————. *The American Heritage History of Antiques from the Civil War to World War I.* New York: American Heritage Publishing Co., 1969.

MASTERPIECES OF THE CENTENNIAL INTERNATIONAL EXHIBITION. Vol. 1: *Fine Art,* by Edward Strahan; Vol 2: *Industrial Art,* by Walter Smith; Vol. 3: *History, Mechanics, Science,* by Joseph M. Wilson. Philadelphia: Gobbie and Barrie, 1876.

TRACY, BERRY B., and GERDTS, WILLIAM H. *Classical America 1815–1845.* Newark: The Newark Museum Association, 1963. Catalogue of an exhibition at the Newark Museum.

TRACY, BERRY B.; JOHNSON, MARILYNN; SCHWARTZ, MARVIN D.; BOORSCH, SUZANNE. *19th-Century America: Furniture and Other Decorative Arts.* An Exhibition in Celebration of the Hundredth Anniversary of the Metropolitan Museum of Art. New York: The Metropolitan Museum, 1970.

WINCHESTER, ALICE (ed.). *The Antiques Treasury of Furniture and Other Decorative Arts.* New York: E. P. Dutton and Co., Inc., 1959.

————. *How to Know American Antiques.* New York: New American Library, Signet Key Books, 1951.

# Index